'A Want of Order and Good Discipline'

'A Want of Order and Good Discipline'

RULES, DISCRETION AND THE VICTORIAN PRISON

RICHARD W. IRELAND

UNIVERSITY OF WALES PRESS
CARDIFF
2007

Published by the University of Wales Press

University of Wales Press
10 Columbus Walk
Brigantine Place
Cardiff
CF10 4UP

www.wales.ac.uk/press

ISBN 978-0-7083-1945-1

British Library Cataloguing-in-Publication Data.
A catalogue record for this book is available from the British Library

The publishers wish to acknowledge the financial support of the Higher
Education Funding Council for Wales in the publication of this book.

Printed in Great Britain by Antony Rowe Ltd, Chippenham, Wiltshire

For Helen

Contents

Contents

Plates

Plate 1. This early nineteenth-century engraving, with its river, bridge and picturesque coracle fishermen, paradoxically demonstrates the dominance of the prison site in the topography of Carmarthen. (*Author's collection*)

Plate 2. The governor's house, moved from the heart of the gaol to its periphery in the later nineteenth century. This latter site is shown here. (*Courtesy of Carmarthen Museum*)

Plate 3. Governor Stephens, his staff and female prisoners (?), 1870s (?). This remarkable photograph, though it presents difficulties in interpretation, is the only known image of the inside of the prison in the nineteenth century. (*Courtesy of Carmarthen Museum*)

Plate 4. Part of James Collard's 1859 plan for the reconstruction of the chapel, showing segregation according to class of prisoner rather than individual separation. Female prisoners were accommodated in an upper gallery. (*Courtesy of Carmarthenshire Archive Service*)

Plate 5. Evan and Hannah Jacob, photographed in Carmarthen prison just before their trial in July 1870. The parents of the celebrated 'Fasting Girl', who had died when claims that she could survive without nutrition were put to the test, were bailed before trial and were transferred subsequently to Swansea during Carmarthen's reconstruction. The mother's garland of flowers eerily echoes those worn by her daughter when she received visitors. From the *Felons' Register*. (*Courtesy of Carmarthenshire Archive Service*)

Plate 6. Birth in the prison: twenty-two-year-old Jane Bowen gave birth to a son at around 6.00 a.m. on 13 July 1864 whilst serving a sentence of six months with hard labour for sending a threatening letter. From the *Felons' Register*. (*Courtesy of Carmarthenshire Archive Service*)

Plate 7. Death in the prison: forty-five-year-old George Adams, 'rag gatherer and gentleman's servant', who died within four days of this photograph being taken, again in July 1864, of 'disease of the heart'. From the *Felons' Register*. (*Courtesy of Carmarthenshire Archive Service*)

Plate 8. David Jenkins, a twenty-seven-year-old farmer, removed to the Joint Counties Asylum and not tried after his remand to the gaol in November 1867. From the *Felons' Register*. (*Courtesy of Carmarthenshire Archive Service*)

Preface

It is time that I finished this book. I write these words sitting in an underground room in the Folkingham House of Correction in Lincolnshire. Bizarrely, but wonderfully, this institution is now let out to holidaymakers. This in itself suggests something about the nineteenth-century gaol in the modern consciousness: its architecture we deem now to be important, whilst, now decommissioned, its function is to fascinate rather than to disturb. It is my second penal establishment of this few days' holiday, for I sought out the cells of the (rather less well preserved) Walsingham House of Correction with, I suspect, almost as much enthusiasm as other visitors seek out that village's spiritual attractions. It is, as I say, time that I finished this book. I have lived with the nineteenth-century prison for too long. Were I given to the language of popular psychology I could not resist, in this context, saying that I demanded 'closure'.

Perhaps the insights of psychology are necessary to understand this deep interest in incarceration, but I hope that those reasons which consciously shaped this study will suffice here. Crime and punishment – the separation of behaviour and of individuals into categories of acceptable and unacceptable, and the construction of that difference and the responses to it – are fascinating things. They mark and floodlight a particular normative boundary; a boundary which changes and which is patrolled by (I don't want to get into difficult definitional issues here, let's just use the word for now) the state. But the main reason I wanted to write this book, and the methodology which underlies what follows, was the desire to write a penal history which expressly went beyond the abstract nouns and theoretical constructions which have dominated so much prison historiography, at an academic level at any rate. Whilst 'popular' history has always recognized the value of the human perspective (though it may concentrate on the more 'atypical' individual, and ignore the contextual background), and whilst I hope that this book will appeal to a non-specialist readership, I want, as an academic legal historian, to help to restore the messiness, the contingency of human affairs to the story of penal development. This is not to say that such elements become simply the reverse side of the Victorian 'penal revolution', a marking of a mere deviation from an ordered ideal. Nor is it to renounce theoretical analysis. Rather it seeks to explore the essential limitations of order, the very essence of the ideal. In a way this book is an extended jurisprudential meditation on the nature of rules. The title, by the way, is taken from a comment on the state of Carmarthen County Gaol by the Inspector, Bisset Hawkins, in his Fifth Report for 1840.

I have many people to thank for their help over the years I have spent in the writing of this book, too many to name here. Colleagues at Aberystwyth and in Victoria (time spent there due to the generosity of McCarthy–Tétrault was important in planning my approach) have been supportive and indulgent. My students too, undergraduate and postgraduate, have tested and added to my ideas. Funding provided by the Sir David Hughes Parry fund was much appreciated. Claire Breay (whose assistance was funded by the Law Department) and Glenys McBurnie proved invaluable in the research. The University of Wales Press (and its reader) has shown a faith in the project for which I am truly grateful. Over the years all the staff at Carmarthenshire Record Office have been more than simply great professionals, but valued collaborators and friends. Their colleagues in the Museum deserve great credit too. Robert Ireland agreed to undertake a meticulous proofreading and preparation of the text for the printers only on the condition that I would not mention him, so I won't. I have, in short, been very lucky.

Lucky too in respect of other sources of help. Imogen, Andrew and Gwyneth won't expect to be here, but will understand why they are. My cat, Tammas, has been an attentive reader, sitting on my shoulder as I typed and sometimes editing the text when I wasn't watching the keyboard. Any errors of substance or presentation are, of course, entirely his responsibility.

There was, however, only one possible dedicatee of this volume. I had worked almost entirely on medieval material before starting this research. I was enticed into the change of direction by a persistent young archivist in Carmarthen. Neither her suggestions that the records merited closer examination, nor my own

willingness to agree, were entirely driven by disinterested considerations of scholarship. I hope that I have not let her down.

RWI
Folkingham and Llanilar

Introduction

Crime, punishment and history

It might be gratifying, particularly in view of the quantity of literature which the interest in the history of the criminal justice system has produced over the last thirty years, to be able to begin this text with a statement of the singular significance of the institution upon which it is centred. Yet Carmarthen gaol does not readily surrender to the modern reader any tokens of particular importance. In the lives of those who lived and worked there, be they prisoners or staff, it was, of course, the location of events of utmost moment – a place where people were born, died, gained and lost status, suffered and sang. The reader will, however, probably expect a little more than a recital of the evidence of those individual events, and for this reason might wish to be offered a distinctive claim, a celebrated event, a famous voice to draw attention to the gaol of a market town in south-west Wales. Carmarthen gaol, however, would not, in the period which this study covers, assist in such a venture. It was not the purpose-built laboratory for a particular penal regime, as was Pentonville. It was not the site of a national scandal, like Birmingham or Leicester. Its governors were not invited to attend significant inquiries as did, say, those of Bristol or Wakefield. Unlike Coldbath Fields, its treadwheel was not carefully engraved to survive through time as an enduring image of past practice. It produced no celebrated chaplain, like Clay of Preston, nor famously articulate prisoners like Michael Davitt or Oscar Wilde: its only noted poetic inhabitant in these years earned his money as a collier and wrote in a language incomprehensible, I dare suggest, to most readers of this book.[1] It was not visited by Dickens or by Mayhew, indeed it was in the last group to be visited by the Prison Inspector for the Southern and Western District when that post was created in 1835. Through its doors, the records reveal, passed a succession of short, sallow-complexioned stealers of clothes and cooking utensils, of drinkers and of tradesmen who could not pay their debts. The treadwheel turned, the prison loaves and gruel were eaten. Carmarthen gaol was not a model institution, nor even a particularly exciting one.

Why then write a book about this prison, or a book which (for this is a truer reflection of its purpose), though it may venture outside, will keep returning to the experience of incarceration in Carmarthen? There is no shortage of books on imprisonment in the nineteenth century, nor are those which do exist all bad, or misguided. As will be considered later, these books are written from a variety of theoretical standpoints and address a variety of different institutions. Indeed the extent of the literature is such that it has now become almost obligatory for an author to comment on the historiography of the subject before presenting his or her own work, a practice not entirely ignored in this text. So academically entrenched has the study of the nineteenth-century prison become that there are now schools of thought to be vindicated, reconciled or dismissed. The history of penal practice in that period now has to accommodate the history of the history of that practice if it is to have academic credibility. It is legitimate to ask who, apart (reviewers and minimal sales permitting) from the author and publisher, wants another book on Victorian imprisonment.

There is certainly a degree of human interest in crime and in its punishment, an interest which is evidenced by its creation as a popular contemporary fictional genre. It may be remarked in passing that not the least interesting of the development in penal affairs occurring in the period covered by this book is the entry of the criminal, and particularly the sentenced prisoner, into many a middle-class drawing room. I have in mind here not simply the journalism of Mayhew but the development of fictional form in the Victorian age.[2] It is a convict who surprises both Pip and the reader in the first chapter of *Great Expectations*; the opening of Wilkie Collins's novel, *The Legacy of Cain*, takes the form of observations by a prison governor; the barbarities of transportation were revealed by Marcus Clarke, those of unchecked local prison administration (a point to which we will of course return) by Charles Reade; the ticket-of-leave system was examined in drama by Tom Taylor, Millbank penitentiary in paint by William Frith.[3] The list could be extended. Yet to highlight the interest is not to explain it, and perhaps that is beyond my powers.

Certainly the extremes of human behaviour and emotion – of greed, lust, anger, desperation and the like – may erupt into crime, and the exploration of those extremes may prove attractive to the artist. Perhaps the respectable reader takes comfort in that respectability when the prison gate closes on the fictional malefactor. Fiction gives distance to the important but unpleasant elements of life; it contains, imprisons, what we fear in others and perhaps in ourselves. It also provides a point of intersection between those who have and can use power (in modern terms we might say 'the state', but for reasons which will become obvious I am reluctant to use that term without explanation here) against those who have none, or those who have abused what they possess. Such a significant moral conjunction can again be addressed and exemplified in fiction.

This concept of 'interest', whatever its roots, is notable because it is selective, and that selectivity has implications for historiography. There must be some reason why the historiography of crimes and punishments (like the subject matter of crime fiction) is skewed towards the more serious end of the spectrum. It cannot be explained entirely by the survival of records (though their geographical location may play a part), though it is true that pre-nineteenth-century petty sessions documentation is often elusive.[4] In the quarter sessions boxes sorted in researching this book some of the offences which occur with monotonous regularity in the 1860s and 1870s are connected with what would nowadays be termed road traffic offences – driving a cart without the use of reins, obstructing the highway, failing to have the name of the cart's owner painted on the side. Yet these offences remain unexplored in academic literature, as do their punishments. Let it not be thought that this is simply because these are recently created crimes, for an important aspect of the criminal law in the nineteenth century was its massive expansion into previously untouched areas. The historiography of criminal justice tells us, from a very early period, much more about felony than misdemeanour, much more about the 'Bloody Code' or the sentence of transportation than it ever does about the fine or the recognizance to keep the peace. It is perhaps unnecessary to state that outside the realm of criminal law itself important elements of the history of power, gender and poverty are structured by land law, commercial law, laws of inheritance and the like. Whilst important work has been and continues to be done by scholars in these areas they are not so numerous as the historians of crime and punishment. The Machinery Acts for the imposition of taxes and the commercial law judgments of Scrutton LJ will never attract an avalanche of scholars, though their social significance is considerable. We like to look at crime, and we like that crime to be serious. These things fascinate us.

It is of course possible to seek to justify the concentration on serious crime, even though the imbalance it creates in perception is less easily defended. This is, one distinguished commentator assures us, 'mainstream crime', the things that contemporaries 'generally had in mind when they talked about crime'.[5] And indeed it was: the events of a murder and its hanging brought together (quite literally – until the middle classes began to make their excuses and leave – in the execution crowd) people of all walks of life. But the 'reality' of petty crime and its punishment was palpable too. People talked about and feared very minor theft in nineteenth-century Carmarthenshire. The loss of washing from the hedge upon which it was drying could be a very serious matter for a household struggling with grinding poverty and in a village which operated generally on an assumption of a degree of trust in its inhabitants' conduct. As will be seen in the next chapter, the phenomenon of wrongdoing was a matter which might impact upon community expectations and norms, not merely upon victims' rights. Nor is the fine imposed on an errant carter or the drunken labourer to be disregarded as trivial, particularly if an employer saw it as a reason to discharge his servant into unemployment. It was said, perhaps with some exaggerations but, as we shall see, with a conviction that demands some respect, that the inhabitants of Carmarthenshire would 'rather die than enter the workhouse'.[6] A 'minor' financial penalty or a few days' imprisonment, which could tarnish 'character' (which was conceived of as given by others, not intrinsic to the self) and therefore jeopardize earning capacity, might make the difference between financial survival and institutionalization of an entire family in the Union workhouse. This is not a trivial matter. The 'interest' which inheres in a study of serious offending can lead us astray.

These considerations lead to a further important feature of the history of crime and punishment, which may reveal another reason for the 'interest' to which the subject as a whole gives rise in academic discourse. For it invites reflection on the use of punishment by those who have power (*ex hypothesi*, for all punishment is an exercise of power, and state punishment is the exercise of power institutionalized and legitimated) upon those who, for the most part, do not. Such a position has been the starting point for some powerful explorations of the use of the criminal law as a weapon of class interest. The literature includes, for example, interesting analyses of 'social crime', important offences like smuggling and poaching, which have contrasted the different perceptions of the lawmaker and the lawbreaker as to which activities might be labelled 'right' or 'wrong'.[7] The 'social crime' discourse has rightly drawn attention to cases in which 'official' and 'popular' normative structures may be in conflict. Yet the position may be more complicated than that. In the next chapter it will be seen that, even where 'popular' and 'official' norms coincided in condemnation of behaviour, the issue of the *priority* of the appropriate punitive agency might still be a live one in Victorian rural Wales. In the nineteenth-century progression towards uniformity – defined laws, impartially administered, resulting in predictable punishment – there was no scope for crime, and certainly not serious crime, to be addressed by self-help, 'vigilante' action, or negotiated compromise. But these elements had long inhered within traditions of decentralized response to antisocial activity, and they were unlikely to disappear quickly or uniformly in a jurisdiction which contained such diverse communities as the slum areas of industrial Manchester and the hill farms of west Wales. The complexity of such relationships demands attention.[8]

An associated point to that of crime and punishment being used as evidence of class interest is that often it is only through legal records that access is available to the words and lives of a whole body of individuals which otherwise would have been lost to us. Whilst the principle of 'less-eligibility' was much voiced in the period covered by this book, that is to say the principle that the incarcerated malefactor should enjoy no greater privilege than his law-abiding brother outside, it is ironic that the privilege of historical survival favours the former. We know that William Evans was no stranger to the law in the 1860s, that his illiterate daughter Sarah had, in 1862 when aged eleven, a 'dark gypsy-like' expression, and that his fourteen-year-old son John was 4 ft 7½ in. tall two years later. We know this because all were at different times remanded to Carmarthen gaol.[9] We know what George Adams, a forty-five-year-old 'rag gatherer and gentleman's servant', looked like in July 1864 because his photograph appears in the prison register.[10] It is improbable that Adams had been photographed before and most unlikely that he was photographed again, for he died within four days of Governor Stephens's capturing both him and his image. We know exactly what every prisoner was supposed to have had for every meal on 24 September 1850 because this was prescribed by the dietary recorded by the Prison Inspector.[11] We know that James Hargrave declined to have a haircut on 22 September 1846, that John Wilson had a piece of cheese in his pocket on the 8th of that month.[12] We know the kind of abuse which might be traded in an argument between women in 1878 because their hasty words are preserved in witness depositions.[13] Of course, as will be shown later, we cannot become complacent about such 'knowledge'. We do not know, for sure, whether the man who called himself 'James Hargrave' was telling the truth, we do not know whether he received his full allowance of food and certainly not how he felt about it.[14] But there remains more evidence than if none of these individuals had brushed up against the law. It may be an overstatement to apply the maxim of forensic science 'every contact leaves a trace', but at least we have some traces.

Such traces of course survive because of the bureaucratization of punishment which will form such an important part of the analysis offered in this book. This too leads perhaps to another reason why writing on crime and punishment has been so popular with historians and also why it has taken the direction that it has. Crime, particularly serious crime, has left copious records, and from the nineteenth century onwards so has the practice of imprisonment. Gaolers, surgeons, chaplains, Visiting Justices, prison inspectors, government committees, journalists and others have left a weight of printed and manuscript evidence for historians to examine. The evidence is not only copious, it is generally legible and almost always in English. This is not to suggest that to write nineteenth-century penal history is easy: interpretation and the construction of any good history is a difficult business. It remains true, though, that the writing of nineteenth-century penal history has a number of practical advantages over the writing of, say, thirteenth-century penal history. Yet the proliferation of academic writing thereby invited brings its own challenges, for each author's interpretation will be considered against a corpus of existent discourse. Across the mighty plains of academe some pretty impressive specimens wander – those writers whose schema of analysis sets an agenda for those who follow. The new author will often find him- or herself sitting like an oxpecker on the back of those creatures, perhaps loosening a few patches of hide here and there but leaving the whole largely untroubled. Or he or she might approach more as a predator, out to destroy the theoretical paradigm. One option which it is naive for the author to adopt is to ignore these creatures altogether. Thus penal history now involves not only an appreciation of the factual discoveries of the historian's predecessors. It becomes necessary to discuss 'Theory'. Such a discussion may irritate or perplex the reader whose interest in the endless disputes of academics is limited. He or she may prefer to ignore the next section, though for others it will be essential.

Penal history and penal theory

S. F. C. Milsom once memorably compared the writing of legal history to the child's game of joining the dots.[15] What brings the evidence (the dots) together is of course interpretation, and interpretation is not in its nature a neutral process: the line is not the dot (indeed, the dot is of course not really the dot, not merely a simple 'given'; the recording, recovery and understanding of all information in itself requires interpretation – but let that pass for a moment). In an academic text, interpretative schemes become articulated, and the articulation constitutes theory and theory demands a position. It is probably no longer possible to write scholarly prison history without engaging in a review of the various theoretical positions propounded by others and locating oneself in the spectrum: certainly it is to risk the wrath of the academic reviewer so to do.[16] Yet this is not the place to engage in a comprehensive discussion of the theories of others, for the reader would be better employed in reading those theories directly (if he or she has not done so already) than in risking the smoke and mirrors of précis and selective quotation. It is hoped, however, that the few comments to be found here will give an indication of the nature of modern penal-historical discourse, in particular that important and controversial branch of it which has concerned itself with the nature of and motivation for penal change. The approach taken to such matters in the present volume will be discovered in the book as a whole, however, rather than within a few sentences.

A 'presentist' analysis, one (that is) which looks back from the present day relating penal change to its linear progression to the present, is as understandable as it is indefensible. It is understandable, *inter alia*, in that its architectural manifestation – the prison building – continues to dominate both modern penal discourse and urban topography. The continued use of prison buildings from the nineteenth century, a fact which allows the adjective 'Victorian' free range in journalistic accounts of contemporary experience, provides a more familiar image of incarceration than more recent constructions have ever achieved. Moreover, prison remains, as it became in the nineteenth century, the focal point of analysis of the modern state penal programme – and this despite the relatively recent proliferation of non-custodial options within that programme. Yet the moral component associated with presentist analysis of history in its most extreme form, that which sees the teleological unfolding of events as a movement from darkness into light, from barbarism to humanity, is particularly difficult to apply to penal history. The continued modern 'crisis' in the prisons (if a condition which has been so termed for so long has not forfeited the right to be called a 'crisis') argues against any complacent idea of a beneficent social evolution. Nor is a benign interpretation of history available to one who, if he or she is willing to examine the evidence of practice rather than the rhetoric of reform, seeks to distance the problems of the present day from a golden age which has been lost; who sees prisons, like other decaying elements of British infrastructure such as railways and sewers, as magnificent in their own day but unable to accommodate the reality of the present. True, the Victorian penal system did not, as did earlier versions, employ blinding and mutilation as judicial punishments, but it did employ prison regimes in which men sometimes blinded or mutilated themselves to escape the pain of labour discipline. The story of penal history cannot be seen simply as one in which far-sighted reformers overturn atavistic cruelty in favour of stern but kind correction. There is probably no penal historian who would now subscribe to such a monochrome assessment.[17]

So is everyone now a 'revisionist', as those are called whose theories reject the ideas of benignity and progress associated with penal change which are still, bizarrely, labelled 'traditionalist'?[18] There are monochrome revisionists as well as monochrome 'traditionalists', and their theories, though they may give insights, need not command unqualified acceptance. There are also different varieties of 'revisionism' to demand attention. A Marxist interpretation would see the criminal law as an instrument of class control[19] and the prison as a particularly appropriate means of its enforcement.[20] There is something peculiarly seductive in the argument that it is only with industrial capitalism that time becomes an asset, something to be 'spent' or 'wasted' and something which could be, by incarceration, forfeited to and confiscated by those, or in the interests of those, who otherwise regulated the time of the labouring poor. Yet such an analysis has grave difficulties to face. For the law might be invoked by those who had very little in the way of material possessions or economic power, although as will be seen in the next chapter it may be wiser to say that *some* of the law was invoked by *some* of these people, for there are a range of different responses to a range of proscribed behaviours. Moreover, although conceptions of time undoubtedly undergo historical change (as work and leisure practices, the greater use of the timepiece and the railway timetable, amongst other factors, produce their effects), there is a whole history of pre-industrial imprisonment, the principal casualty of which remains not time but liberty. The constant repetition of the falsehood (one which has probably arisen because of the distorting effect of the dominance of serious-crime concern in penal historiography) that imprisonment as a punitive measure is a modern invention, does not make that falsehood true. It would certainly not have been accepted as such by those who were themselves caught up in the 'penal revolution'.[21] The penalty for one who repeatedly took salmon illegally was a term of imprisonment not only in 1885 but also 600 years earlier.[22]

That said, there is no difficulty at all in seeing class bias and economic inequality in nineteenth-century law (indeed it would take wilful blindness to ignore it), nor of seeing differences in the use of and rationale behind imprisonment within that period when compared with its earlier employment. These themes will emerge again in the following chapters. Yet if class relations pervade and organize social structure in the nineteenth as in the eighteenth century, they are not the only form of relations which exist, nor can they explain the totality of social structure.

Perhaps more popular in the current climate than Marxist or neo-Marxist analysis has been the work of Michel Foucault. Foucault's *Discipline and Punish* has been a most influential text, so influential indeed that the text itself rather than prisons it describes seems to have become the primary focus of attention of some writers in recent years. Foucault's thesis concentrates on the technology of discipline, and argues that the strategy which underlay the direction of penal change was '... not to punish less but to punish better; to punish with an attenuated severity perhaps, but in order to punish with more universality and necessity; to insert the power to punish more deeply into the social body'.[23] In David Garland's assessment, 'Penality is revealed as having an internal and intimate relationship with power, rather than being its occasional instrument or ally.'[24] Foucauldian analysis sees disciplinary regulation, fuelled by the information which it itself provides, as spreading through the body politic not only via the prison but also through the hospital, asylum, school and other such institutional constructs. Such brief statements may be less than clear to those readers who are not familiar with Foucauldian analysis, and will certainly be less than satisfying for those who are, but for the moment let them hint at the thesis of this complex and layered text.

Foucault's analysis has not escaped criticism, both on grounds of deficiencies in its handling of empirical evidence and, more theoretically, on the basis that for Foucault the issue of the exercise of power is insufficiently related to the identification of those who exercise it and the reaction of those upon whom it is exercised.[25] This lack of specificity in the discussion of both agents and objects of penal change courts the danger of suppressing reasons for actions and resistances to those actions, the narrative becoming thereby determinist and unilinear. Whilst arguments over Foucault will continue, no doubt, for a considerable time, there are important elements in his analysis – the identification of the important drive towards the secure identification and categorization of offenders in the penal complex and the insistence that the prison should not be viewed in isolation from other institutions – which will find echoes in this work. Nonetheless, the principal concern here is with precisely the issues of resistance, with practical problems of enforcement and with the dilemmas of discretion which the smooth lines of theoretical analysis may ignore. Even a 'revisionist' account which fails to give due account of such features must remain haunted by the spectre of Whiggism, for it will be history written from the perspective of the winners.

Such tokenism will not satisfy the committed theoretician. Big theory is always falsifiable by small detail. William Ian Miller has perceptively observed that 'It is a trait of great works to be able to be proven wrong in particular and still manage to offer a truth about the larger picture that would not have been achievable if all the particulars had been right. Many feel such is the case with Freud and Foucault.'[26] This latter himself robustly countered an objection to his use of Bentham's unbuilt Panopticon as an explanatory metaphor for nineteenth-century penality:

> if I had wanted to describe 'real life' in the prisons, I wouldn't indeed have gone to Bentham. But the fact that this real life isn't the same thing as the theoretician's schemes doesn't entail that these schemes are therefore utopian, imaginary etc. One could only think that if one had a very impoverished notion of the real.[27]

The point is an important one. Careful local studies such as those of De Lacy and Zedner have shown that nineteenth-century penal changes were neither consistent nor unilinear. Zedner's observation that 'Evidence from establishments other than a few model penitentiaries suggests that, well after mid-century, the operation of penal policy remained multi-faceted, often contradictory and always problematic'[28] is so obviously true that it does not require the evidence of the present book to exemplify it. Yet it is paradoxically true that the continual accumulation of information about the particular may lead us, if we are not careful, to shift our focus to such an extent as to ignore wider changes, philosophies and perceptions against which, as Foucault's words above indicate, the local experience is to be read and against which it is to be measured. The discourse (to employ that usefully soft-edged term) of prison reform and of reaction was too important a social and intellectual matter, too deeply embedded in the politics and literature of the nineteenth century, to allow us to believe that a 'true' history of the Victorian penal experience is to be gathered simply by the collation of local detail, any more than a 'true' history of religion is to be obtained from the binding together of all the guidebooks to parish churches which are on sale at the tables near their fonts. Michael Ignatieff, in his well-known reconsideration of the extremes of a revisionist position which he had previously espoused, warned of the danger of retreating too far from the rhetoric and concentration on the model institution. 'A counter-revisionist account', he argues, 'which considers only the local institutions which went on the same as before will miss what contemporaries knew had to be explained about their own age.'[29] Whilst Ignatieff's principal period of study precedes that which is undertaken here, a similar need for balance seems necessary in the analysis of the period up to nationalization, in which the tension between projection and reality repeatedly expresses itself in the wording of legislation, committee recommendations and inspectors' reports. Such tension is, in short, not merely an incidental fact but a central issue. The task of this book is not simply to reveal it but to explore it. Yet to do so involves not simply looking at the evolution of penal thought and practice but also at wider questions: the limitations of rules and records and the transitions in the nature and capability of law, government and the nation state.

The 'penal revolution' revisited

It is tempting not to analyse yet again here the transition from corporal to carceral penality which has been identified by so many authors as marking the difference between eighteenth- and nineteenth-century models of punishment. The proposed dichotomy certainly contains an important truth, one too important to be undermined here. Yet the dualism is overstated, and the reasons advanced for it (which are of course the most important parts of the analysis) remain controversial. As has been suggested earlier, an undue concentration upon the most serious offences has downplayed the enduring, though not static, use of non-corporeal sanctions – financial penalties, or their threat (as in, for example, a binding over to keep the peace) in respect of minor crime, and also indeed the long history of incarceration itself in gaols or houses of correction. Moreover, the existence throughout the nineteenth century of the possibility of hanging (notwithstanding that after 1868 it took place inside the walls of the prison), even though it was relatively rarely used, marks not simply an overlooked atavistic survival but a symbolic representation of the final power of the law, the abolition of which had been actively and success-fully opposed throughout the century. Had a descendant of the regicide Damiens, whose grisly death in 1757 is taken by Foucault as an exemplification of the *ancien régime*'s 'theatre of cruelty', been convicted of murdering Queen Victoria in 1857, he too would have died. Admittedly, and the concession is important to the tenor of Foucault's argument, he would have died without the use of pincers or horses, being instead strangled, perhaps slowly, but he would have been just as dead as Damiens. Of course it is true that more people were hanged in the mid-eighteenth century than the mid-nineteenth, but if numbers alone were conclusive of penal significance we would have much more literature on the punish-ment for drunkenness or weights-and-measures offences than upon homicide or street robbery. For this reason the argument in favour of a major transformation must involve, if it is to convince, more than a simple enumeration of the dead.

Yet there was indeed a penal shift from corporal to carceral measures which began during the beginning of the latter part of the eighteenth century and was completed at some point in the nine-teenth. That latter point remains to be determined, and its determination is one of the underlying questions within this book; but it will be suggested that the transformation becomes complete not with the construction of a particular penitentiary, but with the integration of local prisons into a national system, with the suppression of geographical autonomy in the administration of justice and punishment. For a moment, however, the essence of the change must be investigated. Prison moved to the centre of peno-logical debate and became, in theory at any rate, a predictable, more or less uniform response to a wide variety of crimes. Not only hanging but other corporal punishments – stocks, the pillory, whipping – were either discontinued entirely or more rarely and selectively applied. How can this be explained?

It is not necessary to choose between individual initiatives and wider social movements to explain penological change, for both have their parts to play. Individual actors, if they are not to remain isolated eccentrics, must work within, and will have been worked upon by, the cultural possibilities of their time. On the other hand, 'Industrial Capitalism' or 'Power / Knowledge' never – as purely abstract entities – drafted legislation or calculated prison dietaries. It seems reasonable to accept, as do Ignatieff and Garland, for example, that both biography and historical sociology have roles to play in the understanding of the penological shift, though the explanatory weight allocated to each will remain a point of contention for historians. John Howard, for example, is a notable figure in the narrative of transition of which we speak. His work may have come at a particular time in which his ideas may be seen to have fallen on fertile ground, indeed, we may go so far as to assert that they encapsulate some of the dominant ideology of that time. But the stubborn, vegetarian Howard, plunging into ever more dangerous locations in pursuit of a martyr's death, is not merely a cipher through which social forces pass unmediated, any more than is the bullying, manipulative Edmund Du Cane who sits on the other side of the penological divide a century later.[30]

That having been said, it is necessary to look beyond the personalities to establish other motive powers of change. Howard's name could be, and was, invoked by men eager to display Enlightenment values, so directly, indeed, that the dominant image presented of Howard had him taking a lamp into the darkness of the gaols, bearing the purifying light of both science (in particular medicine) and religion.[31] The man may have been unique, but the underlying concerns were cultural, even fashionable. The legal historian John Beattie sees Howard and his fellow reformer Hanway as providing not only a 'program of further development' but also 'justifications and explanations' for an increased use of imprisonment when that process had already begun.[32] This trend, he suggests, had started even before the suspension of the sentence of transportation by the American War of Independence, which suspension produced such problems in respect of the disposition of criminals whose offences had not attracted the death sentence but were held deserving of some substantial punishment.[33] If Beattie's argument is correct then

Howard's role in the process of transition indeed falls to be reassessed. Yet it does not, as Beattie acknowledges, become unimportant. Howard and Hanway could provide the programme, the positive prospectus for incarceration as a potentially socially beneficial sanction which could, in an age in which intellectuals called for scientific analysis and for progress, justify an extension of its use.

It is in a combination of this positive prospectus and the more negative status of the prison (taken to comprise both the county gaol and house of correction) that an important insight into the penal shift is to be found. By 'negative status' is meant that the gaol could be important precisely because of what it was not. Specifically it was not capital or corporal punishment or transportation, the difficulties attached to the use of all of which will require further consideration shortly. Certainly the changing use of imprisonment needs to be explained. Incarceration was certainly not a new penalty in the 1770s, but it was and is in some ways a difficult one. Unlike many other forms of punishment it requires, in any developed form, significant infrastructure and technology which may involve costs and inconveniences which may not all be recoverable from the offender him or herself. The functional paradox of incarceration needs to be explored a little further, though this will involve a departure from the traditional preoccupation of penal historiography in favour of a few paragraphs which may strike some readers as laughably reductivist.

Punishment has, as a practice of social group, a rather limited portfolio of objects (in the simple sense of 'interests or assets which are operated upon'), though it will have a more extensive set of objectives (in the sense of 'states or conditions which it is intended should be achieved by its infliction'). In respect of the latter it may be noted that one of the attractions of incarceration, one which was exploited within the nineteenth century, was the ease with which the institution might be theoretically aligned to suit competing, even contrasting ideologies, as evidenced by the swings between rationales of reformation and deterrence. But the *objects* of penality remain limited – the deprivation of some good possessed by the punished (in the paradigm case this will be the offender): life, bodily security, material wealth, liberty, labour, reputation or society (in the sense of the community of one's fellows). Eschatological punishment – the threat of the damnation of the soul – may be a powerful threat and may form part of a mechanism of social control, but at least in the western Christian tradition it is not within human power to impose.[34] Two further points should also be made. The deprivation of society has been referred to as a form of penality, and I have in mind a historically common form of punishment – expulsion. Yet the penality of expulsion seems rather different from the other forms of deprivation mentioned. It is true that banishment, a penalty which in the Middle Ages in England was called abjuration of the realm but later, and with rather different procedures and organization, was known as transportation, may be seen as the deprivation of the association with known people, places and ways of life. But it has another dimension (more akin in this respect to capital punishment) which blurs the line between object and objective. Banishment moves the offender outside the concern of the expelling society. More important than the repayment of the social debt is the cancellation of the banking arrangement. In its simplest form, banishment concerns itself simply with the matter of 'expulsion from' the punishing society, the destination of the offender being immaterial. Yet in more complex social arrangements the focus of concern changes to consider the perspective of 'expulsion to'. In relatively static and close-knit communities in which people are typically connected by webs of familial and economic knowledge and strangers may be viewed with suspicion, 'expulsion from' may perhaps be sufficient. In more mobile, less integrated social arrangements, and those in which relations with other communities have become more important, a knowledge than an offender has not simply gone, but has gone to a defined and preferably distant location, may be more satisfying.

The second point to be made is that the various penal objects are not mutually exclusive. Loss of reputation in particular is very often to be found as a concomitant of other forms of punishment. Forced labour may be conjoined with loss of liberty in a sentence of imprisonment and hard labour, or with loss of society in a sentence of transportation to work in the colonies (it is in this combination perhaps that the classic sentence of transportation most differs from mere exile). Nonetheless the point remains that there are a finite number of penal possibilities (in terms of objects to be addressed rather than the details of the manner of that address), and all of these were well known by the end of the eighteenth century.

If a paradigm shift in penality did in fact occur (the conditional is used here simply to remind the reader of the danger of underestimating continuities in penal practice which has been adverted to earlier) between the eighteenth and the nineteenth centuries, it remains to explain why the shift was in the direction of a carceral system which in its architecture, maintenance and staffing demanded substantial economic investment. The impressive new gaols built, like that in Carmarthen, from the end of the eighteenth century – enduring visible landmarks of local governmental responsibility – are (unlike the scaffold and cart, or stake and whip) evidence of a prosperous society. Indeed, the society which produced them was a prosperous one. In the period from 1780 to 1860 British national income per head doubled, though it need hardly be said that the economic increase did not benefit all sectors of society to a similar extent.[35] But wealth alone does not account for the rise of the prison. There are other, more appealing ways of demonstrating national (we must return to this word) affluence and the confidence which it carries with it than the building of gaols. Again both the negative and positive penological developments which throw up the triumph of the prison must be considered.

Let us begin with the negative, that is with the decline in use of other penal measures directed at other penal objects The complex narrative of the withdrawal from capital punishment has been brilliantly addressed by Gattrell, and I will not rehearse his analysis here. Drawing from the work of both Foucault and Norbert Elias, Gattrell acknowledges that the analysis of change is a complex one: 'Causes were multiple, and only rash historians would privilege material or political or cultural causes without interrelating all three.'[36] A confident government power, a learned sensibility articulated by the middle classes and the element of political opportunity all played a part in the eventual reform of the system of hanging in the 1830s. So, importantly, did the prospect, as successful prosecution of crime became more common, of the spectacle of execution becoming either an ever-diminishing and increasingly arbitrary consequence of conviction or, if it were to be uniformly inflicted, of an unacceptable degree of judicial carnage. The process is a complex one, and the existence of the rhetoric of humanitarianism should not seduce us into the acceptance of a simple 'revolt against barbarism' as explanatory of penal change. In the same way, the withdrawal from the penalties of public whipping and the pillory (though private whipping was to re-emerge in the hasty Security against Violence Act in 1863) should not be unthinkingly attributed to a 'refinement of manners', a phrase which at most may describe but not explain.

Consider too the other major penalty for serious crime, transportation. Though not abolished as a sentence until 1857 and as a practice until some ten years after that, it was the suspension of the penalty with the outbreak of the American War in 1776 that moved the government to reposition its stance on convicts, through its enforced financial responsibility for the hulks. Even explanations which rely on single causes should be questioned. It was noted above that Beattie has argued that transportation was declining in popularity and being replaced by carceral punishment *before* the war. Taking all the evidence together there remains a proposition easier to affirm than to explain. The penal system, and in particular the objects considered appropriate targets for state action, seem to have been subject to a re-examination which began in the last three decades of the eighteenth century. From then until the third quarter of the nineteenth century the transition in penality may be seen as a continuing process, though one which does not correspond to the model of a simple unfolding of a grand design.

This chronology coincides with the sequence of events still, though with acknowledgement of the crudity of the labelling, termed the Industrial Revolution. It is not improbable that changes in the actuality and the perception of the economic and social base of Britain may have had an impact upon the nature of penality. It may be suggested, however, that the nature of this impact has been on occasions rather too crudely conceived. So, for example, the argument that prison is properly understood as a means of instilling labour discipline, whilst undoubtedly having some truth, is overstated if it suggests that the prison is merely the handmaid to the factory.[37] Certainly there are important grounds for reading the history of both institutions together, and not only in respect of their contemporary connection in the programmes of important individuals like the Benthams, but also more generally in relation to the practical and theoretical importance of structured labour and of its measurement. It will become clear in what follows that, certainly within the nineteenth century, the drive for uniformity of 'product' is evident not only within the factory, the transition from the 'workmanship of chance' to the 'workmanship of precision' being an underlying dynamic in penology as much as in manufacture.[38] As early as 1830 Henry Booth had hailed 'the mechanical principle, the philosophy of the nineteenth century'.[39] Once this underlying dynamic is appreciated, then the fact that one of those closely involved with that celebration of the social benefits of mechanical production which was the Great Exhibition of 1851 was Sir Edmund Du Cane, who later superintended the transition to a nationalized prison system, seems by no means insignificant. Yet despite the relationship between the structure of the convict regime and the inculcation of labour discipline there is a danger in seeing the development of the prison as being merely an adjunct to the changing physical rigidity of methods of production. For one thing, it can be argued that in terms of its pervasiveness the prison was rather more successful by the mid-nineteenth century than was the factory (at least in the common understanding of this latter term).[40] Moreover, in the debates specifically devoted to penal reform, and these were legion within this period, it is difficult to ascribe an opinion to 'business' conceived of as a whole. If the prison's relation to capitalism is construed as breaking the resistance of labour to factory discipline, then we might expect a rather more direct involvement from those who ran the factories. Yet none of these arguments should distract us from the reality of the enormous significance of the changes associated with the revolution in Britain's economic base.

Demographic and social factors and penal structure

Economic and social changes may have contributed to the transition in the matrix of penality in a rather different way from that outlined above. In the explanation suggested here some observations will be offered on very general trends, in a volume which will for the most part discuss the contingent and particular. This is done, moreover, in an area in which even the most skilled economic historians have difficulty in establishing hard data, let alone interpreting it. Yet it is submitted that these factors have been underestimated in most formulations of the history of penal transformation, though they do not wholly explain it. It remains true, despite the broader argument that will be advanced here, that when Howard first produced a vision of positive imprisonment it was science and religion which informed him, not the projection of demographic change. Moreover, in the next chapter it will be argued that such change is neither uniform in its extent nor consistent in its effects. The more specific consideration of demographic and social factors undertaken there will bring to light particular problems and tensions which are apparent within the processes of that transformation. Some very broad observations are necessary at the outset.

There are notable and significant demographic changes in the period which witnessed penal change. Population was increasing: one study suggests that it rose between 1771 and 1871 from around 6.5 million to 21.5 million. Not only did the population grow but it became increasingly urbanized. By 1851 the urban population of Britain had for the first time overtaken the rural, and an important factor in that urban growth was rural emigration, a near constant feature between the 1770s and 1870s. Moreover, those most obviously represented in this emigration were young adults, following the 'urban job pull'. This expansion of the cities did not go unremarked by contemporaries, and as the census provided figures throughout the nineteenth century, the growth of population was clearly empirically demonstrable.[41] Yet even those, like Cobbett, who were unimpressed by the statistics were aware of the changes taking place in the countryside through which they moved.[42] At the same time canal building, road improvement and then, most dramatically, the railway revolution made such movement of both persons and goods easier and cheaper, ultimately changing definitively the understanding of 'relational space', whilst the growth of overseas trade and an increase in shipping did the same for travel abroad.[43]

Some considerable caution is needed here. Firstly, as has been indicated, significant events within the penal transformation occurred at the beginning of this process of growth and urbanization, which cannot have been predicated upon it. That said, the link between demographics, social policy and crime was notably forged by Malthus at the end of the eighteenth century itself.[44] Moreover, the earlier expansion of London may to an extent have operated as a model from which understandings of the nature of crime and reactions to it may have been transferred to the country as a whole. It would not be the only time that metropolitan experience, the experience familiar to those who made and adjudicated the most serious of the penal laws, would influence national policy. Yet political power, even at the accession of Victoria, still had roots in land and agriculture rather than the city street, and it is easy to overstate the importance of the 'urban' for many of the towns so classified in the 1851 census were small, and might be, as Carmarthen was, far from insulated from rural practice and rural mentality.[45] So too it is tempting to assume that notions of geographical mobility change earlier and more radically than was the case – the 1840s was surely the most drastic decade for change in this respect. What follows, then, is merely the delineation of some underlying factors which undoubtedly had an impact on conceptions of crime and punishment in the period covered by this book and which it may be profitable to consider in respect of the major realignment of penality in the period which preceded it. To look for explanatory layers at such a deep level is not, however, intended to replace the detailed analysis of particular changes. Yet such factors as major population growth are not insignificant in altering social relationships, and punishment is a form of relationship. Whilst the details of the demographic trends may be open to debate, the general pattern of such social dynamics is evident. It merits some consideration.

What effects if any did such changes have on methods of punishment? Certainly we will see that demographic factors were discussed in contemporary debates about the nature and extent of criminality and the measures required to combat it. The link with the employment of particular forms of punishment is a rather more elusive one. It would be possible to argue that the impact may have been indirect, in the sense that the result of such significant sociological change was simply an increase in crime. The evidence relating to patterns of criminality in the later eighteenth and nineteenth centuries, and the difficulties in interpreting that evidence, have been admirably discussed elsewhere and will not be revisited here. Nor is it intended to examine the complex question of the nature of the causal, or aetiological, link between changing economic and social patterns and the occurrence of crime upon which link such an argument would depend. The focus here is specifically with the matter of changes in punishment. Such an argument as that advanced above then would maintain that the impact of concern about rising crime rates (and the argument could at this point be joined also by those who are sceptical as to the evidence of rising crime, or of its connection to changes in material culture or both, for the dominant motor of penal change now becomes perception) upon the nature of punishment was to look for newer methods to control malefactors in the face of evidence that the old had failed. Certainly there was much use made of the rhetoric of the rising tide of criminality on many occasions throughout the century, from the general concerns about mounting committal figures in the aftermath of the Napoleonic War to more specific arguments, such as those about the threat of 'ticket-of-leave men' in the 1860s, by which time the dominance of the prison was well established.[46] Some of this rhetoric – the 1860s instance is perhaps the clearest example – undoubtedly did have a direct effect on the nature and extent of punishment meted out to offenders. Yet it is interesting to note that the recognition of difficulty of measuring the true extent of criminality in the country was itself one of the more significant disclosures of the period of penal reform. In a most important report of that most important reforming decade, the 1830s, the matter is presented starkly:

> At the beginning of the Inquiry it became evident to us that the returns of the number of persons prosecuted or convicted, which, in the reasonings in parliament are usually assumed as correct indications of the state of crime within any given district, cannot be relied on for that purpose.[47]

Inadequate knowledge is here portrayed as one of the defects of the existing system, not as an appropriate motor of change. The drive for an increased scientific understanding of social problems was itself one of the constituent elements of the penal revolution. The revolution created the knowledge and the expert just as much as the knowledge and the expert created the revolution. It remains true, however, (as the reference to Parliament in the quotation above indicates and a perusal of, for example, the Report of the

Select Committee on Secondary Punishment of 1832 confirms) that the inadequacy of data is by no means necessarily an obstacle to influencing opinion. Moreover, the resonance of major events such as Peterloo or the Swing Riots (as later, for example, garrotting) may be thought to be more influential than merely their contribution to statistics. Emsley has argued for the existence of a climate of concern amongst the propertied classes in relation to public order throughout the period bounded by the Gordon Riots and Chartism.[48] It is suggested here that perceptions of crime as a particular problem for a society in rapid transition had a major bearing on the associated questions of how and how much to punish it.

Such an argument, however, still fails to explain the morphology of punishment, the question as to why penality took *this* form and not others. The traditional reaction to perceived lawlessness is the call for quantitatively more, not qualitatively different, punishment. Even if we accept Gattrell's argument that it might be regarded as improper or imprudent simply to kill many more people in the name of the law, the fact remains that the emergence of incarceration as the dominant penal measure marks a major realignment in the ordering of penal objects (in the sense explained earlier). Demographic factors may, however, have had an impact here.

The punishment of public whipping, which had been frequently used with a variety of non-capital offenders for a considerable time before the latter part of the eighteenth century, may be considered as an example. Whilst often classified simply as a punishment of the body, public whipping had in fact another important object upon which to operate. As Beattie recognizes:

> One common element, deliberately aimed at, was humiliation. That was the point of the punishment's being carried out in public. The shame of being whipped before people who knew the prisoner and his family was calculated to increase the terror and the effectiveness of the punishment as a discouragement of minor crime beyond the pain it inflicted.[49]

Similar considerations applied also to the pillory, in the use of which the same author discerns on occasions another purpose, 'quite simply to make [the offender's] identity known so as to forewarn potential victims'.[50] If these observations are correct, then it would seem that the efficacy of the penalty was to an extent dependent on knowledge of, or in the second instance recognition of, the offender as an individual. Such knowledge and recognition are easier in conditions of relative social stasis and intimacy than those of population flux and dislocation. It is therefore not surprising that flogging should continue longest in the armed forces and inside prison populations, where the former conditions prevail in the closed disciplinary community. The anthropologist Simon Roberts observes that shaming punishments are likely 'to assume particular importance in small face-to-face communities'.[51] It might be suggested that taken out of such communities the punishment becomes to an extent stripped of its social meaning, and appears more unambiguously as an instance of simple physical pain and as such perhaps less understandable and defensible to a 'civilized' onlooker. This transition need not be articulated at that deeper level in the rhetoric of penal reform. Shame was in any event not the only or even the most obvious element of the penalty of flogging: its very immediacy and brutality were attractive to those pressing for its revival in the later nineteenth century. Moreover, even nineteenth-century opponents still referred to the 'ignominious and indelible disgrace'[52] which accompanied it, though the 'indelibility' would seem, divorced from communal memory, increasingly attached to the offender's individual psychology. Yet the point remains that, increasingly divorced from its community context, flogging's defects, its cruelty and 'unscientific' variability, are thrown into starker relief. This may be one of the reasons why, in Gattrell's words, 'The functions of the old penal ceremony were no longer understood'.[53] The punishment, once shaming, eventually becomes shameful. Shoemaker, studying the decline in defamation litigation in London, comes to a similar conclusion. Public fame as a control mechanism is, he maintains, becoming less significant. Honour is being internalized rather than understood as a public construction, character is being redefined as an inherent rather than a given attribute.[54] It is certainly not contended that all notions of community interaction are swept away by urbanization, that the town becomes wholly and immediately an agglomeration of alienated strangers where notions of shame and public reputation are redundant.[55] Extra-legal communal punishment may, as carried out in industrial towns such as Middleton in Lancashire, lack some of the ritual trappings of rural 'ridings' (discussed in the next chapter), but its source and its motor, the breach of community rules and the assignation of community shame, are similar.[56] There is scope perhaps to consider the positioning of both the agents and audience of industrial shame as within the community of the workplace or workforce rather than, or in addition to, the community of residence, but the idea of local cultural relationship remains, at base, the same.[57] Similarly, Linebaugh's analysis of the London hanged in the 'old' penal regime is suggestive of the drama of capital punishment being performed to selected occupational groups, butchers, sailors and weavers, in the metropolis, though of course trade and residence might overlap.[58] In short, it is not the contention here that the transitions in shaming relations are either total or uncomplicated. An investigation into their precise modalities cannot be undertaken, though the particular case of rural Wales will be returned to in the next chapter. The point remains that the impact of such social changes on punishment practices helps to explain a series of developments representing, if not a complete break with the past, then at least a significant shift in paradigm.

To an extent there may be elements of such communal dislocation in the history of the decline of capital punishment too, though my comments again speak to underlying rather than immediate courses of the transition in this penalty. The scaffold is often referred to by academics as the 'theatre' of punishment, suggesting that hanging was a drama not a spectacle.[59] Such an analogy is a potent one: the hanging itself is only the 'final act' of the law. If things go according to plan, that act will be preceded by an acknowledgement of guilt by the prisoner in which the punishment will be held out as an example to others that they should avoid not only his criminal act but also his flawed life. The drama presented is in the nature of a morality play, or a *tableau vivant* of Hogarth's engravings, and its major role taken not by a random sample but by a chosen one – prosecuted, found guilty by a jury, not pardoned (a process which would involve local, 'respectable' people testifying to character). Throughout this process the criminal may be removed from the narrative if his punishment will be seen to convey the 'wrong' message. Again, however, the meaning of the drama is obscured if those who go to witness it are aware *only* of the final act – the equivalent of running through a video of a performance of *King Lear* on fast-forward to reach the bit where Gloucester's eyes are put out. When people take excursion trains to see a hanging the specificity of its ethical narrative is lost.[60] When hanging takes place almost exclusively in the midst of the urban crowd, then the possibility of identification with the victim as being part of a class (and a class from which alone the crowd itself is increasingly drawn) rather than a part of a moral, or even (in Linebaugh's sense) an occupational community, is a dangerous one. The 'example' of death was intended to be more than an *instance* of death. Its exemplary quality depended on specific forms of knowledge and understanding, forms which depended on the knowledge necessary to link the flawed life to the justified death. Such knowledge, it is true, can be conveyed in printed form, as it increasingly was, as a packaged homily for the literate consumer. Yet this is knowledge at a remove, knowledge which differs from lived experience. Without that knowledge, that sense of place (not merely in a geographical but also a social sense), the body becomes an object of curiosity, or, more alarmingly, sympathy. The well-known unease about the execution crowd which forms part of the call for reform of the capital laws is an acknowledgment of the fact that the audience have come to look but not to learn.

An objection may be made at this point. It is true that, from the origins of state regulation of crime, it is the outsider, the stranger, who is most likely to receive punishment. This certainly was the case, for example, in the Middle Ages. Yet this need not undermine the argument being made here. In a small and static society the outsider is, unless holding a defined status such as that of a merchant, *eo ipso* untrustworthy. If he chooses to remain within the community after a whipping, and there may be reasons why he may not, or may not be allowed so to do, he will be further stigmatized in local knowledge from that exemplary introduction into it. Moreover, the stranger who is hanged confirms a vital moral lesson about the dangers of renunciation of appropriate ties of kinship and locality. The hanged stranger did not know his place. But such considerations, dependent on the otherness of the stranger to confirm the unity of the community, depend on the transient and the alien remaining atypical within society. They cannot survive the recognition of such conditions as, if not universal, or even locally frequent, then at least not unusual as a general feature of social life in a more populous and more mobile nation. Moreover, as will be suggested later, the stranger might in earlier times have been punished by law because other, communal penal measures were unsuited to his position. We will have cause to reflect that such measures became less common as the social basis which underpins them decays. In the nineteenth century all men would be treated as strangers – as autonomous individuals judged on their acts, not as members of local adjudicatory and penal communities.

Transportation too is a penalty which an increase in geographical mobility served both to assist and simultaneously to undermine. As trade and Empire grow, as more ships move more people, it is possible to see the latent problems of 'transportation to' outweighing the relatively constant benefits of 'transportation from'. Again a comment only on general trends will be offered here: for the detailed history of transportation and its decline the reader should look elsewhere. Again, too, the response to these trends need not have been consistent and unilinear – the numbers of prisoners transported to Australia was increasing until 1840[61] – but the underlying obsolescence of the measure is apparent even as its use increases. The argument which connects changing views of transportation with demographic variables manifests itself in a number of respects. Firstly, as colonial territories become more internally settled and the tension between conceptions of a territory as, on the one hand, a penal colony and, on the other, as a colony with prisoners became more evident, they themselves became more vocal. Such a process began remarkably early in Maryland and Virginia, which were both opposing transportation to their territories from as early as 1670, whilst, more centrally to our concerns, opposition from Van Diemen's Land stopped the flow to that destination in 1852.[62] The transformation of the colonies was also evident in their own internal experience of and response to crime. The Molesworth Committee of 1837–8 received evidence about courts and the penal settlements *within* the penal colonies, and discussed the difference between urban and rural criminality *within* the receiving territory.[63]

Moreover, free emigration to the colonies was increasingly conceived as economically more beneficial as a means of colonization. By contrast, transportation understandably suggested comparison with other dark practices now abandoned:

The colonies planted under this system, or rather want of system, have grown up to contain a population of over 100,000 souls, half of whom are free; and the number of criminals we annually export thither has increased from a few hundred to 4,000 or 5,000, while the resources of the country have of late years been so diligently brought into action that their exports are now probably of the value of about 1,000.000 *l.*; at the same time the principles of colonization which suggested the experiment of transportation have been utterly abandoned. The slave trade and slavery itself have been abolished, and in the new settlements which have of late been made in Australia, free emigration has been looked to as the source from which the requisite labour is to be supplied, so that the penal colonies are now an anomaly in politics, and seem to require some very special case for their justification.[64]

But not only did increased communication, the mobility of capital and the familiarity of emigration affect the colonies, they also affected the imagination of those left at home. Travel away from home became less frightening per se; and transportation accordingly may have come to be understood as less punitive for the criminal. He could, moreover, less easily simply cease to exist, as the geography and social condition of his place of exile became more known in the imagination of those at home, whether families, criminal associates, or those concerned with penal policy. The distance of exile was mitigated by knowledge: the prisoner had not simply been lost, but lost to a location the economics, society, topography, animal and plant life of which were becoming more familiar. Again, such a process began early in the established American colonies. The *Annual Register* of 1767 (to take an example from a volume chosen at random) can report for the month of March that five convicts (unnamed) were transported from Gloucester, and also that a fulling mill and some cloth belonging to Captain Gillet had been lost in a flood in Hertford, New England. America was by then a place about the climate and infrastructure of which things were well known at home. In the next century a fictional seducer could use his knowledge of colonial life to insinuate himself into the affections of an exile's lover: 'You were asking me some questions about Australia. I can tell you all about that country, for I have a relation there who writes to me. And I have read all the books about it too, as it happens.'[65] Such specific knowledge of course was, as the examples show, most easily accessible to the literate, but knowledge would no doubt be disseminated to a greater or lesser extent. So too would more direct information. In 1851 the captain of the *Radiant* brings back to Carmarthenshire news of two transports, Frost and Zephaniah Williams, both 'stout and jolly in Van Diemen's Land'.[66] It is interesting to note that the Molesworth Committee suggested that the fear of removal from their homeland existed 'more particularly among the ignorant', reinforcing the point that the fear of the unknown was a potent ingredient in the sentence, but one the potency of which was diminishing. The domestic criticism of transportation which on the one hand condemned its barbarism and on the other ridiculed its luxury despite its divergent manifestations shares the same basis, in that it is predicated on the common feature of life which can be imagined.[67] Herein lie the implications of the recognition of the dimension of 'transportation to'.

There was also the fear that the prisoner may return. In popular literature from *Roderick Random* to *Great Expectations* as well as in the rhetoric of penological debate, the figure of the returned convict was the spectre at the feast. Not only might he return, but in urbanized mobile England he might merge with the crowd, a greater and more anonymous danger than before. The concern about criminal identity, a concern which is certainly evident in Carmarthenshire as well as in London, and is such an important feature of penological debate in the mid-nineteenth century, may be attributable more directly to the fear of the unknown stranger which the abolition of transportation as a penal measure did much to amplify. But the fear was not born then. The laconic entry in Carmarthen's *Felons' Register* that Thomas James was 'supposed transported from Haverfordwest in name of Cushing', or the bemused question of the county's jury foreman faced with a similar case, 'How comes he here again?', evidence a real concern.[68] In an age of mobility even the basic benefits of 'transportation from' are under threat.

The consequences of the shrinkage of the world which have been identified here all counted against transportation as a penalty. The colonizing power had become the colonial power and it would no longer confidently sweep its detritus before it. After Captain Cook revealed in the 1770s that the vast undiscovered continent which geographers had for centuries assumed to exist was no more than a myth, the world could only become smaller.[69] The solution was to turn inwards, and to seek the isolation, control and uniformity jeopardized by overseas exile in the segregation of the prison in the midst of domestic normality. The more that criminality became perceived as mobile, the more that punishment comes to be redefined as a fixative.

It is important to appreciate the limitation of this argument. As was stated, these broad demographic trends do not, on their own, explain the precise chronology or mechanics of penal change. Individual ideas, initiatives, accidents and resistances, as well as the sensibilities of class and the strategies of power may be informed by, but are not rendered redundant as explanations of transformation by such an analysis.[70] Demographics never wrote a statute. It also needs to be restated that the perceived positive benefits of incarceration have temporarily been placed in the background whilst the consideration of other penal measures has been undertaken. Yet this perception of positivity too is predicated on wider cultural understandings, and to such matters reference will be made during the course of discussion. So the idea of reliability promoted by uniformity, such a key element in the conception of social as well as mechanical engineering, could be envisaged in the prison – a closed institution – more easily than in the variability of the outside world. Ideas of psychology, of social learning, were also important in the reformulation of crime as a scientific problem susceptible to scientific analysis and amelioration, which again are techniques facilitated by the controlled environment. Moreover, the very flexibility of the prison sentence, both in its adaptability to different regimes over time and in its capacity, like the gauges and levers of some steam engine, for infinite gradation in amount to measure moral wickedness and administer moral correction, are undoubtedly characteristic of a post-Enlightenment scientific and technological mentality.[71] The argument is merely that demographic and social changes spanning the end of the eighteenth and the first half of the nineteenth century were bound to provide problems for the model of penality, dependent on elements of shame and knowledge or of moving the offender on, which had dominated English attitudes to the formal response to (serious) crime for centuries. In addition, the growing individualistic model of humanity which such changes encouraged, and which may be exemplified in the transition in the idea of 'character' from being something that was socially given to something that was individually owned (but which could be 're-formed' by circumstance, most tellingly by the system of separate confinement, the most asocial of prison regimes which so dominated the discourse of penality in the 1830s and 1840s), in turn supported the ideas of working within rather than upon the body of the offender. Just as the manifestation of vice in sex and drink was increasingly seen as inappropriate in the public street, so too was the correction of vice in whipping and hanging.[72] Yet, for the reasons stated above, that correction had to take place in a domestic not an overseas setting.

Such recognition is important in the framework of the argument which follows. Important too is the recognition that the broad social movements I have highlighted are by no means uniformly distributed throughout the British landscape. As a city, London had already experienced phenomenal growth in the sixteenth and seventeenth centuries, a factor which would account in part for the capital's position in the vanguard of penological change. Yet by the same token other areas of the country, such as rural Wales, saw change take place at a different pace. The 1839 Commission on the Constabulary took evidence on migratory criminality in which urban development was seen as harbouring malefactors. Yarborough in Lincolnshire blamed its robberies on travellers from Hull, Hull in its turn blamed robberies in its own precincts as due 'to persons coming in by the London steam-boats'.[73] Yet the commission also acknowledged rather different problems of law enforcement when offenders were too well, not too little known within highly knit communities. The problem is adverted to in the following synopsis of the Report, though the general air of mobility of both people and goods is apparent in its words:

> We have stated that nature of the evidence as to the state of general insecurity of person and property arising from the *migratory* bodies of habitual depredators and other offenders against the laws; and we have shown the general inadequacy of the security provided against offenders who are *resident* within the rural districts. We have shown in what manner the condition of peaceable inhabitants is frequently impaired by the impurity of those classes, as well as by infractions of their rights by other classes of wrong doers. We have displayed the

state of insecurity of single travellers on the main road, and of property *in transitu* on canals and the inadequacy of the protection
received by strangers or by your Majesty's subjects on the coasts
within the province of inquiry.[74]

The mobility, growth and urbanization of the population might
be increasingly acknowledged as the factors to be addressed in
formulating strategies of application of the criminal law, but
those areas in which such trends are less evident might, as we shall
see, prove more resistant to the strategies thus formulated.

Police, law and state

It is important to realize that not only punishment was changing
during this period. There is a need to place this change alongside
others with which it interrelates. There is a danger in what
follows here that factors which each demand a detailed analysis
may be reduced to a checklist of 'related subjects'. Yet it is necessary to notice elements which impact upon the history of the
prison. The discussion of the particulars of Carmarthenshire's
history which will form the basis of the following chapters will
provide a more concrete sense of the relation of the prison to these
other developments. For the moment some general observations
must suffice to sketch the broad outlines of a complicated picture.

Reference has been made earlier to matters relating to the application of the law and to the change in ideas of policing. Such a
linkage is important in the understanding of nineteenth-century
ideas of crime and its control. The administrative sophistication
and professional autonomy of their modern equivalents,
combined with the academic inclination towards research into
ever more particular areas, tempts historians to consider the
police and the prison as separate elements of the penal system. Yet
when the origins of that system are examined, such subdivision is
less justifiable. The prison and the police in their 'modern' appearance in the late eighteenth and nineteenth century are interrelated.
The modern conception (despite the evidence) of the police as
being primarily intended for the detection of crime underesti-
mates their perceived role as agents of observation and deterrence
at an earlier period, and in these attributes they echo some of the
characteristics of the new penality. When a clamour arose

concerning the introduction of 'French spies' it was evidently not the fear of some proto-Inspector Morse which provoked it, but the resentment that the pub, the lodging house and the pawn-broker's shop would be opened, like the cell, to the eye of the state. As alternative solutions to the same problems, such as the control of recidivists, or as alternative careers for the same individuals (Governors Westlake and Stephens of Carmarthen Gaol came to it from the Metropolitan Police) the early histories of police and prison are best understood as related symptoms of a major social change. Prince Albert in 1845 saw the reform of policing not as an isolated event but grouped it with changes in prosecution procedure as part of 'an immense scheme'.[75] Whilst it is obviously impossible in a book of this nature to chart all the events and implications of policing history within the period under study, it must be borne in mind that the emergence of the 'new' police, operating in some cases as alternative means of ensuring social discipline to the prison and in others as significant filters in the production of the prison population, was a process of immense significance for the study of penal institutions.

Other major social developments also demand recognition, albeit cursory, if the pitfall of assuming that penal history can be written as if it were a self-contained subject is to be avoided. For it must be conceded that to speak, as has been done earlier, of the 'application of the law' and of the 'intervention of the state' is to invoke concepts which are themselves in a condition of flux and which need further investigation.

To begin with the law. The common law had its origin in rural society and its development had, for most of its history, been primarily through the retrospective analysis of judges in case law, rather than the prospective formulation of 'reformers' in the statute. Certainly, medieval and early modern legislation was important, and much of the 'Bloody Code' was based on statute, but the ethos of the law seemed to be rooted more in the declaration and interpretation of, or at the very least the application of law by judges than in its relation to Parliament. Nineteenth-century legal philosophy was to stress different elements of law, elevating the position of statutes in the realm of the law. Utilitarians like Bentham and Austin could formulate a rationale of law in which even custom owed its existence to a tacit sovereign will, whilst later Maine was to elevate legislation to the status

of a peak of quasi-Darwinian social evolution.[76] The influence of
such thinkers is easy to overestimate, and it is clear that other less
rationalist voices leaving less scientific evidence in their wake may
have contributed to a change in the legal landscape for which
philosophy may remain at most an *ex post facto* rationalization.
It is obviously true, for example, that a 'positivist' formulation of
legality stressing the directional power of government authority
might be politically attractive (as was the case in the days of its
precursor Thomas Hobbes) when authority might be challenged.
The traditional non-positivist explanation of the authority of law
was a naturalistic one which in the hands of a Tom Paine or a
Jean-Jacques Rousseau could be a worrying legitimation of
working-class radicalism. But whether the legal-philosophical
doctrines of nineteenth-century England are seen as causes or
symptoms of change, as professionally influential or as academic
embroidery, the direction of the change remains noteworthy. The
dominant Victorian analysis of law was, like other important
aspects of economy and society, based not in nature but in power,
and its authority was discoverable not in metaphysics but in
government. It was also a philosophy of optimism, for law was
conceived of as a tool of social improvement, not simply the
legacy of established practice. The greater intrusion of law into
whole areas of life (health, education, animal welfare and the
like) in the second half of the nineteenth century is certainly a
noticeable phenomenon, and the philosophy which could so
readily serve to underpin it merits our observation. We must be
aware, however, that though such a philosophy may dominate in
the thoughts of lawyers and lawmakers, it was not the only
possible interpretation of the role of the law. Ideas of law as non-
interventionist, and of the 'good old law' as a guarantee of
traditional values and customs were components of a competing
rhetoric which were still available to popular consciousness,
though it might have been less fashionable amongst political
scientists.[77]

Just as we may notice an expansion in the later nineteenth
century in the content of legal regulation, so we should be aware
of change in its orientation and reach in other dimensions which
were related to the demographic trends which have been
commented upon earlier. In the orthodoxy of the common law
the city had always been anomalous; the borough had its own

courts and its own customs and, of course, its own prisons for its own inhabitants.[78] These had developed as tokens of the exceptional status of urban life. As the urbanization of society increased so the legally anomalous position of the town jurisdiction and administration became increasingly a source of tension. The standardizing tendency of the Municipal Corporations Act of 1835 in particular, but also elements of the changes of representation engineered by the Reform Act of 1832 and subsequently the 1867 Representation of the People Act, may be seen in this light. So too should the particular concern with the borough gaols which is evident in the discourse of nineteenth-century penality. Forsythe has argued that it was borough rather than county gaols which came in for particular criticism by the post-1835 inspectorate.[79] Certainly many, including that in Carmarthen, did not survive until nationalization. Such criticism is the more intelligible when it is recognized that urban life, though increasingly a social norm, was ultimately based upon a tradition of legal and administrative variation and anomaly. Certainly it is true that many town gaols were small and might be old. Yet in an age marked by the increase in central control and the drive for uniformity it was difference, not dereliction, which marked out the borough.

Not only was law in transition but so also were constructions of order and government. Keith Wrightson's analysis of the concept of local order in seventeenth-century England reveals much that remains true, as we shall see, in nineteenth-century Wales. Order at a local level, argues Wrightson,

> was less a positive aspiration towards a national condition of disciplined social harmony than a negative absence of disruptive conflict locally ... Order meant little more than conformity to a fairly malleable custom which was considerably more flexible than statute law. The maintenance of order meant less the enforcement of impersonal regulations than the restraint of conflict among known individuals in a specific local context.[80]

Peter King's compelling picture of discretion and negotiation in seventeenth-century English criminal justice again seems not unfamiliar in Victorian Wales.[81] Demographic and economic changes which undermined such local specificity in the maintenance of order necessitated greater impersonality and a more uniform, more national, abstraction of social order. Such a development may be related also to the expansion of the content and ambitions of the legal, specifically the criminal, code, which might seek to regulate not only new activities but also to enter areas hitherto more usually regulated by extra-legal means. Yet, although such changes had an influence throughout Britain, it must again be recognized that the process was neither uniform in extent nor even handed in its progress. At some point the seesaw tips, slowly and imperceptibly, from the dominance of one model of social order to the other. The aberrant becomes the norm and the vestiges of the older norm become aberrant. The retention of an earlier concept of local order can become stigmatized as atavistic and its manifestations as subversive of the Rule of Law (a concept which in its very formulation opposes particularity). Such themes will be considered in the next chapter.

Crucial to the reformulation of law and the guarantee of a new conception of order was the role of government. In the context of penality the role of 'the state' is often regarded as the crucial component to be analysed. Such reasoning dominates to the extent that, in the modern theoretical literature of punishment, questions concerning the use of that technique of control are often elided into those concerning the role of the state, as if agent and agency were the same thing. Such identification may be misleading. Whilst it may be difficult, even impossible, to envisage the carpenter without the hammer, the hammer is not the carpenter, nor is the carpenter the only person who uses a hammer. Yet even this analogy fails to reveal all of the difficulty which inheres in the historical discussion of 'the state', for the power and capacity to govern and to coerce is not a constant to be applied to a greater or lesser extent at will, but is itself subject to evolution. Indeed the term 'state' becomes common currency only as the nineteenth century moves on. Law and administrative process are not simply the consequences of state development: they retorsively mould and constitute that development.

Throughout the early modern period the crucial role in the administration of local affairs was that performed by the Justice of the Peace (JP). Reliance on JPs in the governmental scheme of the 'Old Constitution' invites reflection on certain features of the governance in which they were instrumental. It was local, both in legal form and in social substance, and it was general – Dalton's *Country Justice* of 1619 (note the title, this was not the product of an urban lifestyle) gives a range of responsibilities in respect of matters from sewer regulation to high treason. The 'system' which bound Justices together was not based on expertise or even on direct supervision, but upon class and property. Position in and interest (of a material kind) in the local social structure were the ties that bound magistrate to offender and magistrate to magistrate.

The tradition of local self-government was to be changed during the nineteenth century, such a change making the absorption of local prisons into a national penal system not only possible but acceptable. Traditionally, as Loughlin points out, the division of function between central and local government was seen not in terms of a hierarchy or responsibility but as representing different spheres of influence.[82] Whilst the maintenance of the King's Peace was a matter for the king's judges, the de facto routine administration of justice and punishment was largely a local affair. The Home Office, which comprised in 1815 the Home Secretary, two under-secretaries and eighteen clerks, could not have exercised much detailed control over activities in the localities, even had that been thought desirable.[83] Even in 1870 the Home Office employed only thirty-three permanent officials, of whom fourteen worked for the Domestic and Criminal Departments.[84] Legislation insofar as it related to local matters was frequently permissive only, indicative of desirable trends, but respectful (and particularly so if financial expenditure were involved) of the principle of autonomy. A bridge between the central and local became more apparent from the 1830s onwards. Reforms, such as the crucially important Poor Law Amendment Act of 1834, blended central policy with local administration and mark the transition from a concentration on governmental structure to administrative function. The use of an inspectorate in a whole variety of such functions, as of course under the 1835 Prison Act, whilst theoretically sensitive to local conditions, allowed influence from the centre to pass down, thus feeding the growing craving for uniformity. It is easy, of course, to overestimate the impact of such changes when actual practice on the ground is examined. Apathy and opposition must be acknowledged as powerful and persistent counterbalances to the theoretical advance of reformist legislation policed by specialist inspectors. The workhouse which Lampeter in west Wales was supposed to provide following the 1834 Act remained unbuilt for decades;[85]

the asylum which Carmarthenshire was obliged to construct by the 1845 County Asylums Act was opened only twenty years later;[86] the general provision of separate cells so popular with well-known prison inspectors remained, as we shall see, entirely ignored by the county until after the 1865 Prison Act. Hoppen, examining more generally the changing role of the mid-Victorian state, draws attention to both ideological ('Centralization. No. Never with my consent. Not English.')[87] and practical impediments to increased intervention, and sees as late as the third quarter of the nineteenth century a 'high point of local power'.[88] He acknowledges, however, that 'Perhaps the arena into which the Victorian state spread its influence most dramatically was that of law and order'.[89] It seems that a realignment of government responsibility in relation to 'the enemy' (a traditional state role), taking on those within, criminals, as well as those without, was a less problematic transition than would have been intervention in other aspects of internal affairs.

Social legislation of the kind increasingly popular from the 1830s was also instrumental in the creation of a class of experts who, like the legislation with which they worked, were marked out by the speciality of their subject rather than, as had been the JPs, by the generality of their respectability. The inspector was at the apex of a system which stressed vertical ties of accountability and expertise rather than horizontal community interaction. As Loughlin observes, having discussed the 1856 Police Act which, like the 1865 Prison Act, linked unsatisfactory performance in inspection to withdrawal of central funding,

> Inspection, the technique invented and promoted by Bentham, was the foundation of central supervision not only in relation to the police, but was also applied to the poor law, public health, education and, through audit, to the system of local finance and expenditure. Inspection enabled the centre not only to keep itself informed of the work of local authorities but also directly to encroach on that work.[90]

The mention of finance is also instructive here. The Municipal Corporations Act had altered the nature of the financial nexus in local government in favour of the model of the local ratepayer with a stake in administration. Moreover, the gradual transformation of income tax from a temporary, amateurly administered, quasi-voluntary impost to a professionally regulated and exacted form of finance not only echoes the process of transition evident in other areas of Victorian life but also helped to finance that broader process.[91] It should be remembered, as McConville makes clear, that prison nationalization was essentially promoted as an economic measure, promising (falsely) a better product for a reduced expenditure.[92]

The rise of professionalism in administration, with a series of reforms of the civil service, which began under Lord Liverpool's government following the Northcote–Trevelyan Report of 1853 and the establishment of the Civil Service Commission in 1855 and culminated in the adoption (in principle at any rate) of the open competition policy for position in 1870, are also indicative of the direction of change.[93] The practical effects of these changes may be, as Hoppen argues, easy to overstate, yet they were designed in principle to displace the vagaries of patronage by the operation of an educated career elite.[94] Similar tendencies may be traced in other professions. As Foucault's work indicates, in areas where professionalism is allied to institutionalization the opportunities for the accumulation of information which the institution provides serve to allow the self-validation of the specialist role.[95] In the context of penal administration the roles of prison experts – not only inspectors and governors but also the prison chaplain and the prison surgeon – were increasingly developing as the nineteenth century progressed. The gaoler of old, eighteenth-century local government, living, of course, on his fees, and sometimes with another source of income, was as welcome in the new prisons as a case of gaol fever. He was replaced by the governor who addressed the Royal Commission and wrote books on his penal observations. As will be seen shortly, in this new ascendancy conscious policy finds an ally in a variety of administrative Darwinism, for the older variety of gaoler was often more skilled with the key or the beer tap than with the increasing amount of paperwork which the bureaucratization of the penal experience was to demand as the nineteenth century progressed. His days were numbered, and his replacement was to come, ideally, from another direction. In the new prisons the military man was both example and asset, and one of the attractions of such men was not simply that he could give orders but also that, as one used to hierarchical structure, he knew how to take them. As a report of 1851 noted, 'The class of men who are the best qualified for such duties are pensioned non-commissioned officers, because from their previous habits they not only exercise a watchful vigilance over their different gangs, but are also obedient to any instructions they may receive.'[96] It may also be the case that the military man and the bureaucrat were united in another respect. Both knew the value not only of answering questions, but of doing so in the right way. Though in many ways we know far more about prison life as the mass of documentation grows over the nineteenth century, there is at least some evidence to suggest that some detail becomes lost in that process, as early expansiveness and individuality in records become replaced by terse and cautious bureaucratic formulae.

The ascendancy of the uniform

All of which leads to a consideration of the idea which lies behind so much of the nineteenth-century discourse of punishment: the desire for uniformity. Coincident with the change in the balance of power between local and central government, and with the primacy of function over established structure and the development of specialism, came the clamour for uniformity of penal treatment. Such a statement needs of course qualification; uniformity was construed along legalistic rather than libertarian lines – the anarchic 'uniformity' of the unreformed gaol which threw all, young and old, male and female, together was to be utterly abandoned, in favour of a policy of treating like cases alike. The search for appropriate constructions of 'likeness' became an integral part of the task. Until the latter part of the century, when the concept of the moral individual begins to give way to a scientific model which looked less to similarity than to difference,[97] the 'fetish of uniformity' (in the Webbs' apt phrase)[98] was a dominant motif in penology. Uniformity, after all, was not simply a technique but a value, a mark of progress. The wealth of Empire increasingly lay not in artisan individuality but in the consistency of the quality of the nails and cloth which came out of the factories. In other areas of life – from the time shown by its clocks to the rules of its football matches – the suppression of local variation can be seen as a central element in the emergence of the Victorian nation state, constitutive of it and also made possible by it (and by advances in technology and communication) in a self-sustaining spiral.[99] As government and its experts began to consolidate its position as the motive power of the penal system, so it wished to see less variation in the production process. If the drive for perfect uniformity presented many challenges it also had at its core, for it was impossible to achieve, an excuse for its own failure. The challenges lay in a whole variety of different directions. Geographically and historically the gaols which existed had wide variations in fabric and inmates. Different penal regimes attracted different supporters, as at different times the 'silent system' vied with the 'separate system' and moral reformers vied with deterrence enthusiasts. The debate, despite its consistent invocation of Christian principle (if not the consistent prominence assigned to it), was not one of abstract moral philosophy but of concrete moral science. The identity of the prisoner and his classification – whether he was an old lag or a criminal neophyte – became a problem of considerable urgency which attracted the use of new technology in a fruitless attempt at its solution.[100] Technology too was devised to quantify and standardize that which in other contexts would seem unquantifiable. Bentham's idea of a whipping machine to standardize corporal punishment may never have been used, but the crank and the treadwheel counter were devised to measure the useless and to prevent either an excess or deficit of futility.[101] Another science, economics, also had a crucial role to play in the pursuit of uniformity. For even though it might be accepted in the countryside that government might have a say in the directions of local gaols, while the financing of the institutions remained largely in the hands of those outside the Home Office, it would be difficult to insist on detail – to prescribe a meal for which one did not pay was to stretch intrusion too far. It should be noted again that when nationalization came in 1877 it did so as a result of economic argument.

Yet the difficulty of the pursuit of the chimera of uniformity guaranteed that it would be more enthusiastically pursued. Problems in the punitive complex could be blamed on inconsistency of application, thus postponing the need for questioning initial premises. In 1850 Charles Pearson observed of the penal system: 'A Harlequin's jacket was of a consistent colour in comparison with the variety and discrepancies of the so-called system which prevailed in this country.'[102] As late as 1871 Sir Walter

Crofton could remark: 'There is a want of uniformity in our treatment of prisoners which is fatal to the repression of crime.'[103] Nationalization of the system seven years later would remove this excuse for its failure. Whilst not wishing to underestimate the effects of new conceptions of criminality led by revised scientific and moral taxonomies in the major shifts in penal philosophy evident at the end of the nineteenth century, it should be remembered that the conditions for uniform administration had by then been achieved. Uniformity had proved to be a false idol, yet it was one to which tribute had been paid for a protracted period of time.

A reprise

Having spent a considerable time discussing the context, both historical and historiographical, of the subject matter of this book, it is necessary to return to a question raised at the outset: why write another book of prison history? It will be apparent in what follows that this volume concentrates not upon statutes or Royal Commissions but upon their effects, if any, in a particular location. The focus of this study is twofold. It will begin from a premise which belongs at the beginning of the penal revolution rather than at the end: that the prison is an essentially local institution, not a part of a national system. As such it will place emphasis on the relationship of the gaol to the community or communities in which it was situated, rather than to its relationship with other gaols. Insofar as Carmarthen gaol was affected by the movement towards systemization and the trend to uniformity, then the effect of those changes upon the institution and its inhabitants will be considered. It will become apparent that the local prison and the local prisoner merit more attention than as mere objects of central regulation, for webs of apathy, resistance and negotiation need to be explored to uncover the gap which may exist between the rhetoric and the reality of penal transformation in the nineteenth century. This leads to the second characteristic of the following survey.

It will be necessary to consider the individuals who inhabit Carmarthen gaol to understand such apathies, resistances and negotiations. Even in local prison histories the prisoner is rarely

accorded much interest, and the governor or chaplain is considered as functionary rather than individual. Yet a more detailed
consideration of the characters concerned will highlight some of
the important features of the nineteenth-century penal experience
which tend to be lost in the objectification of the actors in the
penal drama as traditionally presented. It must be remembered
that prisoners are not a given population but a chosen one, and
chosen not, despite the rhetoric, by 'the law' but by people – prosecutors, magistrates and juries, who share a geographical and
possibly a cultural (if not a narrowly social) connection with
those incarcerated as a result of their actions. Prison staff too are
those whose lives take them both inside and outside the institution, who meet other people, stand in crowds, read newspapers.
The real life of the Victorian prison dealt not with categories but
with persons, for even when categorization took place it did so on
the basis of human judgement and decision. The point is a crucial
one, and some examples may clarify it. It is apparent that a
greater distinction is being drawn between the 'mad' and the 'bad'
in nineteenth-century theory and practice – but to which category
was the naked, cell-destroying Eugene Buckley to be assigned?[104]
Scholars have discussed the drive to incapacitate the habitual
offender, but who was the habitual offender – the drunken local
'character' Mary Ann Awberry or the shadowy repeat felon John
Phillips?[105] Such questions are not merely incidental to a consideration of more general trends: they are constitutive of the
understanding of those trends.[106]

The question of regime too will be considered not as an abstract
ideology but as a circumscribed practical technique. The well-
known debate as to the relative reformatory efficacy of the
'separate' and the 'silent' systems, upon which much academic
commentary has been produced, begins to take on a rather
different perspective in Carmarthen, which, despite what the
governor may have told inspectors, had for many years neither
the architecture to employ the former nor the staff to enforce the
latter. Moreover, unless an attempt is made to locate the prisoner
in his or her social milieu, such concepts as a 'separate' or 'silent'
system can only partially be grasped in the twenty-first century,
when communal living – in factories, lodging houses, extended
families, servants quarters, the street, the market, the public house
– is much less the norm than it was in the mid-nineteenth century,

particularly amongst the working classes.[107] To understand the context of the prison it is necessary to understand the experience of imprisonment and the range of perception of that experience. These are not contingent or peripheral issues.

The Welsh experience

The choice of Carmarthenshire as an area of study also adds a rather different dimension to traditional penal historiography. More detailed consideration of the nature of the county will form part of the next chapter, but it may be remarked here that whilst it is true that in its industrialization and the growth of its urban centres, the county town and the tinplate centre of Llanelli, Carmarthenshire mirrored transitions which had taken place elsewhere in Britain, more generally it remained to a great extent an agrarian and rural county. Modes of thought concerning the disciplining of society which were increasingly driven by notions of progress and change were to be applied to an area in which stasis and continuity were still powerful forces. Moreover, Carmarthenshire's experience was a Welsh experience.

Despite the pioneering work of some historians, most notably the late D. J. V. Jones, the Welsh dimension has featured little in accounts of penological development.[108] The historiography is predominantly Anglocentric, although nods towards Irish experience in this area (with articulate Irish prisoners taking a leading role in the debates on prison reform as the century progresses and Ireland's status as a testing ground for initiatives in policing and punishment, as well as its more general political and economic role in the history of nineteenth-century governance) are belatedly more widely incorporated into the literature. A jurisdictional and educational frontier, albeit one frequently misunderstood in the nineteenth century, allows Scotland to be largely left to its 'own' historians. Wales, though its appearance in statistics (as 'and Wales') ensures its nominal appearance in some analyses, seems to oscillate between positions, to be disregarded as strange and different (and therefore left to specialists) or more frequently to be disregarded as unproblematically the same as England. Yet Wales in the nineteenth century was neither Camelot nor Cardiffshire.

The condition of Wales in general in the nineteenth century can be described here in no great detail. Mining and industrialization, which had started in the north but then blossomed spectacularly in the south, provided not only new towns in Wales but the slates for the roofs, the iron for the railway lines and the coal for the engines far beyond. Internal migration disrupted old communities but could also create new ones, which still preserved those great indicia of Welsh difference – language and Nonconformist religion. The essential contradictoriness of the Welsh experience has been recognized by K. O. Morgan: 'Industrialization and urbanization, along with the growth of literacy, could work in contrary ways. They could make the United Kingdom more of an integrated whole, yet also give a distinct national focus to its component parts.'[109] In an enterprise such as the replacement of local variance by national uniformity in the response to crime and its perpetrators, the resolution of such a contradiction becomes a crucial task. It is crucial precisely because the position of Wales posed direct and significant questions for such Victorian totems as the 'common' law and the reformulation of the penal response into a 'national' framework.

Yet the response from outside to such questions and the attitudes which surround them are in themselves contradictory. The Welsh were perceived as very religious, yet their morality was reportedly very lax; Taffy was a thief, yet assize judges might find no cases to detain them on circuit. There was a temptation to ignore the position of 'a small country ... with an indifferent soil, and inhabited by an unenterprising people',[110] yet the experiences of the first half of the century – the Scotch Cattle, the Merthyr Rising, the Newport conflagration and the Rebecca Riots – had shown that Welsh crime could be violent, politically motivated and aimed against industrial capital and old authority. The fear that Wales could become a 'second Ireland'[111] argued against the seductions of neglect.

As the distinguished Welsh historian John Davies has recognized, 'the second half of the nineteenth century would experience nothing comparable with the series of insurrections which had been such a feature of the first'.[112] Whilst he and others have highlighted the role of religion, education and political nationalism (often aspirational rather than oppositional) in the transition of Welsh society in the latter half of the nineteenth century, the changes in the legal, and in particular the penological, experience of the principality will occupy attention here. For, in the half century which lay between the abolition of the separate court which had tried its serious offenders and the creation (in the 1881 Welsh Sunday Closing Act) of a new offence specifically addressed to the morality of its inhabitants, Wales was adapting to new mechanisms of enforcement of the criminal law. The Welsh dimension is an important aspect of the narratives of uniformity, resistance and discretion which will be explored in this text. It is of importance not only for those whose interest lies in the social and penal history of Wales, but also for those who too easily assume that those histories have nothing significant to add to accounts which ignore them. It will be necessary to turn to the Welsh dimension then in the next chapter.

A note on the sources

At the outset of this chapter it was stated that the bureaucratization of the penal system in the nineteenth century has produced a gratifying quantity of documentary evidence out of which its history may be constructed. As such, the generation of records becomes not merely the source for the historical analysis but also one of its objects. Moreover, in such matters as the regulation of antisocial behaviour, the relationship between central and local government or between local government and individuals, we may encounter different and varying normative structures, different definitional boundaries and a range of motivational features in which scientific objectivity is rarely the driving force. It becomes important then to interrogate our sources carefully, to ask questions not only about what information is present but also as to what is, or may be, absent. In addition, the problems of interpretation of evidence may be compounded rather than assisted by modern methods of analysis such as that made possible by the use of computer – a tool which, as will be seen, has been used in the account which follows. For computer analysis can tempt the reader to reach for the *data* and forget the *dator*. An example may indicate the problem more clearly.

Between 1843 and 1871 five men were recorded in the *Felons' Register* as remanded to Carmarthen gaol on charges of bestiality.[113] None were convicted. What do such figures reveal? That bestiality was rarely committed? That it was rarely discovered? That it was rarely prosecuted? That the defendants were innocent of the acts? That sufficient evidence was not available to result in conviction? That juries approved of the offence, did not care about it, disapproved of the penalty for it, were ashamed to acknowledge it? Some of these interpretations may seem more likely than others, but this only pushes back the question one remove – *why* do they seem more likely? What evidence is there for such assumptions? In any event, the temptation to assume that such documentary evidence is capable of rendering an unproblematic 'objective truth' is obvious, even though penal historians may be more ready to repeat such warnings than to heed them. Consider another example. In March 1865 John Phillips was convicted of being concealed in a dwelling house with intent to commit felony. Here at least we have some certainty. Or do we? 'John Phillips' had already been in the gaol in 1853 but was then calling himself George Flynn. In 1870 he was apparently imprisoned as 'John Stanmore' in Merioneth and in 1872, in Montgomery, as 'John Hanley'. Whether such identifications are accurate, and which, if any, is 'correct', are questions which cannot at this distance of time be answered. The important point to note is that the accuracy of recorded information, particularly when it is based solely on the testimony of those who have an interest in the consequences of that record, needs to be questioned. Once this is borne in mind, then analyses of such issues as the extent of recidivism (since it involves either honesty in the offender in reporting a criminal record when it will be to his/her advantage to conceal it, or the detection of identity by prison authorities, a procedure which, although improving through the nineteenth century, was by no means assured), or of the geographical provenance of the prison population, must be treated as problematic.

Nor should it be supposed that it is only the words of those guilty of, or at least suspected of, crime which should be treated with caution. When the prison surgeon reports that instances of diarrhoea are increased due to 'atmospheric change', is this merely a simple piece of reportage, or a casual refusal to diagnose, or a misdiagnosis (and then is it intentional or innocent?) of matters which might reflect badly upon the diet or sanitary condition of the prison, in relation to both of which the surgeon himself had an involvement?[114] When a governor officially reports that silence is observed in the prison, or that categories of inmate are strictly separated, he undoubtedly does no less than would be expected of him. Yet as will be seen, there are times when other evidence may lead us to see such assertions as, at most, statements of policy rather than of practice.[115] Even where the information which we have comes through an 'external' source it need not be any more objective in its reporting. One of the most shocking discoveries in the Birmingham borough prison scandal which was revealed in 1854 was that a government inspector had failed to discover the abuses.[116] Moreover, when inspectors held an ideological stance in respect of penal regime, as most evidently did Crawford and Russell in the 1830s, but as also did less renowned individuals, it is possible that the diagnosis of ills in a particular institution might be led to an extent by the perception of an appropriate remedy rather than vice versa. Nor even at the level of governmental inquiry should it be assumed that evidence given was representative of the whole spectrum of opinion, nor conclusions reached to be the result only of the impartial weighing of that evidence. Sean McConville's excellent work has shown that such seminal inquiries as the Carnarvon Committee's investigation of 1863 were established with the conclusions already in mind.[117]

None of this is intended to suggest that all who leave behind the documents out of which our penal history must be constructed are venal, corrupt or mendacious. Yet records are produced by people for contemporary purposes not by angels for posterity, and should be considered accordingly.

There is, moreover, a dynamic element in nineteenth-century prison record-keeping which should be noted before we proceed. It is clear that as the century wears on the nature, status and background of those running institutions changes. As suggested earlier, when gaoler becomes replaced by prison governor a more bureaucratic approach to record-keeping may be evident. The dismissal of Carmarthenshire's Governor Westlake, a man by no means an archetype of old corruption, but nonetheless one whose neurosis over superintendence and eccentric grasp of literary form mark him out as no easy functionary, fits squarely within this picture. He was replaced by George Stephens. The terse, efficient notes which Stephens leaves in his journal are far less revealing than the detailed, edgy entries of his predecessor. In the Darwinian struggle which sees the bureaucrat conquer, the historian, paradoxically, learns less of the reasons behind decisions, the discretion which inheres in them, the unease which may follow them. The record, in becoming more opaque, gives the impression of the routine application of abstract rules, an impression which conventionally corresponds to the predominant penal philosophy.

Yet whilst such a change in manuscript evidence may record a change in the actual ethos and management of the prison (indeed, such would seem not improbable), the simple truth is that it *need* evidence no such thing. It could of course be the case that it records simply the difference between two individual personalities. While at one level this is clearly true, it need not reveal the whole truth. Forsythe's discovery of a similar change in the character of record-keeping at Exeter suggests that this is part of a transition in the *types* of individuals involved.[118] The point which remains difficult to determine is whether the ascendancy of the bureaucratic governor has more real impact on bureaucracy than on governance. Such questions raise intriguing issues in relation to the sources used in this book, but there are other more obvious problems. On some occasions the manipulation of the record evidence appears patent. In the period before Governor Westlake's dismissal from Carmarthen his journal is, I am sure, being completed by another hand.

The greatest problem with record evidence, however, is not what we have, but what does not remain to us. In some cases it is the accident of history which determines whether information has come down to us. Some material was lost early. On 20 December 1845 Governor Westlake records, with his habitual disregard for the niceties of syntax, spelling and punctuation, that

> T. C. Morris Esqr called with a return to be filled up relating to John Thomas that was Transported at the spring Assizes 1844 which the late Gaoler did not leave is old commitment book with me when he was discharged which I have no other guidance than the calendar when he was tried it does not mention in the Gaoler report when the prisoner left this Gaol for Millbank Penitentiary.[119]

Other material may still exist but its location is unclear – as a sighting of what may be a missing register of misdemeanants from

Carmarthen in (untraced) private hands suggests. Others may have been lost or may never have existed, such as the books which surgeons and chaplains of the gaol were required by statute to complete.[120] Yet others, like the early Quarter Sessions Records of Carmarthenshire with their reports of gaoler, chaplain, surgeon and visiting justices, have certainly been lost. Nonetheless, the records which do survive provide interesting and important insights into the reality of the Victorian penal revolution.

Other records which would certainly have added to our knowledge do not survive, for they were never created. Although the nineteenth century saw the rise of a class of articulate and literate prisoners whose experiences provide a counterpart to the views of those responsible, at whatever level, for their custody, such men (they are mostly men) remain in a very small minority. Carmarthen, around 40 per cent of whose prisoners remanded for felony in the period under discussion are recorded as wholly illiterate, inspired no 'Captain D— S—' or 'Manchester Merchant', still less a Michael Davitt or an Oscar Wilde. The words of its prison population are heard, if at all, only indirectly, as recorded by others who have an official voice. Such a deficiency is a major one in this work, although it is inevitable. Less inevitable is the fact that there may be more information in periodical or diary sources written in Welsh, which through the author's linguistic deficiencies have remained undiscovered. Whilst it is hoped that an awareness of the issue of language is apparent in the account which follows, and use has been made of material in Welsh, it is necessary to accept the view of Russell Davies that

> Unless we learn the language of the people and discover the meaning and nuances they placed on various words and phrases, we cannot understand their talk. In our apprenticeship we have to acquire these linguistic skills and sensitivities before we can hope to graduate in Clio's 'sullen craft'. Perhaps then, Welsh History will cease to be history with the Welsh left out.[121]

What follows is, in this respect, of necessity an undergraduate piece. Nonetheless, though imperfect, it is intended to give an insight into questions not always raised in other penal historiography. Certainly a prison history with the prisoners left out is to be avoided. Certainly too the prison must be related to its cultural context. This latter will be explored in the next chapter.

~ 1 ~

Community, Crime and Sanctions

The commonality of the common law

The expression 'the common law' as used to describe the rules governing citizens in the nineteenth century is an interesting one, for it identifies itself by reference to the criterion of universal or at least non-particular application. The term has its origin in the Middle Ages, when a new conception of royal justice attained precedence over the claims of local laws. It is in essence then a geographical description, albeit one pregnant with other connotations relating *inter alia* to its source, political value, historical associations and propaganda utility. Yet limits to the commonality of law may be sought in two dimensions: vertically and horizontally. Vertically, we may examine the application of the legal rules to the strata of a society, investigating differences among the types of people to whom the rules applied, either theoretically (by which we mean the law in question is directed at one sector of society – employees, say, or vagrants – as opposed to all) or practically (by which is meant the differential application of rules which ostensibly apply to all members of that society, say those restricting the use of violence, in a fashion which is de facto uneven as across social groupings). Analysis of the use of the criminal law in its history has now long embraced this possible vertical deviation from commonality and, although authors will differ as to the extent which they see the social asymmetry of the criminal law as inhering in its very essence or as reflecting a deviation from an accepted ideal, such an axis of investigation seems largely non-controversial. That a social construct, the criminal law and the system which enforces it, should be viewed in isolation from the society in which it is constructed, a society in which wealth, power, knowledge, fear, opportunity and dependence are differentially allocated, would seem to be, despite the rhetoric which may accompany that construct, unacceptably naive. In the chapters that follow, an attempt to relate the law and its application to such factors will necessarily arise as an integral part of the investigation undertaken. For the moment, however, let us consider the other limit, the horizontal or geographical boundary of the commonality of common law, for this is less frequently considered.

In terms of the theoretical boundaries of the common law in the geographical plane it may be noted that by the nineteenth century these had largely disappeared in England and Wales, though the distinct jurisdictions of Scotland and that interesting and fertile ground of penal experimentation, Ireland, set limits to domestic uniformity, while further afield the governance of Empire provided common lawyers with uncommon problems. Yet, even within England and Wales, the difference between urban and rural districts and the change in population balance between the two were not matters of indifference to the nature and application of legal rules.

Wales, the local community and the common law

In Wales, the theoretical commonality of the law (but still not its administration) had been secured in the reign of Henry VIII, after the earlier application of a version of English law to part of Wales under Edward I.[1] The court structure of Wales, however, remained distinct from that to the east of Offa's Dyke until 1830, when the Court of Great Sessions, which had handled, *inter alia*, the trial of serious crime within the principality, was abolished. Such abolition had not been uncontroversial. Though Brougham had stigmatized the Great Sessions in 1828 as the 'worst [court] ever established'[2] and the consequent Commission of Enquiry had used the language of 'assimilation' to justify removal of the separate jurisdiction, the Welsh for the most part opposed the change.

In Carmarthenshire, reaction to the proposed abolition seems to have been hostile. John Jones, the parliamentary representative for the borough of Carmarthen, spoke against the bill in Parliament, and petitions from both the county and the borough urged the retention of Great Sessions. The Welsh-language periodical *Seren Gomer*, in reference to the plan in the original abolition bill to join Welsh and English counties (a proposal subsequently dropped), used powerful language, seeing the bill as a measure which would 'remove the Welsh nation from the face of the earth'.[3] Nonetheless, after 1830 the application and administration of the rules of criminal law were theoretically, regardless of any resentment that might have been engendered, to be the same as those in England.

Practically, however, there may be variance in the use of law and the legal system, which again contains a geographical element. Such a proposition is easier to assert than it is to prove in the absence of detailed statistical comparisons, yet it is by no means an improbable one. The invocation of courts and the law in the event of wrongdoing is not an automatic consequence but one that depends on choice. Clearly, a number of overlapping factors will influence that choice, some 'personal' (how knowledgeable, tolerant etc., is the person who may invoke the law?), some 'economic' (can that person afford, either immediately or with regard to future consequences, to invoke the law?) and some 'cultural' or 'subcultural'. These latter may be further divided into two. This subdivision involves the cultural/subcultural attitude to, firstly, the suitability of the criminal law in general, or to a particular law as a means of redressing the injury, and, secondly (though again the two interconnect), to the availability of, and effectiveness of, other dispute resolution procedures.[4] It has been argued in the previous chapter that such attitudes are not immune from temporal change and that 'the nineteenth century' may have seen the creation of a new paradigm in which the enforcement of the law was generally seen as the equivalent of, rather than merely as one of the means to, keeping the peace. Yet it is also obvious that such important factors as urbanization and manufacture do not affect the whole of the jurisdiction to the same extent at the same time. To this extent, then, models of law and order in the city may be inappropriate to the country; dispute settlement processes may differ in conditions of social anonymity and flux from those favoured in relatively static, face-to-face communities. Even within Wales itself contemporary observers were beginning to distinguish between rural and urban, settled and transient populations in their analyses of the nature, incidence and aetiology of crime.[5] The application of the criminal law at any one period of time, and particularly at a time of 'revolution', which sees the overturning of conventional paradigms, can then clearly be understood as potentially involving a geographical dimension. If on top of such transitional economic and social structures we add differences in such key cultural identifiers as language and religion, we might expect such geographical variants to be enhanced. We must consider here the characteristics of nineteenth-century Carmarthenshire and its population before tracing attitudes to law and order which existed within it.

Carmarthenshire in south-west Wales comprised an area of some 974 square miles.[6] The census taken in 1801, which it must be admitted is rather less reliable than those which followed, gave the population of the county as 55,571, a figure which by 1851 had risen to 94,672 and by 1881 to 111,255. The rise in population was not uniform after mid-century, however, when it began to decline in more rural parts of the county, the growth being in the area of Llanelli, the centre of a thriving tinplate industry.[7] In its degree of industrialization, Llanelli remained an exception to the county as a whole, which remained throughout the century a largely agricultural area.

The county town, Carmarthen, formed a market centre for agricultural production but also itself developed an industrial dimension. It was a busy port at a time when sea travel was much the most convenient means of transporting passengers and freight. The roads in the early years of the century were exceptionally bad, and railway communication, though it had a considerable history in Wales, was late in connecting this part of the principality with others and with England. It would be wrong to see the area as static; its seafaring traditions, military connections and traditional labour practices such as droving and seasonal labour migration, as well as the increasing lure of the higher wages of the mines and factories, meant that population movement was a fact of life for a proportion of Carmarthenshire inhabitants. Yet for many the traditional pattern of face-to-face relationships with people whose families were well known to them, in villages where they had been born, remained a reality throughout the century. Dot Jones's analysis of census statistics shows migration from all areas of the county after mid-century save only for Llanelli. Of those who were counted in the county, however, more than 88 per cent of those replying in 1851 and more than 85 per cent in 1881 had been born there, and the majority of the remainder, in parallel with the opposite movement of those who had been born in the county but had moved away, had not moved particularly far, with neighbouring counties accounting for most of the sample.[8]

The county was also primarily Welsh speaking. Statistics on this matter are rather more difficult both to invoke (no question was asked on the census about use of Welsh until 1891) and to interpret, yet there is no doubt that Russell Davies's observation based on the reports of travellers and officials and church records in the early nineteenth century, is correct.

> The inhabitants of rural areas in the counties of Cardigan, Carmarthen and Pembroke (with the exception of the area south of the *Landsker*) were predominantly Welsh in their social discourse and were overwhelmingly Welsh in their devotions. The Welsh language was firmly embedded in every fibre of the fabric of people's lives. The West was Welsh.[9]

Our best statistical survey before the change in the census, Ravenstein's study of the 1870s, gave figures for the whole of the county which indicated that only 6 per cent of the population spoke no Welsh, some 32.7 per cent spoke only Welsh and the rest had some proficiency in both languages.[10] Whilst Welsh was being abandoned during the century by the Welsh squirearchy, whilst English was unchallenged as the language of officialdom and, of course, law, and whilst amongst some the opinion was held that the only way for the Welsh to progress was to learn English, the linguistic dimension as a fact of everyday life cannot be ignored. Allied with this, as we have seen, was the ambivalent issue of nationality which developed as the century wore on, on the one hand the pressure to assimilate to England, the centre of the world's largest empire, on the other the celebration of difference which was evidenced in cultural, sporting and publishing circles.[11]

It was not only in language that Carmarthenshire found itself differing from the entrenched model of orthodoxy and authority. In religion too the county as a whole eschewed the faith the celebrants of which preached the assize sermons and were appointed as priests within the gaols. As Henry Richard put it succinctly in 1866, 'the Church of England is not the Church of Wales'.[12] Though the figures from the 1851 religious census are again not beyond challenge they clearly reflect the dominance of

Nonconformism in this part of the country. Nor should we accord to religious persuasion in the nineteenth century that peripheral place which it occupies in most, but by no means all of twenty-first-century British social life. Chapels were symbols of communal experience and order and the source of education, not simply the locus for the exercise of personal belief. The political dimension of religion in Wales was also apparent – from the vehement anti-Catholicism of the Anglican, Tory *Carmarthen Journal* to Rebecca's diatribe against the priest of 'the National whore',[13] from the bitterness of the arguments over tithes to the disputes over the appointment of Justices of the Peace.[14] Within this context it is important to remember that those who dealt dishonestly or even violently with their fellow men committed a sin as well as a crime, and an offence against their neighbours as well as against the law. To look at crime and law alone, ignoring other forms of social control, such as those exercised through the chapel or by a village community, is like watching the movement of only one team in a football match – interesting and informative but giving no real understanding of the dynamics of interaction.[15]

The view from the centre

Before passing on to examine attitudes towards social regulation more generally it will be illuminating to consider rural Wales as it was seen by government as a result of four specific inquiries conducted in the first half of the nineteenth century. In a book which takes as its underlying philosophy a degree of scepticism about the value of 'top down' centripetal analysis in explaining local phenomena it may seem strange to begin an analysis of conditions in Carmarthenshire from such a perspective. Yet, as will be seen, even in such 'dominant' discourse in the first half of the century the recognition of 'difference' (as a problem to be conquered) alerts us to the possibility of a much deeper understanding when other information is considered. The Commission on Municipal Corporations and that on the Rural Police were obviously not limited in their geographical compass but provide hints of particular problems. The Reports of the Commissioners of Inquiry into the State of Education in Wales contained observations on the moral status of the country and the operation of the criminal justice system which are as important as they were conceived offensive. The Commissioners on the Rebecca Riots were established to investigate the vastly significant events of rural criminality. All, it will be argued, have a part to play in explaining more general attitudes to criminality and punishment within the period covered by this book.

The First Report of Commissioners on Municipal Corporations of 1835 may seem to be of little significance in this regard. The results of its conclusions in respect of changing the nature and role of local government in general and of contributing to the marginalization of the borough gaol in particular, have been adverted to in the previous chapter. Insofar as the commissioners considered the Borough of Carmarthen itself, however, their findings are significant as providing early evidence of a less than ideal attitude towards the administration of justice at the heart of the county. Carmarthen Borough's political rivalry was notorious, indeed, in the naming of two of the town's thoroughfares 'Red Street' and 'Blue Street' it was topographically inscribed. The antagonism between the factions could break out into violence. The most notorious example, relating to the 1831 election, was laconically recorded by William Spurrell, the town's remembrancer:

> April 29. No return made for borough in consequence of riot: the candidates were John Jones and J. G. Philipps. A currier leaped down from the west gallery of the Hall to the table, and a scene of indescribable tumult ensued. The sheriffs declared themselves in bodily fear, and on the 30th made no return ...

> Aug. 10. Precautions taken to secure tranquillity at the election on the 20th. A large force of constabulary brought into the town; a troop of the 14th Dragoons and the 98th regiment at Llandilo in readiness to uphold the law.

> 1831. Aug. 30. John Jones (274) M. P. for borough: John George Philipps (203) defeated. While being carried in his chair through Dark-gate, numerous missiles were hurled by the mob, one of which wounded the member severely on the head.[16]

This party division permeated the running of local politics. The commission found that borough offices, such as that of gaoler, were in the gift of the ruling party. Moreover, in the main borough court judges, jurors and court officers were appointed by reference to political persuasion.The commissioners found clear evidence of abuse of legal process even in a case of capital felony. In relation to the use of the jury they concluded that verdicts both in the civil and criminal courts 'are frequently given from party bias, against justice and the merits of the case; and a general fear prevails amongst suitors opposed to the majority, that their cases will be so decided'.[17] The findings, albeit in relation only to the county town by a body seeking to overturn the existing structure, hint at the wider issue of jury 'perversity', of the subservience of the criminal law to instrumental status in the pursuit of other ends, which will be noted later.

One of the consequences of the 1835 Municipal Corporations Act was of course the requirement of new police forces for incorporated boroughs such as Carmarthen, where it was duly carried out.[18] As the impetus for police reform more generally developed, some of the characteristics of rural law enforcement may be glimpsed which, though taken from neighbouring counties, fit clearly into a pattern which we will see in Carmarthenshire. The Commissioners on Police in 1839, as we have seen in the previous chapter, concentrated on the mobility of persons and property as undermining traditional methods of law enforcement. In certain areas of the countryside such arguments would carry less weight and so the commissioners changed tack, concentrating on the inefficiency and partiality of those charged with the suppression of crime. Some of the most striking evidence comes from rural Wales, and while it could be readily enlisted to support the cry for a new agency of law enforcement, the stories which the commissioners heard tell of a wider culture of relative disregard for legal process. To police such a society would involve not simply new personnel but rather a new attitude within the locality generally towards the position of the criminal law in the regulation of behaviour. It is difficult, to take an example considered by the commissioners, to discover exactly how the provision of 'New Police' could have prevented the coroner's jury in Llanllwchaiarn finding that Edward Whittaker had died from a fall when the evidence of violence seemed incontrovertible. The commissioners themselves seem to have attributed such action as 'the remaining barbarism of the district' and the 'perversion of popular sentiments'.[19] Such language is intriguing beyond the simple value judgement which lies behind it. For there is a tension evident – the '*remaining* barbarism' speaks of behaviour sanctioned by long usage, whilst 'perversion' bespeaks deviation from the norm. The norm, then, is implicitly a novel one in such localities, and in the recognition of this fact the language is more revealing than in its simple cultural condemnation. A similar suggestion appears in the evidence of Lieutenant Cole speaking of his experience of force and threat in a land dispute at Rhayader (Radnorshire): 'Their feeling is that might overcomes right, and that *custom excludes the law* [my italics]; and they establish the custom according to their own interests.'[20] Perhaps most interesting of all is the evidence of Sir Edmund Head in relation to Cardiganshire, which deserves quotation at length.

> At the present time the magistrates of Cardigan and its vicinity are greatly embarrassed by the practice, called the 'Ceffyl pren' or wooden horse. A figure of a horse is carried at night in the midst of a mob with their faces blackened, and torches in their hands, to the door of any person whose domestic conduct may have exposed him to the censure of his neighbours, or who may have rendered himself unpopular, by informing against another, and by contributing to enforce the law. On the horse is mounted some one, who, when the procession makes a halt opposite the residence of the persons whom it is intended to annoy, addresses the mob on the cause of their assembling, and on the delinquency of the obnoxious party. When the exhibition is directed against supposed domestic irregularities, it is often accompanied with the grossest indecency.
>
> This practice has of late assumed a very serious character; in spite of all efforts made by special constables, and the usual resources of a rural district, it has now continued for several weeks. Two or three magistrates (among them the mayor of Cardigan), were severely maltreated by the mob, and on one occasion the local authorities thought it expedient to write for some troops from Brecon, although they remanded them before they arrived at their destination ...
>
> The right which is thus arrogated of judging and publicly animadverting on, by such means, another man's conduct, is certainly characteristic of a rude state of society; but when the same measures are applied to punishing the discharge of a servant's duty to his master, or to thwarting the operation of the laws of the land they become of much more serious import. The principle is perfectly Irish, and though the practice falls short of the manners of that country in atrocity, it equally contains the germ of resistance to legal order.[21]

'Ridings' such as those described here have their equivalents in many parts of England and have a long history.[22] It might be assumed that in the changing attitudes towards law enforcement evident in the nineteenth century they were inexorably declining in importance. While it is difficult to substantiate independently Head's assertion that such practices were actually increasing in Wales at the time he wrote, the evidence seems suggestive. Moreover, their vigour indicates that elements of shaming and of mass popular participation in judgement were robust traditions in the country. Whatever may have been the earlier relationship between 'popular' and official penalty,[23] Head was rightly concerned about the capacity of such 'rough music' to undermine ideas increasingly dominating the regulation of society in his time: ideas of the rule of law, its enforcement undertaken by professionals and its sanctions institutionalized and reserved. David Jones has suggested that use of the *ceffyl pren* reached its height soon after the Poor Law Amendment Act of 1834.[24] That measure was regarded with immense hostility in Wales, where its bastardy provisions were seen as contrary to traditional courtship practices and its workhouses as dividing families in a way alien to communal morality. If Jones's suggestion is correct, then the capacity of the *ceffyl pren* to represent a model of society in opposition to an increasingly incursive legal order is instructive. So too is Head's use of the Irish parallel, implicitly recognizing the national distinction which statute had sought to erode. Rosemary Jones, in a scholarly analysis of the events to which Head referred and of subsequent manifestations of the *ceffyl pren* and official attempts at its suppression, indicates that the practice was seen as having a specific national basis: '... it was animated by a deep sense of ancient, prescriptive rights, based on the widely held belief that Hywel Dda had sanctioned its usage, a myth which had become so firmly cemented in popular consciousness that it was often reiterated by members of the gentry.'[25] In 1837 for the first time in Cardiganshire an assize judge sentenced a member of a *ceffyl pren* 'mob' to a term of imprisonment.[26]

If proof were needed as to the capacity of rural Wales to kick against the rule of law, and to do so with the trappings of custom and the sanction of community, it was to come on 13 May 1839, when an attack on the tollgate of Efailwen near St Clears in Carmarthenshire marked the onset of a series of disturbances which escalated until 1843 and which are known as the Rebecca Riots. These events have been well documented and thoughtfully analysed by a number of historians and, though their centrality to the consideration of attitudes to law and order in nineteenth-century Carmarthenshire is beyond question, only a few brief observations will be offered here.[27] Firstly, the point must be made that, although the riots were sparked off by a genuine resentment of tolls payable on the county's roads, to see them as *simply* a protest against transport costs in an age of declining rural living standards is to view them superficially. Other objects of complaint, though they too had economic consequences for the rebellious farmers, may be seen as unacceptable not only because they cost money, but because the money was employed for purposes seen as alien or hostile to popular sentiment. Church rates, particularly tithes, were antithetical to a population which was predominantly Nonconformist. Rebecca was no Godless mob, indeed it drew its name from the Bible,[28] but it was by no means an Anglican one. Other grievances were, as has been seen, important too. It is difficult to know which of the responses that rural Wales made to the Poor Law Amendment Act is more notable – Rebecca's frontal attack on Carmarthen's workhouse on 19 June 1843 or the capacity of some areas simply to ignore it.[29]

It was not only the targets of Rebecca's wrath which indicate a distinct cultural slant to what might otherwise simply be dismissed as another rural riot. The methodology of protest drew deep on the *ceffyl pren* traditions, the nocturnal torchlit transvestite processions, and 'justice' and 'right' were its proclaimed objectives. Its genealogy was apparent to contemporaries such as the Carmarthenshire magistrate G. Rice Trevor, who wrote to the Home Office: 'These Cyffil Pren [*sic*] processions were the root of Rebeccaism so far as the *modus operandi* was concerned.'[30] In object too the processions could assert a tradition of customary practice as right in opposition to an order imposed from beyond. The persecution of informers spelled out the message of loyalty to community rather than law, the enforcement of paternal responsibility for bastards underwrote the norms of tradition rather than those of legislation. 'For a few brief months', says Thompson, 'even the poorest and most despised of the people of Carmarthenshire had a glimpse of an ideal of truly popular justice.'[31]

Yet if Rebecca spoke for rural Wales, it was again to a different part of the kingdom that the government's mind was turned by the insurrection. Sir James Graham, the Home Secretary, feared that Wales might become 'a second Ireland'.[32] One of the solutions adopted to control the society whose disorder troubled Queen Victoria herself was that which had been road-tested in Ireland beforehand, a reformed police force.[33] Rebecca stands then at the crux of a major reform which was to have a profound effect on the regulation of Carmarthenshire society. Metropolitan police, as well as over a thousand troops, were instrumental in suppressing the riots. In respect of the county's penal history the introduction of these professional outsiders was significant, for amongst their numbers were Henry Westlake and George Stephens, successive governors of the county gaol. The reaction to the subsequent introduction of Carmarthenshire's own new police was mixed. The authority for the establishment of a county force given by Quarter Sessions in July 1843 which resulted, after some delay, in the creation of a force of 57 men was clearly in line with government policy.[34] Rebecca had provided both a convincing example of why the professional force was needed, and the immediate pretext for its creation. Nonetheless there was, as might be expected, a considerable degree of protest at the alien imposition.[35] Whilst some saw the arrival of the police as removing a source of mischief others saw them perhaps as undermining a tradition of individual and collective restraint. The Revd D. Edwards observed in relation to the year 1846: 'The Police not only enable us to sleep in safety but also have almost eliminated fear in the case of children. Previous to the Rebecca riot I could never venture by myself four miles from home for fear of a drunken man.'[36] But even fifty years thereafter the arrival of a uniformed officer in a rural village could be seen as an adverse reflection on its communal character. 'Plisman yn wir,' remarked Hettie Davies of Cardiganshire, 'be mae nhw'n feddwl ydym ni?' ('A policeman indeed, what do they take us for?').[37]

The Rebecca Riots had shown too that there was a deficit in confidence between a substantial number of the populace and those charged with judicial administration of the law within the county. The social and economic divide between the Justice of the Peace and the majority of those subject to his jurisdiction was, and always had been, an essential element in the relationship between them; the traditional link between property and respectability being sufficient to explain why the rich man in his castle judged the poor man at his gate. It is, indeed, a testament both to the flexibility of the office and the immutability of the principle on which it was based that, though the later nineteenth century toyed with the ideas of training the magistracy and of the use of stipendiaries, the trend was inexorably towards conferring a greater jurisdictional portfolio upon the gentleman amateurs. This apparent exception to the more general trend towards specialization and professionalism evidenced in other areas of the criminal justice system is perhaps the more explicable when we remember that summary jurisdiction advanced at the expense of an even more amateur and, as we shall see, unreliable body, the jury.[38]

Nonetheless, to return to the point, though a disparity in class was an essential condition of the magisterial regime, it was made less palatable in Wales by the sense of partiality or arbitrariness in administration which could only be increased by the alienation of the Justices in matters of language and religion.[39] The presumed social gradient linking those who appeared in court and their 'betters' who judged them was made more slippery when other overt differences between the classes muddled and jeopardized that simple assumption of material/moral ascendancy. A letter of Cardiganshire Rebeccaites of 1843 demonstrated that the crisis was not simply one *for* law and order but *of* law and order.

> The conduct of the magistrates at petty sessions is quite unbearable that we are treated like dogs we are told to hold our tongues or go out of the room, and the law that is dealt out to us is the law of the magistrate's clerk and not the law of the Queen, and the magistrate's clerks charge us what they please.[40]

Such discontent was expressed to the Commissioners of Inquiry for South Wales when they investigated the Rebecca phenomenon. The commission in their report departed from the subject matter of specific complaint to reflect upon 'that frequently-expressed want of confidence in the magistracy which unhappily exists'.[41] Evidence told of sessions held and adjourned to suit the convenience of the Justices, a class commonly having 'an imperfect knowledge of the Welsh language',[42] and excessive and illegal payments demanded by the clerks. The commission even considered the necessity of establishing stipendiary magistrates to restore confidence in the local administration of criminal justice but forebore from a recommendation to this effect, not only on grounds of cost but also because 'we can hardly conceive that the defect would be best supplied by the substitution of strangers unconnected with the country and unacquainted with the usages and manners of the people'.[43] As will be seen later the Justices straddled the line between law and locality. Though criticized from both directions, they at least had one foot on each side.

Still further observations were made by the commissioners which addressed aspects of the lives of the majority of the populace, aspects which were to be addressed again, and with more impact three years later. Faced with the hostility to the 'bastardy clauses' of the Poor Law Amendment Act the commissioners recognized that the law had disrupted traditional canons of sexual regulation in the area. 'Caru yn y gwely' or 'bundling' as a premarital courtship practice was common, despite being frowned upon and campaigned against by Nonconformist as well as Established religion.[44] Pregnancies which resulted from such practice were usually a prelude to marriage. The recognition of the social pressure which lay behind such norms, pressure which could, as we have seen, provoke a *ceffyl pren* but which more often rendered one unnecessary, is eloquently attested in the qualification used by the commissioners in discussing the matter: 'subsequent marriage, – and that not a forced one in the usual acceptance of the term, – almost invariably wiped out the light reproach which public opinion attached to a previous breach of chastity.'[45] The new Poor Law, removing the threat of imprisonment from the father and requiring corroboration of the mother's allegation of paternity, was substituting legal for social regulation, and the result was an apparent reduction in marriage and an increase in the abandonment (some suggested worse) of children.[46] Amendments were introduced into the 1844 Poor Law Act in an attempt to rectify this mischief.[47]

Finally the commissioners commented with regret upon those characteristics which defined the area, its religion and its language. This latter in particular was regarded as presenting obstacles 'to the efficient working of many laws and institutions' and to the administration of justice.[48] The remedy was to lie in a greater knowledge of English, but the poverty of educational provision in south Wales rendered hope of improvement in this respect unfeasible.

Such issues were raised again three years later in the Reports of the Commissioners on the State of Education in Wales. Again the animadversions upon the backwardness and immorality of the Welsh therein contained and the reaction to such charges are well documented elsewhere.[49] What deserves attention here is the official unease, traceable here as in the earlier reports considered above, which persists in relation to issues of law and order in Wales. In what was to become almost a commonplace, one of the commissioners, Jelinger Symonds, described the Welsh as 'peculiarly exempt from the guilt of great crimes' but noted: 'On the other hand, there are perhaps few countries where the standard of minor morals is lower.'[50] The commission heard of the failure of jurors to understand English. Edward Crompton Lloyd Hall, a man with personal experience of the Rebecca troubles, spoke of perjury and partiality in the administration of justice.[51] Again the remedy proposed was the liberation of the people from their old ways by more education and more English language. Though English jurisprudence never espoused the Romantic nationalism of its nineteenth-century German counterpart, the message within the reports was surprisingly similar in its connection between regulation and nationalism: the Welsh would not develop a common respect for the common law whilst their culture and language were so un-English. Building a nation, and beyond that an empire, out of a variety of communities was intimately connected with the construction of an acceptance of a uniform and consistent attitude towards the ideology of 'the Rule of Law'. Economics and communication inevitably eased the assimilation of Wales and England. Some differences might be permitted, even celebrated, but not local peacekeeping, discretionary justice and popular punishment. Such things were no longer good enough.

Yet such practices and the social norms which underpinned them were not easily displaced. They might be denied, and some amongst the literate Welsh middle classes sought to refute the allegations of greater immorality and disrespect for law among their fellows by challenging the premises on which the allegations were based. Either the virtue of the Welsh could be established statistically (as was the tenor of Thomas Phillips's reaction to the Blue Books report)[52] or the balance could be redressed by seeking out instances of worse vice amongst the English. *Seren Gomer* reported in 1849 a case of incest from Hull with the comment 'Pa

le y mae Dirprwywyr y Llyfrau Gleisiau yn awr?' ('Where are the
representatives of the Blue Books now?').[53] Other reactions to the
official criticism within the principality recognized some at least
of the unease over cultural difference. For some the need for more
assimilation, or at least for an emphasis on education in English
was accepted. It was, moreover, difficult for even the most patri-
otic of Welsh Nonconformist opinion-makers to regard courtship
customs which countenanced extramarital sex with equanimity,
and a voluntary association to prevent such practices by
covenants was encouraged.[54] Amongst others, and particularly it
may be suggested amongst the working classes, a less dramatic
response was possible. The attack on traditional morality and the
attempt to engineer a new attitude to sin, crime and punishment
by reference to a 'common law model' of the decontextualized,
rational individual could be responded to simply by ignoring it.

Crime, 'popular punishment' and the courts

It remains the case throughout the period considered in this book
that evidence of a number of crimes was never laid before officials
of the legal system. Such a claim is in itself unsurprising for it
remains true in modern legal systems. Criminologists consider
reasons for the existence of and variation within the 'Dark Figure'
of unrecorded criminality, and victim report studies seek to
provide an index of its extent.[55] It should surprise us not at all that,
in a period in which the onus of criminal prosecution was still prin-
cipally seen as a matter not for official agencies but for the victims
of crime, many offences did not result in process through the
courts. The introduction of the police force heralded a significant
change in direction, of course, but it neither immediately assumed
the guise of a detached investigatory prosecution filter, nor could it
ab initio fundamentally change accepted norms of responsibility. It
also introduced a further layer of discretion into the prosecution
process. In one sense then it is axiomatic that crimes failed to be
reported, or to be officially pursued in nineteenth-century Wales.
Yet the evidence suggests that something more than this is
discernible in the Carmarthenshire experience.

It is clearly inadequate to ascribe the same 'cultural factors' as
explanatory of all under-reporting of all classes of crimes, let

alone all individual instances. To learn that there was only one prosecution for rape in Carmarthenshire, and that unsuccessful, in a period of almost thirty years is to uncover a piece of information the explanation of which demands considerable analysis – analysis which may not hold good for under-reporting of, say, other violent or property crimes. A consideration of particular offences will follow shortly, yet there is evidence that, whilst prosecution was not always considered inappropriate (poor persons being deprived of washing by strangers would possibly prosecute without any sense of impropriety on anyone's part, save perhaps the offender's), in some instances a strong 'popular' perception militated in favour of keeping the offence, even (especially?) when the offender was known, out of the official domain.[56] Such reluctance to externalize wrongdoing might extend even to cases of homicide, even though such 'conspiracies of silence' were condemned by many in nineteenth-century Carmarthenshire. The 'internal' attitude to such a case is suggested in Parry-Jones's memoir of Carmarthenshire life when he describes the consequence of the killing of a woman by her rejected fiancé:

> There was a trial, but the court never knew half of what the unsworn juries discussed in the fields. They could tell you how the murderer ran; at what time and at what farm he re-appeared to establish an alibi; who was with him; who met him in his flight to take his gun, and who made the bullet. They related enough, were it related in a proper place, to hang two or three men. But the trial was in an alien tongue and men became mute as they thought of it. Were it a trial in their own tongue where they could feel at home they would possibly have spoken up, for they had no sympathy with murderers. However a family of considerable means was alleged to have become poor: a few cottagers were alleged to have found it not altogether an ill wind. At any rate they were perfectly happily convinced that retributive justice overtook the murderer, for he never slept again.[57]

Parry-Jones's account, the essence of which there is no reason to doubt, is instructive. It is clear that a reluctance to involve 'the authorities' does not equate to approval of the deed or its perpetrator, or even of tolerance of either. It has been argued elsewhere that reluctance of juries to convict in certain cases has similarly been too readily explained as an exercise of 'mercy' or a product of 'sympathy' on the part of the jury.[58] What Parry-Jones makes clear is that the issue may, rather, involve the question as to the appropriate nature of sanctions and the forum and agency of their administration. He implies in this case ancient methods of dispute settlement – compensation and a belief in superhuman agencies of punishment (in a highly religious community, post-mortem eschatological punishment may be a latent understanding) were considered not simply adequate but proper. In the same text the author expands on the sentiments affected when community norms are infringed but also upon the nature of penal measures:

> Any member who transgressed [rural society's] standards and brought shame not only on his own family but on the larger 'family' as well, had to make the one inevitable recompense and that was to leave it to join the army, the navy, migrate to the coal mines, or else to stay on to receive the full impact of the mounting wrath of the offended society. Oh yes, it applied sanctions![59]

Concealed then within patterns of labour-based migrations, or romanticized in tales of helping offenders to escape their deserts, are instances of structured community ostracism.

The sanctions applicable to those who did not leave could be manifold. Ostracism did not necessarily involve migration, and social and employment status and prospects were ready targets for popular penality. As Peter King has pointed out,

> In a world where neighbourliness was an important buffer against acute distress, and where mutual aid and reciprocity were vital, even the poorer sections of the community had many ways of punishing an offender by withdrawing the right to borrow money, food, tools or means of transport. Integrity and trust were the foundations of the system of neighbourhood exchange which protected many rural families from the vicissitudes of the market.[60]

Nor should we be misled into the assumption that community sanctions were necessarily benign, democratic and lenient. The suicide of a woman who had admitted 'some romping and some familiarities' with a married man is testament to the potency of the shaming society.[61] As its most structured and ritualistic expression (which is not to say that this was by any means its most common manifestation), the *ceffyl pren* remained a potent symbol of community peacekeeping. Despite the prosecutions and the presence of the police it did not easily disappear.

To some extent it seems clear that attempts to suppress the *ceffyl pren* may be linked to those intended to stamp out other disorderly public proletarian assemblies – the fireworks and blazing barrels of Carmarthen's traditional Christmas celebrations, for example.[62] Such suppression represents a complex manifestation of class tension but is rooted to an extent in commonly held bourgeois beliefs in the aetiology of crime. If crime was caused, and this was almost axiomatic, by drink and bad company, it was apparent that occasions which promoted intemperate and indiscriminate company must be controlled. The point was made in June 1852 when the *Carmarthen Journal* reported another such manifestation of disorder:

> Llandybie – On Friday last this village was the scene of a most disgraceful outrage. It had formerly been the custom after the fair to carry what is called the 'mayor'. This year the disgusting practice was revived, and on the day in question a drunken man was carried through the village, followed by a crowd of the lowest characters, all in a beastly state of intoxication, using violent language and demanding money. Those who refused to comply with their lawless demands were shamefully abused. Our correspondent states that the police took no notice of the matter, although they had, on the previous day, been requested to attend.[63]

Such traditions, with their disorder and mocking of authority, were to be suppressed – local boisterousness the more easily to be channelled in acceptable directions, such as the novelty of a coracle parade which preceded the 'rustic sports' arranged to celebrate the marriage of the Prince of Wales in March 1863.[64] Yet the *ceffyl pren* was a horse of a rather darker colour. For this involved an element of representation of a discrete system of social control: a threat – in a direct and profound way – to the model of law and order marks the *ceffyl pren* out as a very particular form of popular congregation. The survival of the institution depended upon the survival of the social conditions which could support it, the sense of community that we have been discussing. This was evident not only in the country, but also in towns and industrial villages with relatively integrated populations. As E. P. Thompson has recognized,

> the essential attribute of rough music appears to be that it only works if it works: that is, if (first) the victim is sufficiently 'of' the community to be vulnerable to disgrace, to *suffer* from it: and (second) if the music does indeed express the consensus of the community – or at least of a sufficiently large and dominant part of the community ... to cow or to

silence those others who – while perhaps disapproving of the ritual – shared in some degree the same disapproval of its victim.[65]

Two observations may perhaps be made at this point. The first is that despite the use of phrases like 'popular' or 'community' punishment the *ceffyl pren,* certainly in the later nineteenth century, seems predominantly an event which involved the working classes. It is impossible to determine the identity of all those who engaged in the practice, still less those who may have chosen to look away when it was raised, but middle-class voices and middle-class newspaper opinion tended to be those most obviously raised against it. Nonetheless the *Carmarthen Journal* could still report in 1852 that the activity was supported even by 'men of very respectable connection and high standing in the parish'.[66] The *ceffyl pren* straddled a fault line within rural society, the integrative forces of geography, religion and language (though this latter also straddled the fault) in opposition to the social divisions of class and its differential conceptions of the 'respectable'. For those who sought self-definition within a particular bourgeois understanding of respectability, sexual misconduct, for example, was obviously wrong, but so was noise, excess, the use of the street as a means of dealing with it. For others, though the numbers were in decline, the tug of tradition or a sense of resignation lingered longer. Yet other social divisions apart from class continued to mark the *ceffyl pren* even in its decline, for women and juveniles remained key protagonists in these assemblies even as they headed for extinction.

The second observation may seem unnecessary or even, if construed as judgemental of past practices in a work which has a descriptive purpose, misguided. Yet perhaps it is in order to observe that *ceffyl pren* processions should not be considered as quaint, romantic survivals of an imaginative fun-loving peasantry. It is true that the ritual elements of the *ceffyl pren* served to control its activity – it was viewed as a form of violence which was not only justified but controlled and contained in its expression. It was also to a degree a 'democratic' proceeding, in that it involved a section of society, many or most of whom would have lacked the property qualification which would have been necessary to serve on a jury. To see in 'rough music' the expression of an unmediated spontaneous *Volksgeist* may however be naive, ignoring as it does the possibility of opinion and action being shaped by dominant individuals or factions within the locality. In any event the menace of the crowd, the fear engendered and the danger of loss of control were certainly real enough. The legal system of the nineteenth century was flawed and unrepresentative, but its increasing rationalization – the increasing emphasis (generally but unevenly) on the primacy of guilt being particular to offence rather than general to offender, the formulation of rules of admissibility of evidence, and the belated recognition of the importance of counsel to the accused – aimed at providing safeguards of a kind which are accepted as essential today. That the legal system failed to live up to such ideals, and we will see that it did, should not blind us to its acknowledgement of the need of such procedural safeguards which, despite the use of 'mock trials' in some *ceffyl pren* events, were not guaranteed under popular penality. The achievements of the legal system in the nineteenth century should not be exaggerated, but neither should the 'wholesomeness' of the torchlit riding.

It is not possible to state exactly how many *ceffyl pren* processions took place in the period covered in this text, and again it should be stressed that such occasions represented only one form (and that the most eye-catching tip of a vast submerged iceberg) of social sanction. Nor are the details of the reasons for such activities always easy to discover. In August 1853 James Jones was fined and twelve others – all boys – were reprimanded and discharged, having been charged with 'riot'. Jones had thrown a stone in a three-hour commotion which had involved blowing horns outside the door of Gwenllian Rees. 'They intended carrying me' was her terse explanation.[67] Some cases, however, are more easily understood and are eloquent as testimony to the conflict between law and 'custom' at this time. In 1851 Elizabeth Gibbs was prosecuted for murder by poisoning at Laugharne before Vaughan Williams J at the Spring Assize and acquitted. Popular opinion had already convicted Gibbs and (the case should be recalled when the representativeness of jury verdicts is discussed shortly) the court's verdict of innocence did nothing to change that view. Action was taken accordingly. A letter emanating from outside the county in support of 'Old English' [*sic*] law rather than 'lynch law', which was published in *The Welshman*, condemned the events:

> That the multitude *pre* judged the unfortunate creature, was too evident from the rude and cruel treatment she received even before a

Coroner's verdict had been given against her. That the same mobocracy (so much wiser that the jury in their own conceits) also *post* judged her is equally evident, from the lawless, barbarous, and stupid aggression against her on regaining her liberty when she was worried more like a wild beast broken loose from a menagerie, than a suffering, long-incarcerated *woman* declared innocent by twelve men on their oaths.[68]

This post-trial treatment had included the burning in effigy of Gibbs outside her house. On the following might the crowd reformed in the same street, by now renamed 'Scape the Gallows', to stage a mock funeral procession. The symbolism did not escape Gibbs, who decamped.[69]

The Gibbs case is interesting not least for the fact that it demonstrates that in the mid-nineteenth century popular penality might operate contrary to official penality, but that nonetheless it by then operated within a landscape which *included* that official penality. Elsewhere the interaction between the Carmarthen crowd and the legal system has been considered in more detail, and study reveals the importance of popular activity around and within the courtroom itself, and also around the prison. It is clear that the official criminal justice system was not conducted outside the realms of wider public commentary, reaction and, quite possibly, influence.[70] The petition raised on behalf of David Thomas in 1853 after his conviction for theft by a Glamorganshire jury ('against the direction of Mr Justice Wightman') is a variant upon such wider involvement.[71] Yet perhaps the most consistent and interesting example of popular participation in the formal legal process is the operation of the jury itself.

Again, the evidence relating to robust 'independence' of Carmarthenshire juries during the period covered by this book has been considered in more detail elsewhere. For more details and a presentation of statistical evidence the reader is referred to those other studies.[72] In summary, though, it is clear that grand juries were extremely reluctant to prosecute and petty juries extremely reluctant to convict in certain categories of cases, in particular those with a sexual or marital component. Such offences may be understood as regarded by at least some contemporaries as more appropriately a matter for the forum of communal shame rather than criminal guilt. As such, the reluctance of juries to proceed to conviction in crimes such as concealment of birth, and sexual or spousal violence is entirely consonant with the suggestion of a sentiment in favour of the propriety of neighbourhood involvement in adjudication and penalty offered earlier. That the 'No Bill' of the grand jury or 'Not Guilty' of a petty jury could fly in the fact of the evidence produced seems undeniable when particular cases are considered. When the grand jury at the assize in 1869 considered the case of Ellen Donoghue it heard uncontested medical evidence that the defendant had recently given birth, that she had left her dwelling, and that a newly born child was found buried near that house. The jury nonetheless found that there was insufficient evidence, not of infanticide but of the lesser offence of concealment of birth, even to allow the matter to proceed to trial.[73] While such 'morals' offences generally failed to produce convictions there are other examples which demonstrate that juries were willing to operate contrary to evidence in accordance with an assessment of the merits of the defendant, rather than those of the case, in other offences including 'ordinary' property crime. When thirteen-year-old Elizabeth Henfield was prosecuted for coal theft by a railway company, the prosecutors, sensing the difficulty ahead, stressed that they would wish only a token sentence. They were denied even that by the verdict of the jury, though the defendant's admonition by the chairman of quarter sessions seems acknow-ledgment that he at least was not unconvinced of her guilt.[74] Such 'contrary' verdicts are by no means unusual, and normally involved an acquittal. On the other hand, a quack doctor, John Harries, was convicted of theft despite the instruction of the chairman of quarter sessions to the jury that there was insufficient evidence to produce such a result. He was apologetically sentenced to one day's imprisonment.[75]

Such instances, and more could be presented, of robust jury 'independence' are significant both in terms of the cases filtered out and those which pass through. A number of points demand attention. Firstly, if the refusal to sanction prosecutions by the grand jury is taken with the reluctance which has been noted on the part of victims or witnesses to come forward, there is again a need to question the stereotype of the Welsh, often repeated and not least by judges, as a people untroubled by serious disorder.[76] Yet the image of the Welsh as free of major crime remained a pervasive constituent in the creation of a national image by both

Welsh and Englishmen. What was conceived of as an attitude towards morality was, in part at least, an attitude towards law.

Secondly, the recognition of the fact that the nineteenth-century criminal justice system in Carmarthenshire did not operate in an objective and depersonalized manner should be remembered when we come to discuss patterns within the prison population in a later chapter. It is obvious that questions such as the geographical origin of criminal prisoners, or of degrees of recidivism, will be determined not only by those who have completed the journey through the official criminal justice system but also by those who have not. Moreover, the complexity of the filtering process through which the prison population has passed may well have had an impact on factors integral to the penal experience prima facie resistant even to approximate statistical measurement – such as the 'atmosphere' within the prison or the nature and quality of the stigma which attached to the status of the prisoner. Yet such matters may be of importance in the context of the nineteenth-century 'fetish of uniformity'. If the criteria of selection of the prison inmate were different in Carmarthen gaol from, say, Birmingham then the consequent experience of prison and life thereafter may well also have been different. As has been pointed out in the Introduction, penal historians have tended to concentrate in their analyses rather too much upon the model convict prisons at the expense of the local gaols. Yet even at the level of the county gaol it may be difficult to generalize from particular instances, for, quite apart from the other variant elements in such gaols, it is dangerous to assume that the same 'sort' or proportion of offender actually arrived there. The simple point merits repetition here. The prison population is, despite the goal of impartial justice and the rule of law so fundamental to the Victorian penal programme, not a given, but a chosen population.

Another point deserves attention for the analysis of jury behaviour above has made no reference to the constitution of juries, assuming them (it might be thought) to be mere mouthpieces of a wider community sentiment. Such a claim, however, would be a dangerous one, for it would ignore not only the difference between individual jurors but also, and perhaps more problematically, the difference between different juries. For in truth there are four types of jury who might speak in court (five if one includes the coroner's jury, whose verdict could be of great significance for subsequent criminal proceedings). Grand and petty juries would operate in both assize and quarter sessions, whilst to complicate matters further, Carmarthen as a borough held meetings of both such courts independently of those which served the county. Whilst it may be credible to assume that petty jurors – typically farmers whose first language (sometimes whose only language) was Welsh – might, in anthropological terms, favour a procedure designed 'to attend to relationships more than rules', it is surely unlikely that the same factors would weigh with the grand jury. Even if the borough grand jury – whose members, we know, might live in the same street as the defendants who came before them[77] – could act in such a way, then surely the county grand jury at assize, composed of the likes of Lord Dynevor, Capt. David Davies and Messrs Henry Lawrence and William DuBuisson – the pick of the county's respectable families and themselves Justices of the Peace – would not do so. Has it not already been established that in the aftermath of the Rebecca conflict it was the division, not the complicity between the JPs and the local communities which attracted attention?

Yet the evidence suggests that even such men were not above the returning of 'convenient' opinions. The explanation for the phenomenon is difficult, but a number of factors may have been at work. It should be remembered that the JP traditionally operated in an intermediate capacity between local community and central government, exercising in so doing a considerable amount of discretion to be tailored to local conditions.[78] The 'Old Constitution' traditionally demanded much more of these individuals than that they serve as minor judicial functionaries. It was a difficult line to walk.

Magistrates, the police and the 'Rule of Law'

Similar considerations arise when the magistracy are observed concluding the trial of minor crime. For whatever reason or combination of reasons – local sensitivity, conservatism, the deference promoted by dispensation – Justices of the Peace not infrequently acted in a manner which shows them using the criminal law as one of a range of instruments in healing social rifts rather than as an end in itself.[79] Cases of assault were not infrequently compromised by monetary payment at the recommendation of the magistrates. In the trial of James Howells for running down two children, an adjournment of the case was ordered for a week so that four counts against the defendant might be settled by compensation.[80]

There are instances of intervention in assault cases by members of the public apparently present in court. Here the magistrates seem to act more in the role of chairmen of a public meeting rather than the dispensers of objective justice.[81] In 1852 Margaret Davies ('evidently a vixen and a scold', according to the newspaper reporter) had refused to compromise despite the bench's efforts to that end, presumably because the assault by her 'former' husband, with whom she was still cohabiting, was not the first such event, a previous binding over having apparently not dissuaded him. Even so the matter was not simply to be regarded as *res judicata*: 'At the conclusion of the ordinary business', the newspaper report runs, 'Mr Jeremy of Cwmdu, Mr Howells, and several other respectable farmers put in a written statement in Welsh, to the effect that the defendant was not to blame in the assault of which he was convicted, as the complainant had, owing to her bad conduct, been the means of "breaking her former husband's heart".'[82] Such communal intervention with its invocation of relationship history outside the narrow criteria of reference of the legal trial shows not only the persistence of communal judgement but also the factors (rightly, to the modern mind, irrelevant) which might inform it. But it shows too the climate in which the justices took their decisions, the sentiments of which they would be aware. In their reluctance to allow penal law through the cottage doorway or to punish a fight when private settlement was possible the magistrates showed a recognition of the principle that keeping the peace and applying the law may be different things.

A further example of compromise will show that not only adjudication but also reparation might be set clearly in a social rather than an individual context. The *Carmarthen Journal* of 2 April 1851 contains this report:

LLANDOVERY. – Last week, Thomas Williams and William Davies, two servants in the employ of Mr James of Llywnjack, lopped off the branches of several valuable trees on the said farm, and upon being threatened with legal punishment by the landlord, Major Rice, they tendered a voluntary fine to avoid the process of a warrant, which offer was accepted and the amount, nine shillings, was handed over, by order of the Major, to the overseer of Llandingad, to be distributed in coal among the necessitous poor of the parish.

If we return to a consideration of the role of the Justices of the Peace we can see that it was not only in the encouragement of financial settlement that the line between legal and extra-legal penality was negotiated. In 1851 E. H. Stacey discharged four-teen-year-old John Jones, alias 'Young Turpin', who had previous convictions, on a charge of stealing apples. Stacey's comments as reported are telling, but hardly serve as a model of due process. He 'had no doubt that [Jones] had stolen the apples but the evidence was inconclusive ... Although he escaped punishment from his [Stacey's] hands, he trusted he would drop in for a good sound whipping from his parents when he got home.'[83] The whip-ping, if administered, was apparently ineffective, for 'Young Turpin' appeared before the bench within a month for the same offence. The court here, in obvious frustration, turned their wrath first upon the prosecutor, who did not wish the case to go ahead ('She and her sort richly deserve to have their gardens well plun-dered'), and then upon the defendant, who was sentenced to two months' hard labour.[84]

Twenty years later, magistrates might still apparently employ a conception of justice which did not always sit comfortably with that of the law. As has been shown elsewhere, an analysis of cases of theft from the railway shows an apparent pattern of refusal to convict in cases where, though the evidence seems clear, it was obtained by private individuals or policemen who had been less than open in their efforts to obtain it. Such an absence of 'fair play' seems to have disturbed the magistrates. In one case the bench acquitted of such an offence notwithstanding the fact that the defendant had actually pleaded guilty.[85]

Other actors too could manipulate the input of the legal system and therefore ultimately have an impact upon penal structures. The role of the prosecutor has been mentioned above, but increas-ingly of course prosecution was being undertaken by the police. Yet, as was suggested earlier, the police too acted with a discretion. The decisions which were made in the everyday exercise of their duty were subject to a relatively low level of visibility and account-ability, but again were such as would ultimately in part determine the type of offender who entered the gaol. Not only, for example, were some offenders released without trial after a night in the lock-up (a variety of custodial 'sentence' which will be considered again in the next chapter), but disorder among certain national or subcultural groupings seems to have been ignored – fights among 'the Irish' or perhaps amongst the railway navigators being apparently routinely overlooked by the local constabulary.[86] Nor, in a force in which examples of policemen being drunk or even of acting as guides to and patrons of the local brothels were well documented, can it be presumed that such decisions were invariably considered, consistent or impartial ones.[87] Even when prosecutions were undertaken, the decision, by whomsoever it was made, as to the nature of the charge laid could be important for the offender's eventual disposition; the possibility of undercharging rape or indecent assault as common assault certainly merits attention.[88] To an extent, however, under-reporting of or failure to prosecute, or to prosecute fully, offences is a commonplace of criminal law enforcement. What I hope I have shown, however, is that in nineteenth-century Wales important cultural factors – the tension between mentality of shame and of guilt, of rule and personal relationship – were in the process of being redrawn. An older pattern of peacekeeping and punishment was being overlaid by new conceptions which predominantly come from 'outside'. The same may obviously apply to a greater or lesser extent to other parts of Britain, even in the absence of the specific variables such as language which have been discussed here, but this is a matter which will demand comparative study by other historians.

The institutional locality – prison, poverty and discharge

In the next chapter the investigation of the prison will begin but, as this chapter seeks to establish, the world in which the prison operates cannot be ignored. Though in sociological terms it may be a 'total' institution,[89] marked by the isolation of its inhabitants, Carmarthen gaol's characteristics were formed as much by those who were outside its walls as those who were inside. Yet the dichotomy between life within and that outside the walls is not even this stark, for the gaol had an interrelationship not only with the 'free' population but also with those who found themselves within other key institutions of the nineteenth-century social order – the workhouse, the hospital and the asylum. Whilst discussion of some particular parts of the relationship will be postponed until later in the text, some general issues may be noted here. The 'institutionalization' which some authors have urged as a characteristic of nineteenth-century social policy, and which has placed the prison within this wider trend, deserves examination from a local perspective.

Whether the Union workhouse was intended, or intended only, as a penal sanction for poverty when it became the basis of the New Poor Law in 1834 is a matter which need not detain us here. Attempts to draw clear distinctions (save for the initial sloganized one between 'the deserving poor' and the rest) between welfare provision and penality is out of place in the nineteenth century. Poverty might in itself be evidence of idleness, the precursor of crime, and of a lack of moral virtue, crime's instant cause. The nineteenth-century criminal code was littered with offences associated with poverty – vagrancy, begging, prostitution, failure to support family members – which might lead to imprisonment. The workhouse, with its timetables, dietaries, segregation (both between sexes on the inside, and from the wider community on the outside), its obligatory labour, its uniforms and its stigma, bore such undoubted similarity to the gaol that the failure of popular opinion clearly to differentiate between the economic principles of 'less-eligibility' and those of criminal jurisprudence seems quite intelligible. As the *Times* reporter was told at a meeting of farmers during the Rebecca disturbances, 'when they are sent to the workhouse the poor think they are going to be incarcerated there, the same as if any one of us were to be sent to prison'.[90] It should be noted, however, that there is a danger of overstating the actual (if perhaps not the symbolic) importance of the workhouse as a response to poverty. In Carmarthenshire the pre-1834 traditions of charitable support, and of outdoor relief from the Poor Rate, remained extremely significant for many decades. In Carmarthen Borough in 1872 the Medical Officer of Health, Dr John Hughes, reported that whilst the inhabitants of the workhouse in a half year numbered 103, some 1,222 persons received outdoor relief.[91]

Nonetheless, in the context of the growing institutionalization (albeit that we have warned of the risk of overstating this tendency), the connection between the workhouse and the gaol merits consideration. In fact Carmarthen as a borough had possessed some institutional provision for paupers since well before the 1834 Act, a workhouse or poor house having been in existence since around 1758.[92] A new building to house 140 inmates was constructed in 1837[93] and other Union workhouses were constructed for the county – at Llandeilo, at Llanelli, at Llandovery and (in Cardiganshire but taking some of the neighbouring county's poor) Newcastle Emlyn. One significant contribution of the Carmarthen workhouse in the history of crime in the county has been noted earlier, for the building was the object of attack by a large band of Rebecca rioters on 19 June 1843. The procession which had been the precursor to that attack had marched under a large banner proclaiming 'Cyfiawnder a Charwyr Cyfiawnder Ydym ni Oll' ('Justice and lovers of justice are we all'), the alternative conception of 'popular' rather than 'official' justice being perhaps never more clearly marked throughout the disturbances.[94] The ensuing cavalry charge by the 4th Light Dragoons resulted in many being taken, but only five individuals were remanded in custody. That flashpoint aside, the link between the workhouse and the gaol was, however, a rather more enduring one.

At the stage preliminary to commitment to an institution the factors which determined discretion to proceed against the homeless indigent as a criminal under the vagrancy laws or a pauper under the 1834 Act are unknown. The bare fact of conviction by a criminal court which formed the official point of bifurcation between gaol and workhouse is not the start of a process but an intermediate point once significant decisions have already been taken. As was the case with those who were subject to the decisions, so too the persons who made them were certainly not all under the impression that the punishment of criminality and provision for paupers were creatures of entirely distinct universes.[95] In 1847 David Davies signed, in his capacity as magistrate, some forty-seven summonses for non-payment of poor rate. He used the magistrates' court as a forum to complain about the improper implementation of the Poor Law, specifically the failure to remove paupers chargeable to other unions – some 200 such cases, he claimed.[96] This same David Davies was the chairman of the Board of Guardians of the Carmarthen Union. In

January 1846 he had sent an order to the gaol, of which he was one of the Visiting Justices, instructing Governor Westlake to release two vagrants two days apart and 'in different directions of the county'.[97] The line between penality and the extra-curial control of the vagrant poor is here blurred, as also, I think, in this case is the issue of its legality. In another case in the same year Westlake reports that another method was employed to combat persistent vagrancy, by advertising in the local press:

> the carmarthen Journal and welshman reporters and the Cambrian do [ditto] called and I gave the particulars respecting Mary Ryves which I consider she is a imposture according to the papers which she has in her possession and she has been Travelling the country so long to obtain sufficient money to carry her to New south wales to her husband as she call him, but as fast as she git it she spend it in drink . . .'[98]

Perhaps the most striking example of the use of the gaol to combat vagrancy above and beyond the simple employment of a penal term was to be found in 1846 and again involves the zealous Davies, this time in association with two other active magistrates. Westlake records that on 28 March he 'Received orders from J. E. Saunders & D. Davies & J. G. Phillipps Esqs to discharge any of the Vagrants that wished to Inlist in the army which I discharged George Brown & Thos Jenkins & they inlisted in the 37 foot'. It is interesting that no official copy of this 'order' is preserved in the 'Magistrates' side' of Westlake's journal. The legal source, if any, of this authority to grant conditional pardons by the magistrates is unknown.[99]

Whilst such a transfer between the gaol and the barrack room seems to be an isolated example there was, as we will see, regular traffic between the military and the gaol for the purposes of punishing military prisoners, though it was one which again raised questions of lawful authority.[100] There was also considerable movement of inmates between the gaol and the workhouses. Offences might be committed in these latter institutions which would entail removal to the house of correction for punishment. Typically these offences took the form of acts of resistance to the workhouse regime – a failure to work or an action causing damage to workhouse property, typically by destroying the uniform.[101] On 28 November 1845 Governor Westlake reports with some satisfaction on the discharge of a prisoner who had

failed to break stones in the Carmarthen Union 'which the prisoner Broke stones in this Gaol according to my orders'.[102] His
discharge was presumably back to the workhouse. This was
certainly the case with Mary Davies, released in March 1846 after
serving a term for refusing to maintain her two bastard children.
The governor remarked that 'the prisoner was very large in the
family way when discharged which the surgeon of the Gaol gave
me orders to obtain a cart to convey her to Llanelly Union which I
did so & paid 2/6d for her conveyance'.[103] Three months later the
recidivist Mary Ann Awberry was discharged and 'sent to the
Union by the police'.[104]

Another connection between the workhouse and the prison
which has been insufficiently addressed by historians is the issue
of 'secondary institutionalization'. If an offender received a gaol
sentence it was possible that an entire family might find themselves in the Union in consequence of the loss of a wage earner. I
have no idea how often such an event might have occurred, not
even simply in Carmarthenshire itself, where workhouse records
do not survive and census information is too slight to allow of any
calculation, but it remains an interesting question. Certainly there
is evidence that female offenders with children considered too old
to accompany them to the prison would face the possibility of
having those children taken to the workhouse.[105] Mary Davies,
remanded and subsequently sentenced to two months' hard
labour for theft, was a widow whose last recorded address was
Cornwall. The *Felons' Register* records that she 'had a child with
her – til 17th May & then taken by Police to Workhouse'.[106]

The pattern of institutional response to wrongdoing is even
more subtle. We have seen that in a society in which reputation
and shame are key elements in social standing, even amongst
those of limited material wealth, informal sanctions might be
important. Amongst these would be the loss of employment and
the prejudice which might jeopardize future employment. For
those unwilling or unable to move to another area where a job
might be secured then the dependency on parish relief, which
might take the form of indoor relief, could de facto result in the
legal institutionalization of an offender for a breach of a legal
norm even where no prosecution were forthcoming. The
'disgraced' female servant about to be discharged from employment for pregnancy might not care to weigh the moral distinction

between a future confined to the workhouse if she revealed the birth and one confined to the prison if she concealed it.

A related point involves the position of a prisoner at the expiry of his or her sentence. Whilst much Victorian time and ink was expended on the issue of employment of former offenders, the question takes on perhaps a rather different character in a predominantly rural county. In cases where a prisoner is a known individual within the community, the willingness to reintegrate that individual into that community on discharge comes to be an issue for the parallel, but as we have seen not identical, punitive sphere of public opinion. When Bisset Hawkins, the first prison inspector to examine Carmarthen and a man strong in his support for promotion of employment for ex-prisoners, found no Prisoners' Aid Society in the county, he perhaps ignored the potential of the county itself to act as a prisoner's aid society – its capacity to give or withhold support less dependent on depersonalized charitable status than an direct knowledge.

Certainly some criminal prisoners (as well as debtors) left Carmarthen gaol with very little in terms of personal property with which to get by unassisted. The governor had discretion to award a sum of money for travel on discharge, but the discretion seems to have been on occasion to have been based on good behaviour during sentence rather than simple need.[107] Henry Evans was discharged in 1846 after serving two years:

> is conduct since Trial was good, the prisoner could not speak english and did not know a word in the Book when he was committed but since he has learned to speak english and read the bible and repeat chapters of the Testament out of the Book which I gave him two shillings when discharged for is good conduct.[108]

Westlake even seems to have applied the rule in reverse on one occasion. John Smith, a prisoner who had some property and perhaps the expectation of more (he was disciplined for tearing a page from the hymn book in chapel to write a note to be smuggled out referring to the location of stolen property concealed in the 'Blue Boar'),[109] had proved troublesome. On discharge Westlake ordered that his money should not be returned to him until after he had been put on the packet *Phoenix* to Bristol, the cost of the journey having been deducted. Again the legal authority under which the governor acted is, at best, unclear.[110]

Some prisoners would find themselves rather worse off on discharge than when ordered to be committed. In relation to Monday 26 January 1846 the governor made the following entry in his journal:

> Rees Thomas came to custody at twenty minutes after eleven o'clock PM in state of Intoxication and the Police Officer John Griffiths was in liquor when he had the prisoner in charge also John Griffiths PC acknowledged that the prisoner had some drink at the Red lion in Priory street prior to his coming to Gaol also drink at the Stag and Pheasant, I have to inform your worships that the police officers are in the habit of telling the prisoners not to take any money in the Gaol with them for that the Gaoler always searches them and take it from them, some of the prisoners not Knowing wether the money is returned to them when discharged.[111]

Of course it was so returned, subject as we have seen to delay and any appropriate deductions.[112] We have seen that transportation costs were reserved in John Smith's case. John Wilson had two pounds taken out of his property to pay his defence solicitor, who had clearly failed to ensure his bill was settled before Wilson's conviction.[113] Other losses of property were similarly sanctioned. Prisoners might have verminous clothing removed and burned on entry. On discharge replacements were supplied at county expense. Such a procedure was, however, carefully checked, for the spectre of 'less-eligibility' might always be invoked by cost-conscious officials. Westlake was criticized by the Finance Committee for buying a shirt for a prisoner, his rather tetchy defence being: 'I was obliged to give him a shirt to cover is knakedness.'[114]

Post-Foucauldian penal theory has acknowledged the nexus between the Victorian gaol and other institutions as the project of observation, categorization and discipline of the working classes moved forward. Yet the dominant orientation of the historiography of such institutions, with its predominantly linear investigations into the history of gaols, or asylums or workhouses, of necessity has resulted in the nexus being formulated at an abstract level. The Carmarthenshire evidence confirms that there was indeed considerable connection between gaol and workhouse, a connection which existed in both popular psychology and more corporally in the passage of individuals between the two. This is not, of course, to deny the real differences

between the institutions or to suggest that they were entirely inter-
changeable in aim or regime. The distinction between the
constituencies which were assigned the workhouse and the house
of correction was important in determining those very differences
of aim and regime. Yet the categories blurred at the edges, not
only at the level of dogma but also in the assessment of individuals. Those, both in the nineteenth and in the twenty-first century,
whose ideology protests that poverty and crime are distinct issues
(they clearly are not entirely so, though the connection of the
former to the latter is complex and not simply deterministic),
ignore a considerable quantity of evidence.

It may be mentioned in passing that whilst penalty and poverty
were related, so too were penality and employment, and not
simply at the level we have noted earlier – namely the deprivation
of employment being used as an alternative or additional sanction
to official penality. The theoretical link urged, as was seen in the
last chapter, by some historians between the factory and the
prison is one which, if it is to be made at all, must be done with
some caution. We have seen that in a predominantly rural area
the industrial developments of southern Carmarthenshire and
beyond could act not simply as a magnet for those (predominantly young men) who could earn good wages, but also as a
destination for those socially ostracized. Yet the link between the
institution of the prison and the contract of employment may be
established more directly in some cases. Prosecutions and convictions for breach of the Master and Servant Act are common in the
records of Carmarthenshire petty sessions, and though the
penalty imposed was a monetary payment it could be enforced in
default by incarceration. In at least one case this measure seems to
have been used before conviction to put pressure on a defendant
to return to his employer.[115] In other cases sailors would be
imprisoned for the offence of failing to join their ships.[116]
Contemporary legal conceptions which distinguish the civil
penalty for breach of contractual obligation sharply from punishment for breach of the criminal law have limited relevance in the
mid-nineteenth century.

On the other hand it would be simplistic to see the criminal law
as enforcing only the rights of capital against labour.
Examination of the records of summary convictions connected
with the mid-century railway development in the county shows

that whilst the formally illegal 'truck' shops apparently continued without interference, there were a number of cases in which navigators pressed for criminal convictions in respect of non-payment of wages by contractors.[117] In the 1860s and 1870s there are examples too of prosecutions of employers under factories and mines regulations.[118]

There were other institutional connections. Clearly the prison had links with the asylum. Whilst the confinement of the mad was a distinct trend in the nineteenth century and one which has attracted its own historiography, it is again one in which more particular studies can reveal resistances and observations. As with developments in the workhouse and the prison on a national level, Wales could show a remarkable reluctance to throw in its lot with the 'Great Confinement', a reluctance attributable in part, no doubt, to the expense to local ratepayers but also again perhaps to older traditions of care for the disordered which persisted in its less atomized social structure. The Asylums Act of 1845, which made county asylum provision for the insane compulsory, remained an optimistic statement of a rather alien faith until the opening of the Joint Counties Lunatic Asylum (which, as the name suggests, also served neighbouring Cardiganshire and Pembrokeshire) as late as November 1865.[119] Before then, aside from the use of the workhouse, a property adjoining the gaol would seem to have been used, or in appropriate circumstances the gaol itself. In 1838 this latter was declared to have a 'large ward used to hold lunatic prisoners formerly'.[120] In the period before the new asylum was built, mad persons were transferred to the Vernon House asylum in Briton Ferry, Glamorganshire, if dangerous, otherwise they were housed by relatives or in lodgings.[121] Both before and after the establishment of the Joint Counties Asylum the distinction between the sane and the insane was a matter of considerable importance not only in the courts but also within the gaol itself. The initial categorization of individuals and their possible subsequent transfer between institutions remained a major problem throughout the period considered here. It will be considered in detail in chapter 6.

Again the link between institutions is apparent when we consider the infirmary. Once more it is clear that connections exist at a far more natural and mundane level than that traditionally considered by the theoreticians of the 'Great Confinement'.

The reconfiguration of social provision which the nineteenth century witnessed was incorporated of necessity into a topography and a community already in existence. When Carmarthen's infirmary was opened in 1847 it did so within the former borough gaol in Cambrian Place. The rationalization of prison provision had freed a public building for an alternative use (in the same way the infirmary had originally been intended to occupy the Barracks in Picton Terrace when new ones were constructed, but they never were).[122] It will not surprise us either to learn that the prominent individuals in county and borough should be involved in the operation of the infirmary, as they were in almost all those projects which touched local pride and local responsibility. Sometimes, as with the workhouse, the closeness of the links on a personal level could muddy the waters on the legal level. Whilst not touching the infirmary directly, an interesting case from 1852 is suggestive. In a case of obstruction brought by an officer of the Board of Health, objections were raised to both the clerk and one of the justices (C. W. Nevill) sitting on the bench, as both were members of the board. The defendant's counsel, who seems to have been responsible for the jurisdictional challenge, was thereafter not allowed to intervene in the case which was ultimately dismissed with 'an understanding' to avoid future obstructions.[123] As has been seen elsewhere, the institutional nexus operates at a level which is personal as well as theoretical.

As with the asylum, the change in direction of provision for the sick generated, by its use, the self-confirming evidence of its utility. The infirmary was making provision for some 620 patients in 1849 (of whom, as with the poor relief, the vast majority received outdoor assistance), and by 1858 a new infirmary was opened on the site of the relocated grammar school.[124] Carmarthen in the 1850s and 1860s saw, then, the construction of a new infirmary, asylum and prison. The topography of the town was significantly altered by the Victorian project of institutionalization. It has been seen that, at the level of local practice and not merely that of theoretical analysis, the connection between institutions might be a real, though fluid one, manifested variously through buildings, personnel and administration. It should be remembered, then, that as we seek to locate the gaol within the local community (the singular noun begs many questions, but we will let that pass for a moment), we must note that

that community is, in its turn, being shaped by a familiarity with and experience of institutions which were increasingly evident in the second half of the century. For some the familiarity remained visual or conceptual; for others, such as its inmates, the institution was constitutive of important and immediate aspects of the very experience of community itself.

Conclusion

Before moving on to discuss the prison, the main focus of this book, it may be in order to consider some of the points which have emerged from this chapter. The nineteenth-century gaol may be seen from two perspectives – the local and the national, or more accurately, the communal and the systemic. The first of these perspectives relates the gaol, its inmates, its staff and its constitutional significance, to the wider geographical and social conditions in which it was found. The systemic perspective relates gaols to other gaols, regimes to regimes, prisoners to prisoners. This latter perspective is perhaps over-represented in current penal historiography. Until the nineteenth century the former would seem to be the more potent explanatory model – that, indeed, was the condition revealed by Howard's *State of the Prisons* – yet it is one which is submerged by changes within that century. These changes were not, however, uniform in their reception. It has been demonstrated in this chapter that developments in penology, in government responsibility and in crime control were not merely projected upon a flat reflective surface. Attitudes, traditions and mentalities evolved markedly in a Britain undergoing industrial, economic and social change. Some characteristics of Carmarthenshire culture have been noted which may have served to resist or refract dominant perceptions of the nature of crime and punishment which we traced in the Introduction. Some of these characteristics, typical perhaps of relatively small and static social groups, may well be found in other rural areas of Britain in the nineteenth century. Others seem more particularly Welsh, for the determinations of a culture transcend the material conditions which lie at its base and will be mediated through (*inter alia*) the conceptions of its eschatological relevance (via religion) and the medium of its transmission and (self-)description (via language). And, as there are differences between communities in the process of change, so there are differences within those communities. If penal history is to chart satisfactorily the nineteenth-century revolution in punishment it cannot ignore the challenges and resistances to, or on occasion the ignorances of, that revolution in particular penal institutions within particular punishing societies. This is not to retreat into a mere catalogue of the particular, to abandon entirely the analytic model, but rather to refine it and to challenge our assumptions about the chronology, nature and extent of the 'penal revolution'. Victorian penal commentators themselves believed that the experience of a prison could challenge ingrained patterns of thought. Perhaps, with this sentiment in mind, it is time to enter the prison.

Controlling the Perimeter

Topography and power

Carmarthen in the nineteenth century was a town of some significance: its market, port and, later, railway junction gave it an economic importance, whilst its long history and traditional association with the Arthurian Merlin attracted the interest of antiquarians. Yet throughout the century the town was dominated not by the architecture of commerce or of religion but by the county gaol. It stood on the mound which rose sharply from the river Towy, overlooking the bridge which crossed the waterway. The armchair traveller who admired a typical topographical engraving such as that by Scott published in 1812 (reproduced as plate 1) would, as they gazed upon the harmony of the scene, the beauty of the river and the grandeur of the construction, have been admiring the residence of its criminals and debtors.

It would be easy to make both too much and too little out of this topographical prominence. The gaol was contained within and partially utilized the walls of Carmarthen's medieval castle, the location of which in such a commanding position was, of course, no accident. The use of castles as places of confinement as well as of defence is as old as their construction, for their physical strength in an age in which 'housebreaking' was an accurate definition of an offence, together with their monumental reification of political power, made such duality of function an obvious one.[1] At the time of Howard's visitations, several such buildings continued to be used as gaols. It is tempting to lay an emphasis on the symbolism for the nineteenth century of such locations which ignores the practical benefits of maintenance of a traditional and otherwise practically redundant site. It is, in view of the discussion in the last chapter, interesting to note that Carmarthen Castle had been built by an English king keen to impose order on a Welsh population, but to suggest that such symbolism was intended, or even apprehended in its employment as a Victorian gaol, is to strain too hard. Its status as county property in the middle of a borough is a far more potent reason for continued usage. Yet to ignore the gaol's position entirely is to ignore the fact that the traditional site was not only used but exploited in the process of post-Howard modernization.

As Robin Evans has recognized, the birth of the modern prison was a process involving not only ideological and practical changes but also architectural ones.[2] Carmarthen's county gaol was extensively rebuilt between 1789 and 1792. The old gaol had been visited by Howard, whose comments upon it reveal a mixture of routine deficiencies and surprising eccentricity.[3] He found both old and 'new cells too close' and the whole 'offensive' with an insufficient water supply. The gaoler, despite the recent construction of a house on site, lived at a distance. Surprisingly, the county and borough gaol both had 'Rules', that is, debtors were allowed to live outside the prison within a designated area, which in the case of the county gaol extended for almost a mile around.[4]

The nineteenth-century historian William Spurrell links the rebuilding of the prison directly to Howard's influence: 'John Howard, the philanthropist, who visited Carmarthen prison in 1774 and in May 1778, suggested plans for its reconstruction, which were carried out, Parliament having authorized the raising of money to defray the expense.'[5] Whether such plans were specific to Carmarthen (as Spurrell suggests) or simply recommendations along Howard's standard themes is unclear, but the task of designing the gaol was entrusted to John Nash, whose later commissions such as Buckingham Palace and the Brighton Pavilion remain marginally better known. 'Nash had arrived in Carmarthen a discharged bankrupt and in the throes of a protracted and bizarre divorce', writes Richard Suggett,[6] and the opportunities which the town's improvement and the patronage of the local gentry afforded him were considerable. The ambiguities in penality so prevalent over the next century are already apparent in Nash's building and its site. Here those of whom the county was most ashamed were presented with civic pride, those ostracized by society located at its very centre. Here religion and science (in Howardian terms of hygiene and ventilation) could not only coexist (a possibility which would be increasingly

contentious a hundred years later) but the hope of reform could
be presented behind a facade which spoke eloquently of deterrence. Carmarthen's gatehouse, with its swag of chains, proudly
echoed Newgate, a name heavy with revulsion, yet this monument to aversion was, as C. R. Cockerell wrote in 1806,
'generally and commonly admired'.[7] The public display of this
public architecture was undoubtedly important. When the county
gaol had been completed the borough gaol, which was also
housed in an ancient structure, the town's East Gate, was demolished, a fact which indicates that antiquity of use, even in
Carmarthenshire, was not always decisive of gaol location. The
new borough gaol when opened in 1810 on the 'Old Bowling
Green' was located in an area of the town marked by new residen-
tial and municipal expansion. It lay close to the new English
Wesleyan Chapel and would in due course be bracketed by the
building of a Welsh Wesleyan counterpart. To an extent, a central
position conferred practical benefits – a gaol was part of a
commercial community, taking substantial deliveries of food,
coal and candles. But quite apart from such considerations it is
clear that gaols were designed to be seen.

There are examples of the very visibility of the county gaol
being exploited quite specifically in the name of deterrence. In
August 1833, the *Carmarthen Journal* recorded that

> The thimble gentry and other notoriously bad characters, who are
> constantly attending the fairs and plundering the unwary in South
> Wales, were taken by surprise and incarcerated during the fair, and
> afterwards escorted out of town, with a suitable admonition and a
> distant view of the treadwheel in full operation.[8]

The newspaper was no doubt proud of this new addition to the
gaol stock, for the wheel had been installed only some four
months previously, but the passage, if accurate, raises the question as to how the treadwheel, located within the walls, was
visible. It is possible that a distant hill afforded a vantage point, or
it may be that part of the wheel machinery extended above the
walls. Certainly in other prisons at this time sails and regulators
of the machinery might be visible for a considerable distance.[9] That
the visibility of deterrence could be used as a wholly conscious
strategy in connection with the wheel in Carmarthen is attested in
a manuscript reference which reveals that at some time during the

nineteenth century a life-sized, painted metal model of a prisoner was maintained on a pole which revolved when the prisoners were at their labour.[10] This was, as far as I am aware, the only example of such a device, but its location above walls which already overlooked the surrounding area would have made its rough theatricality a prominent feature. Its existence should also serve as a caution against ignoring the possibility of elements of symbolic displacement, rather than wholesale replacement, in the transition of public to private for punishment to which modern penal theoreticians often refer. The enduring message of architecture as well as of journalism and the cheap pictorial print and the penological novelty crafted by a Carmarthenshire blacksmith may be less immediately dramatic than the spectacle of a whipping at the cart tail. They ensure, however, that nineteenth-century penality continued to operate in the imagination of those who might have no more direct personal connection with the prison.[11]

The notion of deterrence, however, relies upon the right sort of message being conveyed by the institution. The danger of putting the prisoner in the heart of the community is that deficiencies within the system, the breakdown of the discipline, are hard to conceal from that community. So the escapes which raise fundamental questions about the role of incarceration, an issue to be studied shortly, are escapes not on to some blasted heath but into the immediate neighbourhood of the institution from which judgement, like the fleeing prisoner, will proceed outward. So, too, the message to the outside will be compromised by other forms of unintended porosity of the membrane which is the prison wall; the tobacco thrown over it or the noise which emerges from within. Such failures to control the perimeter could prove difficult problems to those who ran gaols. On 2 August 1846 Governor Westlake records, concerning Mary Ann Awberry

> her conduct up to 9 o clock PM was very bad particularly on a sunday the Inhabitants could here her singing and making such a noise in spilman street and likewise in Bridge Street the Matron Visited her at 9 PM and persuaded her to Keep less noise & she would send her to her own department [she was then in the Refractory cell] but she defied the matron.[12]

Difficult too could be the pressure on the perimeter from the outside. The crowds which lined the streets from court to gaol were regular negotiators of this liminal status, the rioters who attacked public institutions a more obvious but less frequent one. It might not, however, at least in the 1840s, be too difficult to raise a crowd at the door of the gaol. Governor Westlake records in June 1847 that a sheriff's officer arrived at 10.45 p.m. at night, 'drunk and insolent', with a debtor for committal. Westlake was clearly unimpressed by the incident and seems to have objected, at which the officer 'raised a mob of the lower orders around the gaol'. Finally received into the prison, he then had to be evicted by force.[13] Though the apparatus of discipline might be prominent in the population, that prominence could prove a mixed blessing, positive only insofar as its message was appropriately received.

Revisiting the carceral archipelago

If Carmarthen gaol lay at the heart of the town which lay at the heart of the county, it also lay at the heart of the penal system. Orthodox penal historiography, it has been argued, stresses the vertical dimension of the institutions of incarceration, locating the county gaol at the bottom of a penal hierarchy which has its top in the national penitentiary. It has been suggested that such a model invites ignorance of the horizontal relationship of the gaol to other institutions and more generally to networks of community penality. Yet even in the vertical plane the picture is incomplete, for it fails to appreciate the fact that the county gaol stands at the apex of a framework of carceral institutions, the history of which is not static and which to an extent were significant in the selection of the gaol population. These were the local lock-ups to which offenders were taken either as a preliminary to transfer to the gaol or, more interestingly, as a taste of punishment on their own. Again the temptation to condemn such institutions as unworthy of our attention must be avoided. Their history sheds light on aspects of the transition in penality; they are associated with the decline of old, public penalties of a 'minor' kind such as the stocks,[14] and also with the rise of the police, and notably of the police as a de facto agency of punishment. Even in cases of crime which attracted official intervention, and the last chapter shows that this was a contentious category, we should be alive to the gradations in the experience of incarceration. No fewer than 247 prisoners, it was reported in 1851, spent at least one night in Carmarthen's town lock-up. However, before examining the variety of local penal establishments to which Carmarthen gaol is linked it will be instructive to question as to what extent it was connected to a prison 'system', as more widely understood around the middle of the nineteenth century.

In the 1840s, the decade of Pentonville, of Crawford and Russell, Governor Westlake of Carmarthen's concerns seem, to a great extent, stubbornly parochial. He had learned his trade as a policeman, rather than within a prison. His experience of prisons beyond his own was limited. He would meet the staff of other prisons or associated institutions such as madhouses relatively infrequently. Occasionally he would deliver a prisoner condemned to transportation or to the penitentiary in London. In the 1840s this might mean stopping off at other county gaols for an overnight stay, as, indeed, his own gaol was used for the transit of prisoners from other Welsh gaols. As the railway network expanded, so the scope for such contact with other local gaols contracted as journey times decreased. When the sentence of penal servitude was introduced, Taunton, Leicester and Wakefield as well as Millbank and Pentonville became destinations for Carmarthen's prisoners. The theoretical linkage directly to the penitentiary was, to an extent, increasingly assisted by practical considerations.

The other personal contact with other prisons would arise when Westlake or his head turnkey William Williams would go to identify those who had been previously convicted and who were detained for trial in another county. As will be seen in chapter 4, whilst the importance of such identification was receiving much more attention after mid-century, the technological thrust was again decreasing the need for personal visitation, as in the use of photography, which culminated after 1871 in the establishment of a central photographic register of habitual offenders.[15] Again, to a small extent, and in the case of the register as a result of misplaced confidence, changes from outside the penal system may be seen to have assisted the reorientation of the penal hierarchy, from a network of local prisons to a wheel whose hub lies in the capital. Whilst these factors are important in altering the mentality of penality, and in providing some of the tools which both promoted and facilitated the move towards nationalization, if we return to the experience of Governor Westlake we see that all this still lay largely in the future. In 1846, apart from a mysterious absence 'to attend to his private affairs',[16] Westlake only records two trips outside the county. On 5 January he left for Haverfordwest in Pembrokeshire to identify a prisoner, Thomas Hurcome.[17] In August he made the six-day round trip to Millbank to comply with the orders given by the secretary of state to remove the transport Thomas Thomas, who had made two attempts at escape.[18]

As to visits from the centre, the system of inspection established in the 1835 Act was, as has been noted, of signal importance in the process of systematization of custodial provision. Yet its real importance, at least for Carmarthenshire, lay more in the introduction of the mentality of accountability to an exterior bureaucracy than in the imposition of any real degree of immediate control. In the forty years preceding nationalization the Prison Inspectors, successively Bisset Hawkins, J. G. Perry and Henry Briscoe, spent a total of twenty-two days in Carmarthen Gaol, and the tenor of the reports indicate that even then documentary as well as direct eye-witness evidence was relied upon in such visits. These could, indeed, prove to be nervous occasions for the governor – one wonders how George Stephens felt when Perry 'took down a long statement' from Mary Ann Awberry in October 1848, his visit having coincided with her remand to solitary confinement on restricted diet for seven days after a series of events which had begun with her 'refusing to work, using disgusting language and assaulting the matron'.[19] Yet the real and effective immediate accountability, if such indeed it could be called,[20] lay with the Visiting Justices. It is they who superintended expenditure, who oversaw discipline and diet, it is they, ultimately, who controlled the hiring and firing of staff. Despite the increasing influence of central government it would be utterly wrong to underestimate the importance of the nexus between the prison and the Visiting Justices – enduring representatives of a system of local amateur, generalized government, of *old* government, in the period up to 1877. In the resolution of the struggles between centripetal expertise with concomitant administrative uniformity and older models of local autonomy, the victory of the former should not be regarded as either easier or earlier than in fact it was; tensions in the relationship will be explored later in this text. Nonetheless it may be admitted that the direction of change is apparent.

Of course it remains true that, although personal visitation might be rare, integration into a national system did not depend upon it, for written communication could do the job. We have noted earlier that an increased bureaucratic competence was becoming an essential requirement of the nineteenth-century prison governor. So written circulars from the secretary of state concerning imposition of the silent system,[21] the registration of transports[22] and the photography of habitual offenders[23] arrived in the prison whilst the annual returns under the 1835 Prison Act were sent out. Broader trends in the easing of communication, technological, educational and administrative (particularly after postal reform in 1839), diminished the isolation of the local gaol not only from the centre but also from other gaols and economic areas. At mid-century Carmarthen's governor could correspond with his counterpart in Cardiff concerning revision of the dietary,[24] or with a source of ship's rope in Liverpool to provide for his oakum picking.[25] By contrast, however, the writing of letters could, in its turn, undermine local authority. Whilst, as we shall see in a subsequent chapter, the proportion of prisoners possessing more than basic literacy remained low during the period under study, the opportunity, or threat, of taking grievances outside the local community is an important factor in an embryonic development of a concept of 'prisoners' rights', though its content at this time is severely restricted. We can indeed see a shift in the frame of reference of the prison outside its local boundaries, though again we should be wary of any attempt to airbrush the important image of local connections and relationships too early from the picture of penal development.[26]

Rectifying the anomaly: the borough gaol

In the last chapter it was suggested that within the movement towards uniformity and centralism the position of the borough appeared increasingly anomalous. The transformation of England (particularly) and Wales (to a limited but significant extent) into an increasingly urban environment, and one in which new towns arose for present utility rather than ancient distinction, rendered the exceptional status of the chartered borough increasingly difficult to justify. Moreover, a jurisprudential model which operated upon the rhetoric, if not the reality, of the equal protection of laws sat uneasily with the idea that different courts with different entitlements might operate within a borough by virtue of geographical and historical accident. Whilst not every irregularity in criminal jurisdiction was up for grabs in the spirit of reform (the House of Lords with its criminal jurisdiction survived), the legally entrenched anomaly of the borough came under review. And whilst the privilege of special sittings of an assize or quarter sessions within its boundaries might be forgiven as a recognition of tradition and pride – the law after all meted out to malefactors was in general the same as outside – the existence of a variant penal regime was not. If Forsythe is right that borough gaols attracted particular attention from the inspectorate, there would seem to be plenty of reasons which might explain it. In the redrawing of the map of penal connections certain places were doomed to disappear. In Carmarthenshire the borough of Kidwelly lost its gaol. A charter of 1619 had established its right to hold a gaol for misdemeanours in perpetuity, but Howard seems not to have visited it. By 1835 the mayor could report that in his own memory, which extended back thirty years, it had only ever been used to hold offenders against public order until they paid their fines.[27] The county town was similarly to lose its particular carceral franchise.

Howard's visitations had found Carmarthen's eighteenth-century borough gaol easy to criticize. It was housed in the town's East Gate, although, as we have seen, it also had an area surrounding it in which debtors were allowed their liberty – the 'Rules'. In 1788, when rebuilding of the county gaol was proposed, the amalgamation with the borough gaol on the new site was apparently part of the scheme. In 1792, however, statutory authority was obtained to build a gaol and house of correction for the borough on 'The Old Bowling Green', as part of an improvement to the town which was also to include paving and lighting.[28] The land in question was recovered from its lessee, William Lewis, in July of that year for the purpose.[29] The enabling Act refers to the absence of any house of correction in the borough, although there is reference to a 'Bridewell' in papers of 1767.[30] The new gaol was to be surrounded by an area to be kept free of all nuisances and obstructions 'for the more effectively securing a free circulation of pure, wholesome air, and thereby preventing the Gaol fevers and other malignant diseases',[31] an eminently Howardian sentiment. The old borough gaol was demolished but the new one was not built, though a vote of £400 was passed in 1803. The prisoners were transferred to the county gaol. An Act of 1805 repealed the provisions of the earlier legislation in respect of the borough gaol, declaring the site formerly chosen to be 'inconvenient' for the purpose and authorizing that the building might be constructed elsewhere.[32] When Nield visited the town he found that the new county gaol still housed both county and borough prisoners.[33]

In 1810, however, a new gaol for the borough was, as has been noted, opened. This was a development no doubt intended to reflect the confidence of the borough expanding in size and, as its new oil lamps showed, in sophistication. By the 1830s, however, the tide had begun to turn against the institution. In 1832 a riot within the gaol led to doubts as to its suitability, and provision was made for removal of prisoners to the county gaol where necessary.[34] The following year the magistrates ordered that prisoners might be removed to the county gaol at borough expense to be put to work on its new treadwheel.[35] The swingeing attack on the borough launched by the Commissioners on Municipal Corporations in 1835 did not spare the gaol from its censure; they found it 'like all others in the borough towns of this circuit ... much inferior in accommodation and management to the county gaols'.[36] The office of gaoler was in the gift of the political party in power, and the one serving at the time of the report had broken up a large portion of the female offenders' exercise yard for use as a garden.[37]

If this report located the deficiencies of the borough gaol along the axis of administrative inadequacy, very shortly the Prison Inspectorate was to do the same in relation to its penal shortcomings. Bisset Hawkins on his first visit in 1837 found the structure, which comprised a total of nine cells and two day rooms, to have an average daily population of ten criminals and debtors, to be 'dark, ill-ventilated and crowded' and its government 'divided, undefined and uncertain'. The gaoler, a fifty-five-year-old who had been previously discharged from the position, was assisted by his daughter, and no rules had apparently been printed since

1815. No labour was performed within the gaol, though Hawkins noted the recent limited provision for contracting out prisoners to the county. Amongst other major recommendations Hawkins suggested 'with great reluctance' that the gaoler's salary, apparently cut by a third since 1835, should be increased.[38] This had not happened by the time Hawkins made his next report in 1840, though the gaoler had died and been replaced by a non-residential publican. Indeed, a coat of whitewash and the introduction of a dietary (rather than a money allowance) seem to have been the major changes since the previous visit. Hawkins referred to the possibility of amalgamation with the county.[39] By his next report in 1842 Hawkins was observing that 'it is desirable that this gaol should be broken up'.[40] It is interesting, in view of the use of the argument from economics to persuade county authorities to relinquish their powers in 1877, to see Hawkins using the financial argument to convince their borough counterparts thirty-five years earlier. It would be too expensive, he argued, to bring the borough gaol up to standard. The county gaol he had found ill-managed but he nonetheless recommended a rationalization.[41] Hawkins's successor, Perry, produced the last inspector's report on the borough gaol in 1846, but its bare statistical analysis reveals little.[42]

In January 1847 the issue of amalgamation of the two gaols was discussed and formulae for funding and the length of the proposed contract debated.[43] On 10 May Governor Westlake attended a meeting of the 'Town Council' and was ordered to take the bedding, bedsteads and irons from the borough gaol, 'as the two gaols are consolidated this day forthwith and all borough prisoners will be committed to this gaol in future'.[44] The borough officials nonetheless received pay until Christmas.[45] It is possible that some of the maintenance work undertaken in the county gaol shortly thereafter – the repair of grates and of the roof of the Trebanda – was connected with this transfer,[46] as too may have been the purchase of leather for clog making and striped fabric for prisoners' shirts. It is probable that borough prisoners were distinguished in their uniforms from those of the county (whose outer garb, at least in the case of male convicts was probably blue and yellow at this time),[47] for their clothes seem to be made separately.[48] In 1851 borough prisoners were observed to wear fustian clothing, county ones cloth.[49]

In truth, the process of amalgamation of the two gaols had been in progress for some time before the final closure of the borough institution. Thereafter, the responsibility of the borough for its prisoners was to be, as was also the case with the borough of Kidwelly, a financial rather than a properly punitive one. The county gaoler was instructed to draw up the accounts for maintenance of convicted borough prisoners,[50] and officers of his gaol supported their claims for a pay increase by reference to the extra work created by the amalgamation.[51] Forty years earlier the distinctiveness of borough penality had been a matter for local pride. By mid-century it is increasingly thought that punishment should be more uniform, more centralized. Punishment was bureaucratized, a matter for penal experts not ostentatious burgesses, whose interest became a negative one, a fiscal burden. By August 1847 the borough gaol was being used as a storeroom for building material.[52]

A penal microcosm

There remained within the borough one remnant of penal property – the lock-up house.[53] As we noted earlier, the lock-up was, despite its general neglect by prison historians, an institution of some importance. It not only operated as a de facto place of punishment for those guilty of drunkenness or public order offences, but did so at the discretion of the police rather than the conviction of the court. One example from many recorded by Carmarthen's PC Williams will illustrate the point. Williams, in his diary entry for 2 January 1858, states: 'From information I received I locked up William Jones Collier native of Saundersfoot. Who I found begging on Monument Hill and exposing a sore arm.' On the next day he reports: 'at 11 am I took William Jones from the lock up to the St Clears road by the orders of my Supert.'[54] Such practice was recognized by the prison governor as jurisdictionally appropriate, as Westlake's refusal to accept a drunken dragoon in the gaol rather than the lock-up makes clear.[55] Recognition of the widespread use of discretionary, though temporary, incarceration alerts us not only to the process of filtering which determined to an extent the population of other penal institutions, but also to questions concerning the controversy over the role of, and the reaction to, the 'New Police'.

Lock-ups too are important to penal history, for they demonstrate just how thoroughgoing was the Victorian effort at systemization. Originally, temporary detention in rural areas was probably arranged on an ad hoc basis until transfer to a purpose-built institution became possible. Payments made in Carmarthenshire in the 1820s show daily rates being granted to the constable of the hamlet of Gwynfe for the detention of one Jane Jones on suspicion of concealment of birth. I think it improbable that Gwynfe had a lock-up of its own, and it is most likely that the custody was devised for the specific occasion. Certainly this was true of Ann Griffiths, taken for concealment of birth in 1840 and held for six days and nights in a public house.[56] More substantial towns, however, would have some kind of accommodation even before the reforms of policing. Llandeilo, for example, needed a place of detention not only for its own malefactors but also to hold county prisoners transferred to the town when quarter sessions were held there. Carmarthenshire's gaoler and his charges might be obliged to stay overnight in the town until the sessions held there were concluded. Yet even these places of temporary confinement were not to be excluded from the Victorian penal revolution.

J. G. Perry in his report for 1851 discussed the conditions in the lock-ups of Carmarthen, Llandeilo, Llangadog, Llandovery, Newcastle Emlyn and Llanelli.[57] It seems not to have been his first visit to at least the first mentioned, though it was his first formal report upon them. The information given on these small buildings (Llangadog, Llandovery and Newcastle Emlyn had two cells each, Llanelli three) is terse, but interesting as forming a mid-century snapshot of penal evolution. Some new work had been done at Carmarthen, Llandeilo and Llangadog (the latter building was only two years old but had never been used), but the report is generally critical. The evidence of older models of incarceration was revealed in these smaller satellites of the emerging 'penal system'; the drunken gaoler at Carmarthen, the drunken prisoners at Llandovery (beer was passed to them on a pole from outside), the insecurity at Newcastle Emlyn (where rotten doors meant that only drunks could be kept there, those charged with felony being taken to the constable's house).[58] Yet the inspector's continuing dependency on local cooperation was also evident. Perry had assumed that his reporting of the Carmarthen keeper's intoxication on the previous visit would lead to his dismissal. Not only had this not been the case but the 'keeper's condition and violent conduct' meant that the inspector was unable to get any information from him on his return.[59] Interesting too is the increasing association between the new police and the lock-up: this seems to have been institutionalized at Llanelli where the building was also the police station, but the absence of such connection was specifically mentioned by the inspector in the case of Llandovery.

Perhaps, however, it is the sheer ambition of the attempt to reform the prison system by the inspectorate which is the most striking element of Perry's investigations. In the introduction to this volume, arguments which link the overhaul of nineteenth-century penality to broad social and demographic changes were considered. Such issues were obvious to Perry, who remarks in respect of Llanelli: 'The rapidly increasing population of this thriving town and neighbourhood renders [his recommended] alterations imperatively necessary.'[60] The factors which led to the call for alterations included dissatisfaction with the heat of the kitchen and the inconvenience of the privy. If it were either necessary or possible (it is not) to mark a significant moment in the story of penal transition, I would place it not at the opening of Pentonville as a model penitentiary but with J. G. Perry's laconic observations on the temperature of the cookhouse of the Llanelli lock-up.

On the brink of nationalization some twenty-five years later it is possible to see how the trends evident in Perry's report had developed. The Newcastle Emlyn lock-up had been rebuilt, apparently not long after Perry's critical report, and part of the cost of the rebuilding had been borne by the county of Cardiganshire, the borders of which ran close to the town. The significance of this rather obvious arrangement is easy to overlook. Not only had the special status of the borough been overtaken in the cause of administrative efficiency, but so too has the integrity of the county, albeit at the counties' own instigation. As with the lunatic asylum and as with the post-1877 gaol, the institution now serves a population rather than a local government area. Demography had triumphed over tradition.[61]

By 1875 the new Newcastle Emlyn lock-up was considered deficient. The mechanics of central government intervention were by then, however, even more sophisticated than at mid-century. A 'request' from the office of Mr Cross, the under-secretary of state at the Home Office, was forwarded from Whitehall, to the effect that the cells at the lock-up should be put in 'proper condition' and under 'adequate supervision'. This letter was accompanied by a report made by the 'Medical Officer of Health for the Kenarth Division of the Newcastle in Emlyn Rural Sanitary Authority' to the Local Government Board, and another from Captain Willis, inspector of constabulary, written from Cheltenham. Willis had examined the cells, as he admitted, on dubious authority, since strictly they were 'not in the possession or keeping of the Police'. This disjunction, indeed, was central to Willis's report: 'I am of opinion that it is extremely objectionable that prisoners whilst in the temporary custody of Police for examination before the Magistrates should be handed over to the charge of persons totally unconnected with the police or gaol establishments.' Policing, though of course still locally organized, was systematized, professional and accountable.[62] At around the same time new lock-ups were being recommended by the local police committee to serve Burry Port and St Clears[63] and a plan considered to annex a room, the 'Old Mad House' adjoining the gaol in Carmarthen itself, for a combined police station and lock-up. The chief constable observed: 'I am informed that when the Government takes possession of a prison, no prisoners will be allowed to be remanded there.'[64] A night in the cells for a drunk was now an experience clearly within the purview of the Victorian criminal justice system. Fifty years previously the events described within this paragraph would have been inconceivable.

The county gaol – security

At some points earlier the porosity of the membrane which was the prison wall has been noted. The most vivid example of such porosity was of course the incidence of escape. The prison escapee occupied an ambivalent position in the public imagination, or at least in sections of it. There was of course an element of fear implicit in the concept, but also, in a strand of thought discernible from the eighteenth century onwards, with the tales of Jack Sheppard, Caleb Williams or Magwitch, of the heroic, of the person who beats the system.[65] Escape is of course of more than literary interest. As prison predominates in the penal system, different criteria for its success – anecdotal evidence, moral reform, mathematical analysis of reconviction rates or whatever – were variously put forward. But escape *is* failure, immediate and obvious, in the primary function of imprisonment. Analysis of escape is important for what it reveals about the architecture and technology of prisons, the deployment and commitment of staff and the resistance or passivity of the prisoners. It is necessary to examine how people were kept in.

It may be instructive first to consider how, and to what extent, things might be kept out. Contraband is a problem *in* prison because contraband is a problem *for* prison. In a penal sanction which employs elements of isolation, depersonalization and disempowerment the possession of prohibited goods indicates a breakdown of the first of these and a threat to the other two. It also provides the possibility of undermining particular elements of the sentence (a nail was a tremendously important utensil in a Victorian jail which employed oakum picking as labour, whilst food or tobacco could mitigate privation),[66] or even of prematurely ending it (materials which could be used as tools or weapons could aid escape). Whether or not it was ever elevated to such a theoretical status by the governors of Carmarthen gaol is doubtful, but as a practical matter it certainly occupied their attention.

Tobacco was a favoured form of contraband, it being prohibited to criminal prisoners. There were exceptions to this rule in cases where the surgeon was willing to certify that tobacco was necessary. So in March 1847 Surgeon Jenkins wrote that seventy-six-year-old Lewis Lewis should be allowed a small quantity of tobacco daily 'as he fancies he cannot exist without it',[67] and in January 1849 he requested that George Rowlands be granted the use of 'a little Cephalic or other snuff for his eyes to which he is accustomed'.[68] Such exceptional cases were insufficient to account for much contraband, yet illicit tobacco did find its way into the gaol. Occasional searches of individuals or of the buildings revealed smuggled tobacco but not necessarily its origin. It is unclear what prompted such searches and how often they were undertaken. Governor Stephens seems to have 'gone over' the prison deliberately if infrequently, on occasions doing so in the early hours of the morning.[69] In one search he detected the smell of tobacco but could find no pipe.[70] Governor Westlake, his predecessor, makes reference to only one search. This was undertaken two days after he made this entry in his diary: 'John Rees in the refractory cell for having a lighted rag in his pocket when going to bed and I searched him and found a pipe in his pocket likewise.'[71]

The source of the contraband tobacco was not always clear. Some attempts to breach security seem rather crude and potentially non-specific in their addressee, but they serve to remind us of the relationship of those within the walls to those outside. On 27 October 1845 Governor Westlake recorded: 'I discovered a paper of Tobacco thrown over the wall at the back of the wheel which it lodged on the top of the wheel.'[72] More generally, however, it would seem that the contraband problem was a risk associated with the presence in the same gaol of a body of prisoners enjoying considerably greater privileges than their colleagues. Debtors, as will be seen in chapter 4, remained a small but problematic presence within Carmarthen gaol throughout the period covered by this book. Whilst segregation of categories of prisoners was a key element of nineteenth-century carceral theory, it depended for its accomplishment on either architecture or vigilance. In the central convict prisons, particularly in the struggle over regime between supporters of the separate and silent systems which respectively relied upon a different admixture of these elements, the success of segregation might be, if not perfect, at least credible. Within many local prisons it was less readily manageable. In such county gaols, not only was the debtor presence a real one within the mixed population but both the condition of the buildings and the number and salary level of the prison staff remained (though subject to the comments of the prison inspector) at the discretion of the county authorities. In this respect, as in so many others, Carmarthen was no Pentonville. In January 1846 Westlake prohibited delivery of tobacco to the debtors pending instructions from the visiting magistrates after Charles Vaughan, a debtor, had been detected trafficking it for bread over an internal wall with a convicted felon.[73] In August 1847 the Visiting Justices ordered a door in the debtors' yard to be sealed up to prevent communication with the trial yard which had a door opposite.[74] Even if debtors were not actually involved in the supply of contraband, suspicion of them could be exploited by other prisoners. In June 1846 David Davies received tobacco from a female visitor who had dropped it in the lodge. When it was discovered in his pocket he claimed that he had been given it by one of the debtors, a man called Pendry who was to be discharged the next day. Davies was sent to the refractory cell for the false accusation.[75]

Other commodities for illicit exchange are occasionally met. In one case a prisoner, William Owen, testified that William Davies, remanded for trial at the same quarter sessions as himself in respect of a different offence had revealed to him that he had swallowed money before entering the gaol, where it was then recovered by means of 'operating pills'. The same case also suggests that untried prisoners' clothing could be a marketable commodity within the walls.[76]

The nature of the prison diet made food an obvious object of trafficking, and again the debtors' privilege of having their own meals from outside suggests a source of supply. Carmarthen's records are, however, inconclusive on this matter. When John Wilson was found to have a piece of cheese in his pocket in the Trebanda (the yard of which, we have seen, was convenient for communication with the debtors) he refused to say where it had come from.[77] An alternative source of contraband food was, if anything, rather more alarming for the governor than liaison between supposedly separated prisoners. In August 1850 three prisoners accused the head turnkey William Williams of conniving at two others' taking dough, presumably from the prison kitchen, and making it into puddings. Williams, the governor's right-hand man, was reprimanded by the Visiting Justices.[78] It was, though Governor Stephens probably did not know it at the time, not the first time that Williams had been implicated. At New Year in 1846 a debtor, Charles Vaughan, was found drunk by Governor Westlake, whom he then abused, apparently through Williams's 'Neglect of duty ... in allowing the drink to pass in to the Gaol a gainst is rules laid down for his guidence'.[79] Williams was, however, apparently more vigilant than some of his colleagues, as Westlake acknowledged following one of the few cases of prisoners' removing material from inside the gaol to the outside. In terms of personal belongings, of course, there was little for prisoners to seek to smuggle out, although a letter or, in one interesting incident, a note giving the location of stolen goods might be intercepted.[80] Yet in June 1847 Thomas James on discharge from the prison managed to take out with him one of the uniform waistcoats. The incident led to James being taken by the Swansea police and returned to Carmarthen, though the Justices there declined to prosecute. Within the gaol, however, Westlake decided to redeploy his staff, moving Francis the turnkey to watch the wheel and Williams to supervise the gate 'as I do not consider Francis so active as Williams'.[81]

If we examine the instances of escape, or attempts thereat by prisoners for which evidence is available, we find, as we have seen in relation to illicit property dealings, that staff might be implicated. Not all attempts fell into this category. So, for example, Thomas Thomas, described by Governor Westlake as 'tired', nonetheless made a rather desperate escape attempt by endeavouring to crawl out of the privy.[82] Clearly this was an attempt to exploit deficiencies in the prison itself rather than in its employees. Structural weaknesses within the buildings attracted the prison inspector's notice in 1842.[83]

There were cases in which officers of the gaol were in some way implicated in escapes, their culpability ranging from apparent inadvertence to the possibility of collusion. In 1849 David Rees the turnkey was reprimanded following the escape of William Thomas, who was subsequently recaptured in a nearby lead mine. Thomas had used a ladder being used by another prisoner for work, and which had been left during the meal break, to escape over the wall of the coal yard. This was a weak spot within the gaol and Rees had neglected to lock the door to the yard.[84] A year later Rees was dismissed after another incident. He had failed to lock a Yorkshireman, John Vickerman, in his cell but had instead locked him out in the yard. Here Vickerman had succeeded in under two hours in taking fifty-three paving slabs from the yard, and by piling them up to a height of five ft and placing a bench on top had succeeded in overcoming both the yard wall and the *chevaux de frise*. Rees was replaced and an alarm bell ordered to be installed.[85] Ironically, Rees had gained his position after his predecessor, John Francis, mentioned earlier, had been dismissed and charged with assisting the escape of a remand prisoner, Thomas Davies, who had prevailed upon Francis to leave open a door for this purpose.[86]

Other escape attempts showed the capacity of prisoners to combine together to breach security. Clearly the fragmentation of inmate subculture envisaged by the separate and silent systems would tend to suppress such combinations, but in gaols such as Carmarthen, where the regime was inadequately enforced and (among remand prisoners in particular) where the rigour of the regime was necessarily relaxed, they remained a possibility. In June 1848 five remand prisoners were ordered to be put in irons after a homemade screwdriver and a rope made from a torn quilt were found in the bed of one of the men, Joseph Eagles.[87] Three weeks later (and the day after a letter was seized which one of the five was involved in trying to smuggle out),[88] two of the remand prisoners again attempted to make tools for escape.[89] Successful escapes in 1858, 1862 and 1866 all involved more than one prisoner.[90]

The appearance of turnkeys as culpable persons in cases both of trafficking and escape at mid-century should make us pause for a moment. Carmarthen was a gaol which, as the next chapter will explain, had few staff and they were poorly paid. The extent of the wage bill in a local gaol was determined by the local Justices, who were concerned to limit regular expenditure on incarceration, a theme which will become common throughout this book. Even after nationalization Captain D— S— was able to boast of the ease of corrupting the underpaid staff of London's Coldbath Fields.[91] Central government directives, such as that requiring the silent system, demanded much from such a poorly staffed institution: one man, for example, would be obliged permanently to monitor the treadwheel in order to maintain silence. Whilst the illustrations in Mayhew and Binney's *Criminal Prisons of London*[92] show veritable armies of officers supervising working prisoners in the showcase gaols of the capital, the pressure on a prison staff who numbered only a handful was to prove much greater. To such considerations we shall have cause to return later.

The problems of trafficking and escape have been considered at some length, not simply because they are of everyday importance to the administration of the prison. It has become clear that the control of the boundary is a matter of importance if the prison were to achieve the aims, no matter how divergent they might be, of the class of penal experts – the Crawfords, Russells, Jebbs, Du

Canes – whose views increasingly dominated the penal discourse of Victorian England and Wales. Trafficking and escape conjured the shades of the pre-Howardian gaol, with its strong inmate subculture and its venal staff, at a time when they were supposed to have been left behind. The dislocation of that subculture by silence or separation was difficult enough to achieve within the convict prison, the atypical institution emerging as the tail to be found wagging the typical dog. Within local prisons it was much more difficult. The local prisons had a much broader spectrum of inmate, with a different range of privilege than did Pentonville or Millbank. Debtors were a historical anomaly within the county gaol. The persistence of the problems caused by that anomaly, together with the change of penal paradigm which was precipitated by the construction of the penitentiaries, may have played a role in the review of the suitability of incarceration as a result of debt within the nineteenth century. The reconfiguration of the 'civil' inmate within the system, as we shall see in chapter 4, tells us much about the reappraisal of prison, as well as the reappraisal of debt.

Nor was this the only traditional feature of the local gaol to be brought into focus by the smuggler and the fugitive. For as long as the crucial but constitutionally delicate issue of funding remained with the counties (and boroughs), then the salaries (and by implication the quality) of the staff and the state of the building (with its consequent constraints on disciplinary regime) ran the risk of being driven, ultimately, not by new professionalism but by old parsimony. More detailed consideration of the architectural history of Carmarthen's gaol will illustrate this point further.

The topography of the prison

We have noted that Carmarthen's county gaol was located within the bustling normality of a busy market town. Paradoxically, the gaol had, situated near its own centre, a microcosm of the supposed normality and respectability of the world outside its walls. The 1851 census reveals that resident within the gaol were the families of both Governor Stephens – his wife Mary (the matron), his children George (7), Marcus (6), Celeus (4) and Augustus (2) and their domestic servant Elizabeth Arnold – and

Head Turnkey William Williams – his daughters Frances (22), Jane (16), Catharine (13), Harriet (11) and Margaret (7).[93] It seems that Stephens's family inhabited the large house which seems to have been a product of Nash's rebuilding of the prison, whilst Williams's occupied the 'Turnkey's Lodge', which was probably within the castle gatehouse. It was there that Williams's wife had died in December 1845. Williams was excused duty for four days and Stephens's predecessor Henry Westlake ordered the treadwheel to be stopped for an hour whilst the funeral took place.[94] The vulnerability of the domestic quarters, if ever the prisoners combined together, was a subject of some concern to the chaplain following disorder in the mid-1850s, and as we shall see, the governor's house was eventually relocated (see plate 2).[95] Also within the walls of the prison was another token of domesticity, for open spaces were used for gardening and also possibly contained a mulberry tree.[96]

The perimeter of the prison contained a number of other buildings and associated yards intended to serve the various categories of inmates. As we shall see at different points of this account, the theoretical lines of segregation which formed such an important element of the practice of incarceration might be blurred on occasion in the practical administration of the gaol. Two principal buildings were the house of correction and the Trebanda. This latter probably, in spite of its exotic and mysterious title, was the part of the edifice properly known as the county gaol at the time before the increase in the availability of the carceral penalty had eroded the distinction between the two institutions, a process which was completed linguistically when the term 'prison' came to dominate the language of incarceration. The Trebanda then, in theory, held prisoners remanded for trial and convicted felons, whilst the house of correction held those convicted of misdemeanours. As we shall see in chapter 4, however, such separation might be compromised in practice.

Both the Trebanda and the house of correction were two-storey buildings. At mid-century the Trebanda had survived the expensive enthusiasm of the previous two decades for separate confinement, and its inmates slept, as they worked, in association. Such 'cells' as there were had not been constructed on the Pentonville pattern. The convicts also had a day room. The Trebanda also contained the 'itch ward' for the isolation of

prisoners with scabies.[97] The house of correction did have separate sleeping cells, twelve of them at mid-century, measuring 9 ft
10 in. × 7 ft 2 in. × 9 ft in. height. This building also housed the
oakum room and, below ground level, 'dark cells', unheated and
unventilated boxes 7 ft 3 in. square and 7 ft high.

Apart from the itch ward, medical provision seems to have
been limited for some time. One room seems to have been set
aside at an early period for lunatic prisoners, but a cell within it
was by the late 1830s being used for sick male prisoners, there
being no infirmary.[98] This absence was noted by the prison
inspector on his first visit to the gaol, and the county authorities
seem to have moved quickly to respond to the criticism, or at least
to look as if they intended to. By 1842 infirmary provision had
been projected for both male and female prisoners and a budget
of up to £500 approved.[99] By mid-century an infirmary
containing separate apartments for male and female prisoners,
approached by different staircases, was provided, though the
commitment to health was a limited one: the infirmary was damp,
possessed only one bath, and the drains and water closets of the
prison were described as 'offensive'.[100] It was only after the
rebuilding of the female part of the prison that separate infir-
maries seem to have been provided.[101]

Provision for female criminal prisoners was long a source of
complaint at Carmarthen. The remedying of these complaints,
indeed the very fact of their being voiced, may be construed as a
recognition of the idea that, as the 'new prison' developed, its
female inhabitants were no longer to be regarded as atypical and
peripheral but as objects of control within the same extensive
penal paradigm as men. That is not to say, and we will return to
this point in a later chapter, that the female experience of gaol,
and the gaol's response to the female prisoner, ever became
wholly assimilated. The only known photograph of the inside of
the prison from the period considered here (see plate 3) is of
Governor Stephens surrounded by a group of women. If these are
prisoners, and the question is a difficult one, it suggests that by the
1870s women have become an integral, if (as the very presence of
the photograph indicates) a rather special, part of the prison
population.[102]

In 1838, women were housed in four small cells adjoining the
gaoler's house. They had a small yard but were obliged to use the

privy in the gaoler's yard. Women's imprisonment was apparently anticipated to be not only of short duration but also unproblematic, for no infirmary or punishment cell provision was made for them, Bisset Hawkins remarking that they lived 'as though they were in a private house'. Two years later the women had apparently been provided with a privy, and, at least in theory, untried and tried female prisoners were housed and exercised as distinct groups.[103] By 1852, however, it was clear that the women were sharing a single day room and had three sleeping rooms with five beds.[104] It should be pointed out that, here and elsewhere in the discussion, the number of beds referred to does not necessarily correspond with the number of prisoners confined. At one time in the year 1856–7 no fewer than thirteen adults and two children were obliged to share these five beds. Whilst it is true that in the homes and lodging houses of the Victorian poor the single occupation of a bed might be regarded as unusual, such overcrowding within a government institution, and one which was ostensibly dedicated to the elimination even of verbal communication between inhabitants, was intolerable. The committee of justices described the provision for female prisoners to be 'no less discreditable to the county than repugnant to every feeling of propriety and decorum'.[105] In the light of adverse comments from prison inspectors stretching back some eighteen years such repugnance had apparently required a protracted incubation period.

The crisis over women prisoners' accommodation necessitated a major alteration to the topography of the prison. Hitherto those changes which had been pressed upon the county by the inspectors – the infirmary and the provision of a kitchen for the gaol independent of that of the gaoler – had been accommodated by redistribution of the internal space of the prison. The same principle was mooted again with the suggestion that a new house should be built for the governor and the old one converted to a female prison. Yet this expedient would 'curtail the free circulation of air' within the institution, and the Visiting Justices were obliged to recommend the purchase of more land, a part of the so-called 'Cursitor's Garden' which belonged to Lord Cawdor. Two points are notable in respect of the proposal. The first is that deficiencies were expressly stated by the magistrates to have been 'severely animadverted upon by Her Majesty's Inspector of Prisons', and it seems clear that a major change in the prison fabric with considerable expenditure had for the first time been precipitated by pressure from the penal bureaucracy. Secondly, it is interesting to see that the option of removing the governor and his family to a house outside the prison was not yet an option for the local authorities. The absentee gaoler still bespoke old corruption. The 1823 Act and its successors had been clear on the residence requirement. The oasis of normality at the very heart of the gaol would continue, at least until increased central government intervention displaced the local official to the edges of the approved, functional fabric.[106]

In October 1857 the Visiting Justices were lamenting that the new female accommodation was not near completion. Indeed, it seems that the land had not been purchased until August and the building not begun until December. It is interesting to note that the motion to adopt the Gaol Committee's report was moved by Lord Cawdor despite the fact that he himself stood to gain by it. A sum of £1,000 was allocated to the project, the result of a ¾d. in the pound rate,[107] and some £30 of it was paid to Cawdor to purchase the necessary land.[108] Work was delayed in part through a remarkable and late exhibition of local autonomy. The plans for the rebuilding had been submitted to both the prison inspector, John Perry, and the director of convict prisons, Joshua Jebb. They had not approved the design; Jebb had sent back his own which was based on the separate system. Despite some support for that system (Lord Dynevor declared that his experience of such prisons showed them to be 'really splendid places'), a combination of arguments, at first economic and then criminological, led to the rejection of separation in principle and Jebb's plans in particular. A version of the local plan was to be pursued.[109] At this point it is necessary to point out again the very real limitations on central government power when it came to implementation of its intentions.

At the quarter sessions of 1858 the Gaol Improvement Committee, to which the superintendence of the work had been delegated, proudly reported the completion of the work. The construction, with the local architect R. Kyrke Penson certifying it satisfactory,[110] had resulted in an increase in the area of space allotted to female prisoners from 3,304 cubic feet to 20,526, comprising six dormitories, two punishment cells and a separate laundry. The accommodation was intended for sixteen prisoners and involved the doubling in the number of day rooms to allow unconvicted and convicted prisoners to be segregated from each other. The work, together with an enlargement of the governor's house, cost £994. 4s. 1d. The committee, full of pride, invited the magistrates to view the work 'which not only will materially conduce to the Health of the Female Prisoners, but also be a lasting evidence of the Humanity and Liberality of the County'.[111]

Not everyone was so impressed. The snubbed J. G. Perry, the recent Birmingham gaol scandal not having dimmed his view of the merits of separate confinement, marked in his report for 1859 the contrast between local pride and thrift and the icy Olympian world of professional expertise. Whilst welcoming the new building as 'a great gain', Perry remarked that it was the only new prison building that he had come across in the previous fifteen years which had not been constructed on the principle of the separate system, and he regretted the continuance of the 'exploded' system of association.[112]

The rectification of the problems with women's confinement seems to have spurred the imagination of the chaplain of the time, Thomas Williams, whose reports, as will be seen, show him full of zeal in his approach to his office. In 1857 he had drawn attention to the unwholesome state of the refractory cells.[113] By 1859, he had turned to the chapel itself, writing to the visiting magistrates that the current conditions were unsatisfactory. Convicted felons and misdemeanants, he said,

> are crammed together like sheep in pens, and in hot weather the foulness of the air arising from the breath of so many cooped together in so small a space is almost intolerable to the Chaplain. I have occasionally found the greatest difficulty in speaking. Indeed, my health has been affected by much speaking and I have no doubt the closeness of the Chapel has contributed in a great measure.

Furthermore, Williams condemned the necessity of having to use the chapel as a schoolroom, not only as it was too small but also as this reduced 'the feeling of reverence' which was its appropriate ambience.[114] Plans were drawn up by the local architect, James Collard of Queen Street, Carmarthen, for internal alterations to the chapel (see plate 4) and the construction of a new schoolroom to the rear. Collard had been the only one to tender for the job and in October 1859 a contract was signed with him, the cost being £108. 11s. 6d.[115] The improvements were noted by the prison inspector without much comment. Even Perry was not an adherent to the principle of separation in chapel, a principle which had been carried out at Pentonville and elsewhere through some of the most bizarre architectural constructions of the nineteenth century. That he favoured, or could be pressed by the Carnarvon Committee to favour,[116] separation in the schoolroom seems, however, not to have been a source of difficulty to him at Carmarthen.[117]

Perry's regret regarding the failure to provide separate cells for women was not to last long.[118] The 1865 Prison Act provided the impetus for the most substantial reconstruction of the gaol since the time of Nash. In the period between the 1863 Carnarvon Committee Report which had urged separation and the Act which implemented it, Perry was left to urge that prisoners should eat in their cells and, in the case of untried prisoners, exercise singly when not in them. He knew, however, that, the cells being of a kind that could not be certified for separate confinement, there were limits to his capacity to enforce the regime.[119] The 1865 Prison Act was a momentous piece of legislation not only for Carmarthenshire but for all local prisons, this latter term becoming more current hereafter with the abolition of the ancient distinction between gaol and house of correction. Designed to promote an increase in both severity and uniformity in the prison regime, the 1865 Act differed from precursors such as those of 1823 and 1835 in providing a direct mechanism of enforcement. Section 35 allowed that if the provisions of the Act were not complied with, state aid in the maintenance of all prisoners would be removed.[120] In Carmarthenshire this aid had amounted, in the half-year ending 31 March 1865, to the not inconsiderable sum of £80. 10s. 10d.[121] Moreover, in the event of non-compliance with the legislation for four consecutive years, the government was ultimately empowered to close a prison.[122] In effect, the right and duty of each county to operate a gaol, a right subsisting since medieval times, was now explicitly linked to compliance with standards established outside the county itself.

The reaction to the Act within Carmarthenshire exhibited a mixture of defiant local pride and a recognition of the practical impact should funding be withdrawn. It was the first of these elements, together with a touch of self-justification, which was to the fore at the October 1865 quarter sessions. Following the customary reading of the Visiting Justices' report, Sir James Hamilton addressed a clearly excited court in the following terms, according to a newspaper report:

> The Justices had asked him to say that the Carmarthen County Gaol could now challenge competition with any gaol in the country – (*hear, hear*) – and that if there was anything wrong or unsatisfactory about it, it was owing very much to the fact of the visits of some of the justices being so infrequent. (*Hear.*) He wished to say that the new Gaol Act [*sic*] would come into operation in the early part of the ensuing year, and would probably be brought under discussion at the next Quarter Sessions. He, therefore, took the liberty of asking them to endeavour to make themselves acquainted with it. It was voluminous and rather complicated, and he believed its provisions could not be carried out without a large additional outlay. Perhaps, however, it might not be necessary to carry them out at their County Gaol.

Whether the rebuke to the absentee Justices was a real one or not, it received a reply from the acting chairman which was greeted by cheers. The other Justices had not visited the gaol, he said, because 'they knew perfectly well that it was in perfectly good hands, and that they could not improve the condition of affairs'.[123]

The issue fell to be considered at a time when the county's primary attention was focused elsewhere, for the spread of cattle plague in 1865 and 1866 was a matter of immediate and considerable concern to Carmarthenshire's magistracy, as it was for the population generally. Yet the successful double escape of a ticket-of-leave man, Charles Williams (alias Owen Pritchard, or 'the modern "Jack Sheppard"' as he was dubbed by the local press), and John Reed from the Trebanda increased the pressure upon the magistrates to give consideration to rebuilding the gaol.[124]

At the next quarter sessions the regular chairman, John Johnes, had recovered from one of his persistent bouts of illness and presided over a rather more pragmatic discussion than that which had gone before, he having declared himself in favour of the principle of separation. There was some urgency in the matter, for Perry had inspected the gaol a few days previous to the court's sitting and had warned Governor Stephens against using the uncertified refractory cells after the end of the month. Johnes suggested that the court should petition the secretary of state to discover how long the county gaol had before it was obliged to comply with the terms of the Act. Lord Dynevor proposed remitting the question of the manner of compliance to the Visiting Justices, raising the possibility of transforming the debtors' area into separate cells and building a new gaol for that class of prisoner elsewhere.[125]

Thereafter, the rebuilding of the gaol was considered by the Visiting Justices. The expedient of adapting the existing debtors' prison and building a new one was considered but rejected as being insufficient to provide the forty new cells which, by virtue of the method of calculation laid down within the Act, were needed, together with exercise and stone-breaking yards.[126] The county surveyor, Mr George, was dispatched to examine the gaols at Swansea, Cardiff, Gloucester and Reading as an apprenticeship which seemed, at the time, preferable to calling in 'foreign assistance'.[127] It seems clear that some extra land on the Castle Green would need to be purchased from Lord Cawdor, whose name had, interestingly, recently been placed on the list of Visiting Justices.[128] George submitted plans in April showing the current state of the gaol and in June 1866 had produced a proposal for reconstruction.[129] At the July sessions, however, the plans were referred back, the scheme of buying the whole of Castle Green, rather than a parcel of it which would cost £300, being now considered.[130] This more radical proposal was to carry the day.[131]

The reference to 'foreign assistance' seems perfectly in harmony with the general mood of offended localism which marked the early debate. At the 1866 summer sessions the ratepayers were to be left under no illusion as to whose was the responsibility for spending the thousands of pounds which the work would cost, nor as to the merit of the existing gaol. 'It was right to state for the information of the County generally', said Johnes from the chair of the summer quarter sessions, 'that the Court was not altering the gaol for motives of their own, but simply in response to the voice of the legislature (*Cheers*).' Sir John Mansel declared at the following session that 'There is not a more healthy gaol in England' than that currently in use in the county, a declaration which drew cries of 'Hear, Hear'. Nonetheless, Mansel urged swift action for fear of losing the government fees.[132]

Yet problems began to present themselves and to provide the opportunity for the internal squabbling at which the Carmarthenshire magistracy excelled. The purchase of the Green would involve not simply the eviction of the cottagers who lived there, a point which apparently disturbed no one but the tenants themselves, but also the obstruction of a right of way. Initially this seemed to be no great problem, the Visiting Justices declaring it to be 'very little used' and 'almost impassible' at one point.[133] Yet at the January sessions in 1867 Captain David Davies revealed that he would, in his capacity of chairman of the Carmarthen Highway Board, object to the plans which he was presenting in his capacity as one of the Visiting Justices. The loss would be not only of a pathway but of an open space and (a most powerful argument indeed) one upon which John Wesley himself had preached.[134] For a while the issue threatened the expansion until Davies was prevailed upon to withdraw his objection, at which, it was reported to laughter, it was expected that everyone else would do so. At the next sessions permission was quietly granted to block the footpath.[135]

It has been noted that the plans and the estimates for the rebuilding work had been drawn up by the county surveyor, Mr George, who clearly thought that the work would be entrusted to him. It emerged, however, that not all the Justices, notably Davies, were in favour of such a plan. The Justices put out the work to tender in the autumn of 1866 and the Birmingham architect William Martin became interested in the project.[136] He was described as a man 'who gives the whole of his time and attention to gaols'[137] and was also approached by Cardiganshire as it too struggled desperately to bring its gaol into conformity with the 1865 Act. Martin submitted his plans for Carmarthen in April 1867.[138] The snubbed George was apparently outraged and submitted a bill for £233. 1s. 6d. for his services 'as architect', a sum which included £200 commission on his estimate of £8,000 for the reconstruction. In an attempt to pass the buck someone had told George that the initiative to use another architect had come from the prison inspector, and the Justices were presumably surprised when the surveyor wrote to J. G. Perry to establish that this was not the case. Sir John Mansel brazened out the issue at the quarter sessions, variously citing the rudeness, inexperience and unoriginality of the surveyor, whose reputation was not so low as to prevent the county granting him, rather guiltily, a 'gratuity of £100'.[139]

The obstacles having been surmounted, it was decided to proceed with Martin's plan, at an estimated cost of £17,700, £15,000 of which was to be borrowed in instalments from the Public Works Loans Commissioners, a procedure provided for in the 1865 Act.[140] The plans had to be approved by the Home Office, and, as a preliminary to this, the plans were despatched to the inspector for his opinion. Perry considered the edifice larger than it need be and suggested diminishing the number of cells (by now sixty-two were proposed) by removing one tier of the building, leaving it at two storeys. This would result in a saving of £2,000. However, the bench, for reasons unknown, did not accept that cell provision be reduced to Perry's suggested level and it was agreed that provision be made for forty-eight cells. Plans were reported as being approved by the quarter sessions in July and by October 1868 construction of the new prison had begun.[141]

The work necessarily disrupted the operation of the existing gaol at a time when it was under pressure from an influx of prisoners which was being blamed on a greater than normal number of committals for vagrancy.[142] Both county and borough prisoners began to be removed to Swansea from May 1869, the contract being for all the female prisoners, those on remand and those serving more than three months. The cost of each prisoner was set at 10s. 6d. per week.[143] The logistics of such an exercise were complicated. It was to last for some time and might involve removal of a prisoner out of the county for remand, return to Carmarthen for trial and then, if convicted, a return to Swansea for sentence. Conveyance of the prisoners, though of course much easier in the age of communication to which the systemization of prisons in part owed its existence, involved expense in the provision of a prison van,[144] the purchase of railway and omnibus tickets, and in staff time due to the need for an officer to escort.[145] It was an expense which, even if affordable by the county, was probably beyond the means of many of the friends and relatives of the prisoners. It is ironic that amongst those prisoners to complete their sentences outside the county were Carmarthenshire's most famous Victorian criminals, Evan and Hannah Jacob (see plate 5), whose daughter Sarah, the 'Welsh Fasting Girl', had achieved national celebrity before her death under medical observation had dispelled belief in her miraculous powers.[146]

For those prisoners who remained in Carmarthen and also for the staff of the prison the construction work represented a change in routine. Governor Stephens, living in temporary rented accommodation,[147] employed inmates in excavating the foundations and cleaning the bricks which were probably recycled from the parts of the structure which had been demolished.[148] This 'alternative' to the forms of hard labour insisted on by the 1865 Prisons Act, though it presumably compromised the separation principle which underlay the Act, was recognized by the governor as having an economic advantage.[149]

The rebuilding was contracted to local builder George Thomas, who was paid by instalments, under the superintendence of a clerk to the works, Joseph Burch. The work was slowed by factors such as severe weather and the difficulty of obtaining materials including ironwork.[150] In addition, there were some changes in plans, the Visiting Justices urging extra work in accordance with the architect's proposal to raise walls, add railings and repaint the remaining section of the castle as the project neared completion: 'it would not be judicious to losing [*sic*] this opportunity of having the work thoroughly well done.'[151] As parts of the old building came down and the new one went up, the prisoners were moved round the gaol, convicted prisoners at one point sleeping in the debtors' quarters. The delays which inhered in the bureaucratic control of the work by the quarter sessions seem to have frustrated the architect Martin. Having given directions to a local firm, Victor and Company, to install the gas fittings in the new governor's house he found that his actions had not been authorized by the Justices. In consequence, he urged for tenders for similar work together with the supply of locks, bells and the like to be invited 'without much delay'.[152] The successful tender for the heating of the gaol came from a firm, Haden and Sons, in Trowbridge.[153] With a Warwickshire architect and a Wiltshire engineer involved, the notion of the local foundation of the ancient county gaol was exploded by the 1865 Act in relation to its infrastructure as well as its regulation.

By the summer of 1872 the gaol had been rebuilt, and following certification by the inspectorate it was soon receiving prisoners. The contract with Swansea was terminated and a gratuity of £10 proposed for Governor William Cox of that gaol, who had housed Carmarthen's offenders for nearly three years.[154] The 'substantial and well-finished structure'[155] which was the new building sat alongside the refurbished old part of the prison now used for women. Money had been spent on the treadwheel house and in sinking an elaborate well, a step perhaps necessitated by cases of 'English Cholera' being detected during the renovations for which the state of the cesspool had been blamed.[156]

All should have been well, but was not. The contractor seems to have been reluctant to complete his task. Imperfections in the work were to prove remarkably resistant to rectification and problems with the heating and ventilation of the women's prison persisted for years, as did the leaking cupola.[157] Martin, whose visits during the construction periods had resulted in 'a large sum' being claimed for travelling and out-of-pocket expenses,[158] seems to have been rather less assiduous when it came to rectification of the defects.[159] Moreover, it was apparently only after the work had been completed that the absence of a lock-up for the temporary detention of county prisoners seems to have been recognized as a problem.[160]

More alarming than the physical deficiencies was the question of finance. A dispute between the architect and the contractor, who had failed, *inter alia,* to include the cost of some materials as well as labour in his estimate, delayed the presentation of the accounts. They reached the Building Committee only a day before the April 1873 quarter sessions and Sir John Mansel, whose desire to see the work 'thoroughly well done' had in no way diminished the costs, was obliged to submit them after only a limited examination.[161] By the next sessions he was compelled to report that the balance due was 'considerably in excess of what we anticipated' and stated that Martin would be asked to attend the next sessions to defend the account, which apparently totalled over £20,000.[162] The embarrassed bench, unwilling to return to the Loans Commissioners to be bailed out, were obliged to deploy moneys directly from the rates to meet the bills.[163]

Yet perhaps the most interesting aspect of the rebuilding programme was the message it carries of the lack of clear direction in government policy in the period between the two Prison Acts of 1865 and 1877. There seems no doubt that Carmarthenshire's Justices had seen their task, and it was one which they had resented, to be the construction of a new gaol for the county. In neighbouring Cardiganshire, however, work had not been so swiftly undertaken. As early as 1868, Cardiganshire quarter sessions had discussed the possibility of a three-counties gaol on a similar principle to the lunatic asylum, only to be told that Gathorne Hardy, the secretary of state, was opposed to the idea.[164] Yet its failure to build a new gaol did Cardiganshire little harm. Central funding might be withdrawn by virtue of the provisions of the 1865 statute, and, indeed, such a step was threatened, but one of the great weaknesses of the Act was that in the final result the reliance on the old local government structure meant that central government had no power to compel the acceptance of one county's prisoners by the gaol of another.[165] In 1871 the government informed the Cardiganshire bench that the threat of withholding funds would be suspended until the Judicature Commission had reported on a possible consolidation of the county structure.[166] Whilst Carmarthen's prisoners washed the bricks for the construction of their new accommodation, Cardiganshire's magistracy sat tight. Nationalization achieved the redistribution of prisoners which the 1865 Act had lacked the power to do. In 1878, Cardiganshire's prisoners began to be moved to Carmarthen, its own gaol having been closed, to the relief of the county's bench.[167] Pembrokeshire was more antagonistic towards the loss of its gaol and secured a respite of its closure before the Home Office finally took that step.[168]

It is inconceivable that Carmarthenshire authorities remained unaware of the debates from the late 1860s about consolidation. Yet it seems clear that their understanding, as they planned and executed their new building, was that they were constructing a prison to serve their own county. Within six years of its opening as a reformed institution, the indolence and parsimony of its neighbours and the vacillation over and ultimate reversal of central government policy placed it under great strain. By May 1878 the inspector delayed the transfer of further prisoners from Cardigan, the gaol at Carmarthen being rather full.[169] In August of the same year, anticipating the arrival of prisoners from Pembrokeshire, the *Carmarthen Journal* made the point succinctly. 'Some years ago', it said, 'the County of Carmarthen incurred great expense in providing separate-cell accommodation for each prisoner – is that work to be undone and our criminals to be huddled together as they were before the days of Howard and Elizabeth Fry?'[170]

Dramatis Personae 1: The Staff

This chapter and the next will consider the individuals whose lives, or significant portions thereof, were spent inside the walls of Carmarthen gaol in the period under study. All that has been said concerning the methodology of this book to this point should indicate why such consideration is necessary. The experience of prison may be structured by rules, ideologies and systems, but it remains at a fundamental level an experience of human interaction. Human beings then become an indispensable element within the narrative. To restore individuals to the history of the gaol is not to add interesting local colour to the theoretical or statistical discourse which surrounds nineteenth-century penal history, it is, rather, to grapple with the essential nature of that history. Of course, a familiar argument resurfaces at this point. The investigation of the personalities of those within a particular institution will, of necessity, render dubious the claim to generality which is the essence of thematic historical analysis. Yet only by that investigation can we be adequately alerted to those elements of discretion, variation and contingency which must be reintegrated into the analytical paradigms.

Yet to insist upon the return of the individual to the description of prison history is by no means to engage in an unproblematical task. The basic biographical data, the records of their major life events, let alone the details of character or opinion, of many of the individuals to be mentioned here are often elusive. To this extent the historian may, paradoxically, be more successful in pursuing the chimera of the 'mentality of an age' than the mentality of an individual, in that the general, unfocused reflections from many different individuals may produce rather more light than the occluded image of a few. Yet the point remains that a concentration on particular events relating to particular individuals in a particular gaol will oblige us to accept, and to accept as essential rather than as an introductory truism, that the particular, in all its human complexity, must be incorporated into our construction of the general. The people who enforced rules or who were subject to their effects were not, could not be, programmed automata, even though some penal policy-makers might have wished that they were. 'Hard labour' and 'religious instruction' were not mere elements of a penal regime but exchanges which involved elements of negotiation. And it should not be forgotten, despite the seductive shorthand of theory, that 'opinion' or 'ideas' about crime, criminals or punishment were not necessarily any more consistent and uncontroversial a century and a half ago than they are today, although part of the story of this book is of a movement to privilege certain opinions and ideas, or at least the opinions and ideas of certain types of persons, over others.

The recognition of the individual actor in the penal narrative, however, does not prevent the making of general statements about the past, any more than the recognition of individual DNA inhibits discussion of human beings in general. It simply makes the questions more sophisticated. Moreover, the movement into the realms of the particular actor(s) does not necessitate that we should ignore the constraints on their individuality. On the contrary, it is the boundary between the individual and the constraint which will inform much of the following discussion. By 'constraint' no philosophical notion of determinism as against free will is being invoked. Nor is it intended to explore the issue as to how far opinions are temporally and culturally determined rather than individually derived. As to this latter point, the reader will recall that chapter 1 explored the idea of cultural identity to which ideas of community, language and religion can contribute. Such factors, of course, in themselves will have effects upon the constitution of individual identity, though. What is intended by the idea of 'constraint' here is simply that the individuals within a prison live within a framework of rules and expectations and occupy a space which is not merely personal but also symbolic. This remains true even as rules, expectations and symbolism change, as they do during the nineteenth century. Some reflections may help to clarify the issue.

The prisoner is indeed an individual, but he or she is also a prisoner. It has been seen that it is wrong to equate the terms 'prisoner' and 'criminal', for the former category is only a subset of the latter. Even if the categories of debtors and the untried are discounted, there remains a class whose presence within the institution depends on elements not only perhaps of chance (for example, of their offence having been discovered) but also of choice (in prosecution or conviction). In this study, as in the world, incarceration results in the ascription of a particular status in addition to the existing characteristics of the individual personality: the status of prisoner. This label has a symbolic meaning, not only for specific purposes (for instance, the prisoner may now have a role in deterring others from crime) but also by the very fact of selection for social exclusion. Individual actions and motives have become processed through the instrumentality of generic systems. The processes through which the individual has passed necessarily for some purposes shift the balance between individual and symbolic existence in the direction of the latter, and this shift is deliberately accomplished. David Davies of Llanelli becomes firstly 'the prisoner at the bar' charged with a general offence and then the numbered, uniformed, crop-headed participant in silent regulated labour. Of course, this does not mean that the penal system can simply ignore the personal qualities of those who enter it. Such oversight would be impossible within institutions on practical grounds and may even be undesirable on ideological ones. As to the former, as will be seen, issues of health, strength, compliance and the like will problematize the performance of the symbolic role. As to the latter, then ideas of individual reformation, and accordingly of susceptibility to it, remain of importance to many throughout the nineteenth century. It will be suggested, however, that the increasingly centralized prison system inevitably diminished the engagement, at policy level, with actual individuals rather than with a penological construct of 'individualism'. The inevitable tensions between the personal and the symbolic become important areas of study in the ensuing analysis.

So too with the staff. They also, as has been noted earlier, are to be constructed as inhabitants of a symbolic as well as an individual world. They too become clothed in a uniform[1] and participate in an enterprise in which they will increasingly be seen as the representatives of government (local or national) authority rather than as self-regulating entrepreneurs. When Henry Westlake is dismissed from his position of governor of the gaol for drunkenness it is not merely in reaction to a moral or physical weakness but for actions incompatible with his status.

It is individuals, then, who will form the subject of this chapter and the next, but they are individuals who work within a matrix of rules and an architecture of symbolism. For reasons of convenience rather than any logical priority we will begin by considering the staff.

From gaoler to governor

At the heart of the redrafting of the role of the prison in the nineteenth century lay the transition from gaoler to governor. The former term had been that used, for example, by Howard to describe those responsible for prisons in his pre-reform survey; the latter is common form a century later.[2] The change of terminology, as we shall see also in the retreat from the brutally functional 'turnkey' as the descriptor of junior staff, was intended to signify a change in function and in status.[3] Unlike the hangman, whose basic and ancient title remained unaffected and whose personal notoriety seems to have increased as his performances became rarer and less public,[4] the prison governor was generally not a man of great public renown, although of course in a small town he would still be a recognized figure. The role of prison staff was to be functional and respectable rather than to be celebrated. Their clothing throughout remained more muted than that of the prisoners over whom they presided.

The position of governor conferred upon its holder both power and responsibility. Yet even leaving to one side the individual issues of personality which would complicate the exercise of that power or the undertaking of that responsibility, there were tensions inherent in the role which required resolution. The governor had power over the prisoners, and in a small prison this was exercised often in face-to-face encounters rather than at a bureaucratic remove. He also had power over his subordinate staff. But who were his 'subordinate' staff? The turnkeys (or 'warders' or 'officers', as they became) clearly fell into this category. So too did the matron, though her position was complicated by the fact that in a gaol like Carmarthen she was also likely to be married to the governor. But in respect of 'servants' of the gaol, such as the university-educated, socially superior surgeon or chaplain, upon whose cooperation the practical functioning of the gaol or its essential respectability might depend, the hierarchical relationship would have been more obscure and difficult.[5]

On the matter of responsibility too the governor's role was complicated. Appointed,[6] paid and having his budget decided in the main by local government in the years before nationalization, he was undoubtedly accountable to the county (or, in appropriate cases, the borough) authority. He reported regularly to quarter sessions. The Visiting Justices, a subdivision of the local magistracy, were the immediate sources of his support or censure. Yet in several of his responsibilities, in respect of particular legislative provisions and in his dealings with the prison inspectors, he was answerable also to the Home Office. It has been seen in the discussion of institutional change in the last chapter that the interests and opinions of these two tiers of administration need not coincide. Furthermore, the governor knew that defaults on his own part might bring down criticism not only upon himself but also upon his immediate superiors. It was a difficult line to tread. Moreover, it is clear that prisoners might themselves try to exploit the division of authority to their own ends. Appeals, or threats of appeals, to the secretary of state could discomfort both the governor and the Visiting Justices, whose routine support for their appointee against a prisoner could not be guaranteed and would at least have to be considered.[7]

Henry Westlake

Henry Westlake was appointed governor of the Carmarthenshire county gaol on 4 July 1844, replacing John Burnhill, who retired with a pension following nineteen years in that position.[8] Burnhill had employed his wife and three sons in the prison as matron and turnkeys respectively, but it seems that the whole family lost their employment when its head quitted the house within the gaol. That one of the sons subsequently appears to have secured a position on the staff of the workhouse is a further indication of the close institutional relationships within the town to which reference was made earlier.[9] When Westlake was appointed, his own wife, Harriet, assumed the position of matron and a new turnkey, William Williams, also took up his post.

Henry Westlake was at this time forty-two years old. He came to the job from an immediate background of policing in Carmarthen, having elected to remain with the new local force established after the Rebecca Riots. It was Rebecca which had brought him to Wales as one of the London policeman drafted in to suppress the disturbances.[10] This background marks him out as different in kind from the older tradition of less 'respectable' gaolers, one of whom, a publican, could still fill the post in respect of Carmarthen's borough gaol.[11]

It is improbable that either Westlake or his wife could speak Welsh. That an outsider would learn the language is implausible, and Westlake's spelling of local place names in his register suggests ignorance. It is worth remembering that Welsh would be the first language of many, and the only language of some, of those prisoners placed in his charge. Yet Westlake's phonetic spelling and shaky grammar in writing in his native English remind us that he fell short of the ideal of the superior, bureaucratic governor. Appointed on a salary of £150 per annum, he also received £1. 15s. in fees, as well as the house, garden, coal and candles. Yet he also had to provide a bail bond in respect of his position, and out of his salary was to be provided not only the salary of the matron[12] but also £50 per year pension payable to Burnhill.[13] These financial arrangements would leave the governor comfortable, but by no means well off in contemporary society.[14]

In return for this salary it should be remembered that the governor's employment was for twenty-four hours a day, seven days a week and fifty-two weeks in a year. On those few occasions when he was absent from the gaol for any extended period, as for instance when he escorted convicts to Millbank for dispersal, his duties would be performed by the head turnkey. If, on the other hand, the chaplain fell ill (a frequent occurrence in the early part of Westlake's successor's governorship), the governor would himself be expected to add to his duties by reading prayers, though not by taking the school.

The records which survive him suggest Westlake to have been a man rather nervous about his authority. It is probable that his concern for correct procedures is indicative of the difficulties confronting one who found himself an actor in a penal system which was making the exercise of personal judgement and discretion generally a less comfortable matter, rather than simply the manifestations of a personal neurosis. Such a hypothesis remains, however, ultimately unprovable. He was undoubtedly capable of acting with resolve on occasions when he found himself dealing with persons he thought to be acting improperly in respect of the regulations. He refused to allow an improper visit to the gaol even though it had been sanctioned by one of the Justices,[15] and refused assistance to both the chief constable[16] and a local solicitor[17] in circumstances where he believed that to do so would be to act outside his authority. Yet if he were unsure of his position Westlake would refer matters on to the Visiting Justices, carefully recording the details of their replies as insurance against future challenges to his own actions. To his subordinates he could display a tolerance of failings, as long as these were neither too grave nor too frequent. It is not clear whether in this he was guided simply by pragmatism, by loyalty, or by a disposition towards the importance of forgiveness. This latter certainly seems to have had a role to play in his dealings with prisoners. Whenever an inmate had been confined to the refractory cell for an infringement of discipline Westlake released him after some sort of formula or ritual of forgiveness, which is, as we shall see, routinely recorded. Such an idea is not unprecedented, but I am not aware if it was standard practice.[18] Certainly Westlake's successor does not routinely mention the practice, and it may have been for him a less significant process, although the occasional references should remind us that absence of evidence is not the same as evidence of absence.[19] To Henry Westlake however it seems that the ritual was of some importance.

As an apparently enthusiastic gardener Westlake experimented with growing potatoes under glass, and his interest in that vegetable as an element of the prison diet is, understandably perhaps in the light of wider events at this time both in Ireland and closer to home, recorded more than once.[20] He also, it seems, enjoyed a drink.

The circumstances surrounding Westlake's dismissal in September 1847 are somewhat mysterious, though the records state that drunkenness was the cause, and make specific mention of an incident on 29 July.[21] The local newspapers are strangely silent on the affair, and the air of mystery is compounded by the fact that the Gaoler's Journal, ostensibly kept and signed by Westlake, appears to be in another hand for some days preceding the governor's suspension.[22]

George Stephens

Westlake's successor had also been brought to Carmarthen by the Rebecca disturbances. George Stephens had joined the Metropolitan Police in 1837 and was promoted to sergeant two years later. His work in the riots had earned him a further promotion to the rank of inspector, which rank he held at the time of his appointment to the gaol.[23] As was to be expected, his wife, Mary, replaced Harriet Westlake as matron, and she also brought to the institution, as well as their children, a domestic servant, Elizabeth Arnold, who was probably her sister.[24] When Mrs Stephens became ill in 1850 Arnold apparently took over her post temporarily, but after his wife's death Stephens seems to have married another sister, Sarah, who in turn became matron. His daughter Emily also secured a position in the gaol, taking over as female 'warden' in 1874.[25] Stephens retired in 1878, having presided over the last days of the gaol as a local institution.

Stephens was engaged on the same terms as his predecessor, a salary of £150 per year plus extras, though his obligation to pay Burnhill's pension, if it continued at all, was short-lived.[26] We learn, from a memorial submitted by Stephens to quarter sessions in 1850 in opposition to a committee proposal to reduce the salaries of officers of the gaol by 10 per cent, that this salary was the same as that of the governor of Brecon, but less than those of Pembrokeshire and Glamorgan.[27] It would seem that the resistance to the salary cut was successful and, indeed, within a few years the stipend was increased to £200.

Despite the apparent similarity of their backgrounds and conditions of service, Stephens was of a rather different character from his predecessor. Again we should note the inability to speak Welsh, but Stephens's record-keeping – confident, terse, grammatical – stands in stark contrast to that of Henry Westlake. A journal entry such as that of Stephens for 26 September 1847, 'Nothing particular occurred, All Well', would have been unthinkable to his predecessor. As has been suggested in the Introduction, the significance of such a change in the nature of the archival record is unclear. It may reflect no more than a difference in personality, yet it may be that Stephens corresponded more closely to the preferred type of bureaucratic governor than had Westlake. The further question of whether a less idiosyncratic, more functional form of record-keeping can be read as indicative of a generally more uniform and structured penal practice is a difficult one. It is certainly tempting to take it as such, in the light of wider contemporary changes in the prison system, but we should be wary of the limitations of our evidence.

There is, however, another respect in which Stephens does seem to represent the progressive mood of his time. Where Westlake's interest lay in potatoes, Stephens embraced the new technology of photography. After first taking a portrait of James Jones, sentenced to hang in 1858 for a brutal attack upon his sister-in-law, Stephens soon realized the potential of photography for the identification of recidivist offenders. Thereafter he began regularly to paste photographs alongside the details of offenders within his register. His efforts in this direction and their significance will be considered later.[28]

In the figure of the disciplined, bureaucratic, scientific figure of George Stephens Carmarthenshire seems to have caught the spirit of the wider changes taking place elsewhere in the penal system at this time. But we must exercise some caution, lest we fall into the trap identified earlier of assuming change to be everywhere predetermined and uncontested. Let us remember then that Stephens, no less than Westlake, had to negotiate the boundary between local power and economics and central direction. His everyday routine brought him up against the same sort of problems and involved him in making the same sort of decisions as had his predecessor. That he did so apparently with more confidence, a greater economy of record and the aid of a camera may indeed mark him out as a representative of the trend of national change. Yet he had been appointed by a body of Justices still capable of entertaining views of law and justice which at best might be described as 'traditional'. Moreover, as has been suggested earlier, it is at least possible that the changes in record-keeping may *constitute* the major difference in the running of the gaol rather than be evidence of it. With the benefit of hindsight the replacement of Westlake by Stephens seems charged with symbolism, but we must be wary of looking too hard to make our facts match our theories.[29]

From turnkey to warder

It has been noted that the changes in the nineteenth-century prison system were evidenced linguistically. The medieval 'gaol' becomes the more modern 'prison', the purely locative 'gaoler' becomes the more resonant 'governor'. So too in 1865 we see the term 'warder',[30] with its connotation of care as well as custody, being used in place of the traditional and functional description 'turnkey'.

It was not only the nomenclature that was to change, for so too was the appearance of the inferior officers of the prison staff. In Carmarthen in 1851 the prison inspector described the turnkeys as having 'a very slovenly appearance being indistinguishable by dress from the untried prisoners'.[31] Indeed, as has been mentioned in the previous chapter, the social distance between these men and those in their charge might not be great either. In 1845 George Davies, the gaol porter, was being paid only 9s. a week. In the next year David Davies was appointed as turnkey at 16s., only to have his pay cut two months later. He resigned in consequence, to be replaced by John Francis who was willing to work for only 12s. per week. The danger of poor pay opening the door (perhaps literally!) to corruption was noted in the previous chapter and it was adverted to directly by some of the staff. In their petition against a proposed reduction of their wages in 1850 William Williams and David Rees urged that they 'ought to be paid at least the full Wages of a Mechanic in Towns and that to give them a less or a scanty payment would not only expose your Memorialists, but every one who would have to fill the same situation to unnecessary temptations which every public servant entrusted with heavy responsibility should be protected from'.[32] The low pay, and the 'unnecessary temptations', were responsible for a high turnover in staff, certainly in the 1840s. This in itself would prove an obstacle to the realization of an ideal of a dedicated, professional prison personnel.

Despite the animadversions of the inspector, the issue of uniforms was not addressed in Carmarthen until some time probably between 1857 and 1859.[33] As with the provision of uniform for prisoners, its use for officers of the gaol had a symbolic function, even when, as at Carmarthen, they might have to pay for it themselves.[34] As Thomas observes, the dress code serves to 'emphasise the uniformity of role of all the people wearing the same clothes, and emphasises the disparity of role of people wearing different clothes'.[35] The 'fetish of uniformity', to which we have so often referred, was here given its most simple and direct expression.

It is difficult, because of the deficiencies of our sources, but instructive, to try to reconstruct the working regime of the prison staff in our period. Again the fuller records of Governor Westlake allow us a rather clearer view than those of his successor, but the possibility of change over time counsels against an uncritical reliance only on the former. The long-serving head turnkey William Williams lived with his family inside the walls of the gaol.[36] He was clearly a man generally trusted, even though not always above temptation.[37] As a native of Llanguthon he was probably the conduit for conveying the governor's orders in Welsh. He claimed to work sixteen or seventeen hours a day during a seven-day week and to be additionally liable to be disturbed at night.[38] In addition there was, in the 1840s, generally one other turnkey in employ, although a third was taken on for a while in 1844 and this became the norm in the 1860s.[39] By 1865 there are three male 'warders' and a night watchman, and the complement was augmented again in the 1870s, when, amongst others, an 'Engineer' was appointed.[40] It is clear that there had been a movement away from a minimal staff of mere 'turnkeys'. It is clear too that the local authorities were gradually being obliged to increase not only the staffing but also the expense of the institution.

The reasons are obvious. The deployment of the staff when there were only two turnkeys on duty seems to have been that one would watch the treadwheel to ensure that the prisoners kept to their task and to enforce silence, whilst the other would be on duty at the gate.[41] If we allow that the matron, assisted in later years by one female turnkey, took charge of all classes of female prisoners (though in instances of discipline the governor's authority and presence was necessary), that the chaplain was running the school for a brief period each day and the governor took a peripatetic role when not otherwise engaged, then we find that whole groups of prisoners – the debtors, remand prisoners, those not serving hard-labour sentences or performing tasks like cooking, the sick in the infirmary, or those confined to the refractory cells – were not under constant supervision. If any of the officers of the gaol were absent, sick or required elsewhere, then pressure on resources would be considerably increased.[42] In May 1846, when he was reliant on only one turnkey, the Finance Committee having dismissed the second, Westlake made it clear that the discipline of the gaol was in peril, pointing out that the three work parties could not be supervised. He was championed by David Davies JP, who pointed out that Westlake himself had 'numerous books to keep and could not always be watching the prisoners'. Davies was in no doubt as to where the blame lay. The Finance Committee, he said, 'thought of nothing but economy' and 'were wrong nine times out of ten'.[43]

It is no surprise, then, to find that prisoners at this time were regularly pressed into service to perform tasks such as tending to the sick. Whilst even in the centrally administered convict prisons inmates occupied positions of trust and engaged in work such as cooking and hairdressing, their supervision would be rendered easier by adequate staffing. It was also desirable that such prisoners would be drawn from amongst the less disruptive of the population. In Carmarthen again we find that models which were defensible in model penal establishments broke apart when confronted by the stark reality of local conditions. Though the governor may on occasion have been able to employ a 'good' prisoner, such as David Joshua,[44] to tend the sick, his choice at other times was more circumscribed. Notorious prisoners whose names will recur elsewhere in this book, such as Charles Hunt, James Hargrave, Mariah Thomas and Ann Awberry,[45] all find themselves at different times serving as attendants in the infirmary.

In such circumstances the 'silent system' enjoined by the Home Office was impossible to maintain. But even in ordinary circumstances it could be, as Westlake frankly admitted, impossible to police adequately.[46] Such deviations from the desired regulation of employment and regime are very important, for they hit hard into the official desiderata of the Victorian prison project. Whilst the chimera of uniformity was being enthusiastically pursued by the penal 'experts', the existence of understaffed (because still largely locally financed) gaols such as Carmarthenshire's must have been a constant irritation. Gradually the staffing was increased more adequately to meet not only an increasing gaol population[47] but also the expectations of the mentality which produced the prescriptive 1865 Prison Act. It is easy to see how the consequent increase in local expenditure could provide a potent argument for the acceptance of nationalization, with the attraction of central government funding, in 1877.

The surgeon

The position of the surgeon in the administration of the nineteenth-century gaol has, I believe, received less attention than it merits.[48] This is due perhaps to the assumption that, as at the present day, doctors are to be sought out to deal with occasional and specific instances of disorder and that their interventions are individual and technical. Yet the role of the gaol surgeon in the period under investigation here was much wider and occupied a space of both symbolic and actual importance in the daily operation of the institution.

For the prison reformers who took their lead from Howard the sentiment that cleanliness was next to godliness was much more than simply a commonplace. The 'gaol fever' endemic in some pre-reform gaols, and the 'dysentery' which had come close to aborting the first central government experiment in penitentiary confinement, were evils incompatible with an 'enlightened' system. Even as ideals of reformation gave way to the avowedly punitive regimes of the convict establishments of the 1850s and beyond, the atavistic and arbitrary misery of disease formed no part of the acceptable conditions. Moreover, even in a local gaol the surgeon in many ways patrolled the boundary between the life led inside the prison and that outside. It was the surgeon's examination which determined the prisoner's initial disposition and company within the gaol, for if the inmate were suffering from scabies, a very common complaint amongst those remanded, then he or she would be sent to the 'itch ward' specifically provided for them.[49] This diagnosis might also determine when the symbolic transition to wearing the uniform took place. In cases of severe or intractable illness the recommendation of the surgeon might even result in an early release from sentence, or even an exemption from trial, decisions in which principles of humanity seem to have been more important than a mere cynical desire to avoid the consequences, both administrative and in terms of adverse publicity, of death in custody.[50] During the sentence itself the surgeon's role was central in the administration of the disciplinary regime. It was within his dispensing power to exempt a prisoner from labour and/or to order extra diet. This ability might impact not only upon the ideal of uniformity of punishment, but even (by producing results which might run counter to principles of 'less-eligibility') on the question as to whether the experience was perceived by the prisoner as punitive at all, that is, whether it was worse than he might expect outside. These dispensing powers were exercised upon the surgeon's 'judgement', a matter of discretion necessarily in tension with a system increasingly based on a belief in the importance of abstract rules. And the prisoners knew it. Here as elsewhere they sought to control elements of their own prison experience, rather than act as mere recipients of it. The issue of feigning illness, physical or mental, or even of manufacturing it, was a real and current one for the Victorian prison surgeon. The first chapter, and it is a substantial one, of Beck's *Elements of Medical Jurisprudence* is devoted to the means of feigning maladies and their detection.[51]

Here again we may detect a potential source of tension in the surgeon's role. For his responsibility to his patient as an individual might be, or be perceived to be, at odds with his responsibility to the institution. It might be difficult, for example, for the surgeon to take the side of the prisoner against the governor, and even more to take it as against his social equals or superiors the Visiting Justices. In this section I will consider only those aspects of the surgeon's task which raise starkly the issues of dispensation from regime and the problems which inhered therein. A more detailed consideration of the health of the prison population will be postponed until a later chapter. First, though, it is necessary to see what sort of men held the position of surgeon in Carmarthen gaol.

John Jenkins was appointed as gaol surgeon in 1823, the year in which Peel's Gaol Act had provided for the office,[52] having already served for three years in that capacity in the borough prison.[53] He remained in office until his death in January 1850. His salary, £80 per year in 1846, would have supplemented his earnings from his private practice. Out of it he provided medicine and bandages, but not larger items such as trusses.[54] Duties at the gaol involved regular visits to the institution.[55] In addition, he would be summoned if any medical problems arose within the gaol. It is clear that much of the routine work was performed, in Jenkins's name, by his deputy David Jones, although there may have been some unease about this.[56] When Jenkins died, the mantle of public beneficence was assumed by an even greater pillar of the Carmarthenshire establishment, James Rowlands, a Tory, JP, and also the chief surgeon of the Infirmary.[57] Such public offices, their unification in one man pointing yet again to the de facto connection between different institutions on an individual level, seem clearly to have been regarded in the town as the expectation of public position rather than the training school of professional criminological expertise.

It has been suggested that as a representative of the institution the surgeon might be expected to take the side of the governor against the prisoner. So, for example, we find that in the acrimonious and potentially damaging series of disputes between Governor Westlake and a number of prisoners centred on the persons of Charles Hunt and James Hargrave in 1846–7, the surgeon provides reliable support. Not only does Jenkins approve of the haircuts which the men, in an overt challenge to local authority, dispute, but he also finds himself summoned, in the absence of a Visiting Justice, to testify as to the merits of the soup ('it was excellent soup & plenty of it for any working men').[58] Nonetheless, when Hunt was sent to the refractory cell for refusing to cooperate with the surgeon the latter was clearly rather put out, subsequently sending a note to the governor asking for the punishment to be curtailed.[59]

If the surgeon was inclined in such matters to take the side of the governor, the issue of diagnosis, as has been suggested, could be rather more difficult and productive of tension. Certainly the simulation of disease, though it was unpopular with fellow prisoners as well as with the staff,[60] does seem to have been practised at Carmarthen, as elsewhere. In 1875 Rowlands noted that George Morgan, who had been drinking to excess, 'assumed insanity. A little watching proved him a malingerer.'[61] Regular weighing of the inmates was practised in the 1860s in an attempt to detect the simulation of disease.[62] Twenty years earlier the expansive Governor Westlake gives us an insight into the clashes that could occur concerning issues of a prisoner's fitness to work in the gaol. It is perhaps significant that in these cases it is

Jones, the surgeon's assistant, rather than the surgeon himself who finds himself on the wrong side of the governor's intervention. In January 1846 the case of John Wilson provoked some disagreement:

> D. Jones asst surgeon called and he considered it was to could for John Willson a blind prisoner to remain in the wheel during the hours the wheel was at work, which I informed Dl Prytherch esq. [a JP] of it the prisoner was sentenced to twelve calendar months hard labour by the court of quarter sessions, which I placed him in one division of the wheel and their is sufficient Room for him to walk a bout.[63]

A year later a similar disagreement led to a more direct criticism:

> D. Jones Asst surgeon called and ordered John Roberts a vagrant extra diet as he was of opinion that the prisoner was weak and not fit for labour which I Informed the asst. surgeon that the prisoners was deceiving him as many others had in my time, the prisoner was very well yesterday when he was doubtfull of not receiving is meat diet.[64]

In such circumstances the surgeon's judgement was responsible for the resolution of conflicts which involved directly the nature of the regime to which a prisoner was to be subjected. There were other occasions where he seems to have had influence in whether an individual was to be punished at all. The number and nature of such interventions are difficult to determine, but some evidence does survive. In July 1846 Jenkins reported to the Carmarthenshire bench in respect of the 'hysterical' remand prisoner Frances Anne Jones: 'Her liberation I have little doubt would prove the best remedial mean that could be employed.'[65] The grand jury in the case subsequently declined to sanction the prosecution. In the most remarkable and difficult case, that of Eugene Buckley in 1846–7, a similar result was achieved. Buckley, facing an indictment for highway robbery, had caused considerable difficulty during his remand by a range of conduct which included nakedness, violence and destruction of property. The question as to whether he was feigning madness had involved bringing in medically trained JPs to add their own opinions to that of Surgeon Jenkins. The decision to release Buckley without prosecution was pragmatic, but hardly fits well with the 'due process' model which underlay the idea of the Victorian criminal justice system and the scientific rationalism of the pioneers of psychology. Buckley was either 'bad' or 'mad', and the resolution of that question was a matter for medical decision and then appropriate process. Yet he was allowed simply to go on his way as he might have been two hundred years before.[66]

There is no clear pattern of cases evident in the records subsequent to Buckley's. It may be that the paradigm was shifting away from the discretionary at this level of penal decision-making, or, more accurately, that the results of the exercise of the inevitable discretion were to be circumscribed further. The belated building of the lunatic asylum around the same time as the rebuilding of the prisons may suggest a more thoroughly institutional response to such difficulties in future. The time of Governor Stephens and Surgeon Rowlands was not that of Governor Westlake and Surgeon Jenkins. It would appear that things were gradually changing in rural Wales, that new models were becoming dominant. Yet it seems clear, as suggested earlier, that 'local and particular' interventions sometimes still occurred. The prison inspector reported, as late as 1873, that a female remand prisoner had been 'given up to her friends and by them sent to an asylum' without, apparently, even the technicality of an appearance before the grand jury.[67]

The chaplain

In his third annual report, delivered to the Michaelmas quarter sessions in 1858, Thomas Williams, the prison chaplain, gave an indication of the nature and limitations of his work. 'I have endeavoured', he wrote,

> to perform my ministerial duties faithfully. The services on Sundays and Weekdays have been regularly attended to. In private conversation with the Prisoners, I have laboured to impress upon their minds the evil of sin, in its nature and consequences, and the benefits of a moral and religious life, and I hope that my services have not been altogether in vain. I have perceived in most instances, at the time, the softening influence of the Gospel; but as to its lasting effects, I am not, from past experience, very sanguine in my hopes. However, 'The bread has been cast upon the waters', trusting 'it may be found after many days.' The use of the means is ours, the blessing is God's.[68]

The chaplain enters the Journal of Carmarthen's governor less often than the surgeon, though his visits to the gaol were more frequent and his contact with the prisoners, or at least with some of them, was more regular and structured. As Rawlings has pointed out, the role of the chaplain is not central to the disciplinary task of the nineteenth-century local gaol, notwithstanding the protestations of contemporary holders of that office like the celebrated John Clay of Preston. But that is not to say that elsewhere such figures regarded themselves, or were regarded by others, as marginal characters in the institution.[69] From the Penitentiary Act of 1779 the three elements of prison discipline, separation, labour and religion, all remained essential components until at least the Gladstone Committee of 1895. What changed was the recipe, not the ingredients. Yet the period during which the effects of religion were the chief concern of those close to the centre of the national penal programme – the days when the Revd Nihill became governor of Millbank, the Revd Russell became the most influential of prison inspectors, and when the word 'penitentiary' makes a transitional appearance in the movement from 'gaol' to prison – was the first half of the nineteenth century. This, as we know, is when the drive for uniformity within the counties was still struggling to have tangible effect. The chaplain had never enjoyed so much power in the local gaols. Moreover, a model premised, like Pentonville's, upon the re-formation of the individual (the hyphen is supplied so that the novelty of the exercise is less likely to be lost in the familiarity of the word), needed, as even its most ardent supporters argued, time to work. In the local gaol, where sentences were often in weeks or even days rather than months or years, such regimes could never achieve dominance. There is an argument to be made that it was not the insanity figures alone which finished the dominance of the 'separate system' in its original manifestation as a spiritual bludgeon. It was overtaken by the greater project of uniformity, for which it could never provide a feasible model.

This is certainly not to say, however, that the role of the chaplain declined in local gaols in the period up to nationalization. The contrary appears to have been the case. The explanation for this apparent paradox lies in reading Thomas Williams's report alongside Philip Rawlings's contention. The chaplain's role in such circumstances is personal rather than disciplinary. Its success is a matter to be measured by the occasional triumph rather than mass conversion. This did not make it unimportant. A local prison without an active chaplain in the 1850s or 1860s would provoke unease in a way which it would not thirty years before. But the shock troops of the penal crusade had been replaced by patient missionaries.

Curiously, this 'semi-detachment' of the chaplain may have given to his role a sense of perspective which, together perhaps with a desire to show a more tangible return on his salary, seems to have led him to expand upon his reports. This certainly happened in Carmarthen and has been noted elsewhere.[70] The phenomenon could again be accounted for by a change in the nature of the bureaucratic record rather than the mentality of its keeper, but there may well be more to it than that. For the chaplain began to leave his thoughts on the nature and causes of crime and on the characteristics of offenders. Such nascent criminology, the more interesting because it is locally derived and unpublished, will occupy us in this section. Again, though, it is necessary to introduce the individuals.

Thomas Jones was appointed chaplain to the gaol in October 1823, an event no doubt connected with the Gaol Act of that year.[71] He took on the responsibility and salary of schoolmaster in 1837 but continued to hold an additional living outside the gaol for a short while. He remained in the post until his retirement upon a pension in 1856, shortly after the prison inspector had rather pointedly observed that his 'very advanced age' (he was by then in his eighties) meant it was desirable that a younger man should take over the teaching function. His salary on retirement was the same as it had been for many years, £80 per annum for the priestly and £20 for the tutelary responsibilities. When he was, as we have seen other officers were, threatened with a reduction in salary he pointed out that his workload had been added to by the amalgamation of the borough gaol, whose spiritual needs had previously been attended to (inadequately, for the chaplain lived at a distance and the chapel was 'unfit') by another. Jones certainly thought he earned his salary. He held divine service twice on every Sunday with a sermon at one service, and attended daily to read the liturgy and catechize the prisoners in their wards and converse with them in their cells. By the early 1850s he reported that his weekday school duties took two hours, though his teaching practice at weekends seems to have varied over time. He was, in addition, responsible for ordering books for the prisoners, although the Justices kept an eye on this process. In a period of retrenchment in 1846 Captain Davies ordered some books to be returned, the prison being, in his opinion, sufficiently well provided for.[72]

From the outset we should notice that Jones, and I think both of his successors, used Welsh as well as English in their religious duties. This is a point of some significance, for we have noted that bilingualism seems not to have been required of the governor. The use of Welsh is explicitly mentioned in the reports of the prison inspectors, Hawkins in 1842 giving the clearest account of the linguistic code-switching when he noted that if the prayers were in English then the sermon would be in Welsh and vice versa.[73]

Jones was succeeded by Thomas Williams, who also, it seems, served the workhouse and who held the post of chaplain (though for a short period not also that of schoolmaster, perhaps in consequence of interim arrangements made in Jones's final year) until he departed the prison service sometime around 1860. Though his period of office was brief he seems to have made an impact. It has been noted in the previous chapter that Williams had pressed for the rebuilding of the chapel. In addition he seems to have begun the process of analytical, indeed statistical, annual reports which was to be continued by his successor. This was Aaron Roberts, Oxford educated and born in Denbigh. Both Williams and Roberts were new faces at the time of their appointments, and both seem to have brought a degree not only of enthusiasm but also of intellectual curiosity to their position. Nonetheless the status of their office seems not to have been increased, for in 1870 Roberts was still in receipt of the same combined salary of £100 as Jones had been over thirty years earlier. It is interesting to note that in an unsuccessful claim in 1866 for an increase in salary Roberts claimed that his work had been increased by the implementation of the Prison Act of the previous year, a measure usually taken to be emblematic of the trend of renunciation of reformation in favour of deterrence which marked the second half of the century.[74]

It was not only in relation to language that the position of chaplain to Carmarthen gaol differed from that in many English locations, for many of the prisoners admitted to the gaol were not members of the Church of England. There were the occasional 'exotic' visitors, amongst whom we may number the four Deists

and one 'Mahometan' (an Egyptian, James Washington, whose
conversion is a matter of great pride to Revd Williams) who were
in the gaol in 1857–8, some at least of whom would have arrived
by virtue of the town's significance as a port.[75] The same attraction, together (as will be seen) with the presence of the army, may
also have been responsible for the more constant proportion of
Roman Catholics, at least some of whom came from Ireland. The
Revd Roberts took pleasure at receiving no fewer than six Irish-
language New Testaments in 1875.[76] But the largest body of
prisoners outside the Established Church were Nonconformists
whose numbers could, particularly in the earlier part of the period
under consideration, form the majority within the gaol,[77] a fact
which in the light of the demographics considered in chapter 1
will not surprise us. The prison inspector noted in 1840 that most
prisoners did have 'some religious knowledge',[78] but we must of
course be careful not to assume that the profession of a particular
religion by a prisoner indicated more than a nominal adherence to
it. The Revd Roberts was well aware of this. Tabulating, as was
his custom, the professed religions in his annual report for 1870
he produced a total for the year of 141 Church of England, 69
Nonconformists, 33 Roman Catholics, 2 Presbyterians and 1
Lutheran. He went on to state:

> With regard to the apparent preponderance in the number of persons
> professing to belong to the Church of England, I have to remark that
> they are mostly of the vagrant class, who, if asked when they had been
> last time in Church, generally reply that they have not been in *any*
> place of worship for 3 or 4 or more years, unless it may have been in
> some other prison chapel. Not one fourth of the number would be
> what we call members of the Church, and there is *not one of them a
> communicant*. The same remarks would apply, though in a lesser
> degree, to the 69 Nonconformists. I should be equally sorry to call any
> one of the 69 a member of any Nonconformist denomination, as I
> would to say any one of the 141 would be a communicant of the
> Church of England. At the same time I am of the opinion that more of
> the 69 are regular hearers than there are members of the Church out
> of the 141. It should be borne in mind that the Nonconformists do not
> call their regular attendants members unless they are communicants,
> whereas the Church of England calls her baptized hearers members,
> though they be no communicants.[79]

Certainly the administration of the sacrament was a very rare
occurrence, meriting particular mention.[80] Whilst Catholic

prisoners occasionally took advantage of the opportunity to see a clergyman of their own faith, this was almost unknown amongst the Nonconformists.[81] It is unclear to what extent religious affiliation affected the participation in the school work, as opposed to the services, undertaken by the chaplain. The lessons given by Jones and by Williams certainly seem to have been predominantly scriptural in nature, the latter in particular going through the books of the Bible in turn (though apparently avoiding too much emphasis on Revelation) to stimulate both reading and discussion.[82] Women apparently did not attend school,[83] nor those sentenced to very short terms,[84] but the only figures which are available suggest an average school group of only nine or ten prisoners at mid-century.[85] The case of the Muslim, James Washington, mentioned earlier, does, however, suggest that basic literacy education was available to all, irrespective of religion.[86] It certainly seems to have included teaching English to Welsh prisoners such as Henry Evans, who otherwise had none.[87]

As the content of the preceding notes will have made clear, it is very tempting to quote from the annual reports of Carmarthen's prison chaplain. Those produced by Williams and Roberts are amongst the most interesting documents relating to the history of the institution, more discursive than the bluntly factual quarterly reports of the governor, surgeon and Visiting Justices which were also submitted to quarter sessions. Although Williams in particular seems keen to show himself supportive of the governor,[88] these were men whose role was largely autonomous within the prison. The unrealistic expectation of routine conversion having been removed from them, they could employ information gathered from their regular contact with prisoners to offer analyses of the incidence and even the causes of criminality. It is clear from an extensive quotation from 'a Brother Chaplain' which Roberts includes in his report of 1875 that some contact, at least in the form of written material, existed between the Carmarthen incumbent and his counterpart elsewhere. The development of a class of published criminological 'experts', which Foucault rightly links with the presence of a captive body of experimental subjects, was replicated on a local level by these men.[89]

William Williams's report for 1857 – his second, but the first of his which it has been possible to trace – is, in the Carmarthenshire context, groundbreaking. Not content simply to describe his duties, Williams produces a handwritten, five-page document together with a tabular appendix.[90] The report is comparative, both as to figures from different parts of the year in question and from the previous one. The observations on the causes of crime are familiar,[91] but it is their appearance in the first place, not their originality, which is notable, as is the chaplain's acknowledgement of the limitations of his impact:

> as to the religious effect produced, it is difficult to give a decided opinion, as I have been disappointed in some of whom I thought favourably; but it is a source of satisfaction, that some have, on their release, when they could have had no motive to deceive, spontaneously acknowledged their gratitude for the attention shown them – for the endeavours made to promote their temporal and spiritual welfare, – and for the instruction which they had received, promising, that, with the help of God, they would reform.

Williams concludes critically, urging the ventilation of the refractory cells ('not fit for human beings'), a greater separation between hardened and less experienced offenders, and the substitution of productive for unproductive labour.

In his next report Williams broadens his discussion, tabulating also the offence categories, ages and educational attainment of the gaol population, or selected elements within it. He urges the use of reformatory schools to combat juvenile crime, and the utility of education more generally as a means of countering offending behaviour. In describing a general trend of decrease in convictions in the following year, however, rather different causes are assigned:

> This pleasing state of things is doubtless attributable in a great measure to the prosperity of the times, to the excellent manner in which the law is administered, and the efficiency of the Police. I hope I may add, to our becoming with the blessing of God a more moral and religious people.

One figure which caused particular concern to him, though it too had declined from the previous year, was that of deserters. These could prove to be difficult prisoners, some of whom 'caused such anxiety to the Governor, which, at one time, I grieve to report, affected his health'. Williams explained his approach to such men, and salvaged a modicum of national pride from the position:

CAERMARTHEN.

Plate 1. This early nineteenth-century engraving, with its river, bridge and picturesque coracle fishermen, paradoxically demonstrates the dominance of the prison site in the topography of Carmarthen. (*Author's collection*)

Plate 2. The governor's house, moved from the heart of the gaol to its periphery in the later nineteenth century. This latter site is shown here. (*Courtesy of Carmarthen Museum*)

Plate 3. Governor Stephens, his staff and female prisoners (?), 1870s (?). This remarkable photograph, though it presents difficulties in interpretation, is the only known image of the inside of the prison in the nineteenth century. (*Courtesy of Carmarthen Museum*)

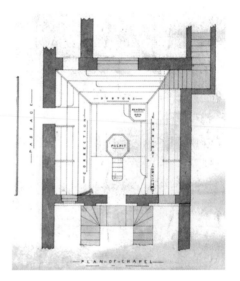

Plate 4. Part of James Collard's 1859 plan for the reconstruction of the chapel, showing segregation according to class of prisoner rather than individual separation. Female prisoners were accommodated in an upper gallery. (*Courtesy of Carmarthenshire Archive Service*)

Plate 5. Evan and Hannah Jacob, photographed in Carmarthen prison just before their trial in July 1870. The parents of the celebrated 'Fasting Girl' who had died when claims that she could survive without nutrition were put to the test, were bailed before trial and were transferred subsequently to Swansea during Carmarthen's reconstruction. The mother's garland of flowers eerily echoes those worn by her daughter when she received visitors. From the *Felons' Register*. (*Courtesy of Carmarthenshire Archive Service*)

Plate 6. Birth in the prison: twenty-two-year-old Jane Bowen gave birth to a son at around 6.00 a.m. on 13 July 1864 whilst serving a sentence of six months with hard labour for sending a threatening letter. From the *Felons' Register*. (*Courtesy of Carmarthenshire Archive Service*)

Plate 7. Death in the prison: forty-five-year-old George Adams, 'rag gatherer and gentleman's servant', who died within four days of this photograph being taken, again in July 1864, of 'disease of the heart'. From the *Felons' Register*. (*Courtesy of Carmarthenshire Archive Service*)

Plate 8. David Jenkins, a twenty-seven-year-old farmer, removed to the Joint Counties Asylum and not tried after his remand to the gaol in November 1867. From the *Felons' Register*. (*Courtesy of Carmarthenshire Archive Service*)

I have invariably endeavoured to impress upon their minds the sanctity of an oath, the sin of the violation of it against God, their country, and their own souls, and the sad consequences to the nation if all our soldiers were as unfaithful as they had been, and I trust that my labours have not been altogether in vain ... In this sad picture there is one pleasing feature, of the 36 convicted of desertion only 2 were Welshmen. Most of the others were either English or Irishmen.

Aaron Roberts's reports, some of which he submitted in printed as well as manuscript form, continue this analytical, statistical tradition established by his predecessor. To a certain extent it would seem that his own reflections were prompted by the fear of recidivism and the mobility of criminality,[92] which as we shall see was growing in the 1860s, and by the changes in the gaol (which during the rebuilding process included the demolition of the existing chapel and school)[93] to which that fear had indirectly contributed. It was vagrancy which Roberts picked out as a particular concern, writing in 1874 that

After an experience of nearly 14 years among the inmates of a County Prison, I would most respectfully beg to be permitted to remark that some stringent measures should be enacted to restrain the growing effects of Vagrancy, so as, if possible, to diminish the number of those sturdy, able-bodied, idle Vagabonds and Impostors, who get committed to Prison for practising any expedient but work for their living.

He returned to the same subject two years later, noting that

out of a Total of 264 Prisoners received in our own Prison during the past year 77 males and 3 Females, or a total of 80 persons, were committed for Vagrancy. This is an offence which appears to me to have some fascination grasping its Victims with so firm a hold, that once indulged in, Vagrants seldom, if Ever, renounce it. I have known several instances in which confirmed Tramps have been offered work at 1s per diem and have declined it, preferring to go to Prison. Too idle to work, but to beg they are not ashamed!

As will be seen in the next chapter he had decided views also on juvenile offenders.

Roberts was enthusiastically supportive of the cellular separation of the rebuilt prison. 'The separate and silent system,' he reported in 1873, the elision of the two competing regimes concisely illustrating the by now antiquated nature of the controversy, 'as now fully carried out, works well, and is a manifest improvement on the necessary partially associated system which existed in the old prison. The improvement in the mind of several prisoners at the time of their discharge has been very marked.'[94] He repeated his praise in his next report. In 1873 he had also noted a rather more immediate improvement in conditions following the reconstruction: 'The services in the new chapel have, I believe, been much valued by the prisoners. The music has lately been considerably invigorated and improved by the introduction of an harmonium – the kind and munificent gift of Sir James John Hamilton, Bart'!

Conclusion

The study of the Carmarthenshire evidence does reveal the transition in the third quarter of the nineteenth century towards a more 'professional', rather higher-status staff that we might expect. The photograph of George Stephens and his uniformed staff, taken towards the end of our period, tells a rather different tale from that of the earlier records. So too do the criminological discussions of the active and intelligent prison chaplains. To an extent it may be that the 'bureaucratization' of the prison, the change in the nature of record evidence, may help to explain this. The chaplain committed rather more to paper, the governor, paradoxically, rather less, but both seem more at home in the new prison (new both architecturally and linguistically) than in the old gaol. Perhaps the relative continuity of the surgeon's report, terse and functional, conceals wider changes within his role, though the fact that he remains in no way dependent on the institution for his financial autonomy is perhaps a potent argument against radical transformation.

Yet it becomes clear too that the changes we expect were neither necessarily rapid nor uncontested. They involved changes of personnel which depended on individual staff leaving, voluntarily or otherwise, and others taking on the work. Insofar as changes involved financial expenditure they were unlikely to win the easy approval of the local authorities – salaries were pegged for years, staff increases slow to materialize. It is perhaps only that compression of perspective which the telescope of historical inquiry produces which allows us to talk of a penal revolution, rather than the, at times, rather stately evolutionary process which closer examination suggests. This should not really surprise us, for mindsets and affiliations often do take rather longer to change than prison uniforms.[95]

There is another factor which may distort our picture of the operation of the gaol. This discussion of those within the gaol has opened by concentrating on the staff. This makes some sense in the structuring of the account, for the staff, and other officials in the criminal justice system, are those who are predominantly the persons who produce the records through which we learn about the prisoners. It is well for us to know who they are when we are about to consider what they write. Yet the creation of record, the control of the register, is part of the wider differentiation of power that exists within the prison, and indeed outside it. It is necessary now to consider the prisoners themselves, for, of course, without them none of the other officials would have been necessary.

Dramatis Personae 2: The Prisoners

After his final inspection of Carmarthen gaol in 1842 the prison inspector, Bisset Hawkins, offered a rather curious observation. 'This prison throughout', he wrote, 'is certainly insecure for the confinement of desperate active men but is apparently safe for the population of this county, whose habits are simple, compared with those of some other districts.'[1] It is not simply the reflection on the character of the prisoners that is notable, but the assumption that the inhabitants of the county gaol would come from the population of that county. Both of these implications, and many other ideas about the inmates to be found within the gaol, will be considered in this chapter.

Some points, however, need to be repeated before we begin our exploration of the prisoner population of our institution. The first is one which was explored in chapter 1, namely that that population was a chosen not a given one. The commitment to prison, whether on remand, for sentence, for debt or for any other reason, was a product of a series of choices and decisions of considerable complexity, decisions which involve elements of personal judgement exercised within a community context. The second point, as has been noted in the Introduction, touches upon the methodology to be employed within this chapter. Since some of the information considered here is susceptible to computer analysis, it might be tempting to produce a statistical survey of the inmate population and let it speak for itself. For a number of reasons, however, such an undertaking, without more detailed analysis, would be dangerous. Firstly, then, there are classes of prisoner, misdemeanants or debtors, for example, about whom the same depth of quantitative information does not survive as is the case with felons. Secondly, it must be remembered that not all of the information which does survive is necessarily impeccable. To rely upon statistics of prisoners' previous criminal records or geographical origin would be dangerous when, in many instances, the only source of that information is the word of that prisoner. Even the production of a table with an appropriate disclaimer is open to some objection, for it may be that the table carries more psychological weight than the disclaimer. But there is another reason, integral to the purpose of this book, which argues against the reduction of information concerning prisoners to numerical composites. It has been argued throughout that the reality of Victorian prison life was not an engagement with a statistical mass but with the messy reality of particular individuals. In this chapter, then, an attempt will be made to recover the experiences of named prisoners to sit alongside the more general observations. In the combination, it is hoped, it will be possible to glimpse a rather richer picture of the diurnal operation of the institution by incorporation of information which is unquantifiable or unquantified.

As a scheme of arrangement, however, it is wise, at the outset of the discussion, to categorize the types of prisoner which were to be found in Carmarthen gaol during the period under study. This categorization is roughly along the lines which determined the conditions, regimes, rights and liabilities of the prisoners in contemporary official taxonomies. It will be appropriate to omit, however, those categories which seem never to have attracted any members in Carmarthenshire (there is apparently no record of a 'first class misdemeanant' in the county. It would be interesting to discover to what extent such a privileged individual was a creature only of metropolitan or urban criminal process).[2] This chapter must also be read together with the next, in which will be included others, such as insane prisoners, who posed particular problems to the gaol, yet strictly speaking were not a recognizable official class, as the insane were not supposed to be held in prison in the first place. In discussing the inmate population it has been decided not to group women (misdemeanants, felons, remands, debtors) as a separate category, but to consider them along with men when discussing the particular classes of prisoner. This has been done after much consideration. The historic experience of women's imprisonment has, to an extent, been neglected until recent trends in historiography provided a more fertile environment for consideration of the experiences of this class of largely voiceless women.[3] It is undeniable that these experiences are different from those of men, a difference discernible, even if we leave aside psychological factors, in mundane matters such as labour and regime. Here, then, is an argument for a separate treatment. The archetypal nineteenth-century prisoner was male; the 'prison revolution' was, to an extent, based on that premise of masculinity, and one of the results of that premise was that women were often fitted into the buildings and regimes which developed from it. Yet this does not explain the decision to avoid a separate categorization. The intention of this book is to try to recover the individual experience of prisoners, all of whom still remain largely voiceless. Where women's experience differed from that of men this form of analysis should reveal it. It probably does not matter in this context (though it may in others) whether we choose to discuss Mary Ann Awberry as a recidivist woman or as a woman recidivist. What is important is to try to tell her story. It would be impossible in a study of this nature to ignore women's experience and how it differed from men's. That difference should be as important to those who seek to recover the daily reality of the gaol as it was to those who lived it.

Debtors

It may seem almost wilfully perverse to take as our first category of inmate to study the one which at first glance was becoming increasingly peripheral to the prison experience as the nineteenth century moves on. Imprisonment for debt had been a feature of gaol experience since the fourteenth century and was still one of the indicators of county gaol status. When it was decided, as late as 1867 (presumably in connection with the 1865 Prison Act), that the old county gaol at Monmouth should be relocated in the much more 'advanced' penal establishment of the house of correction at Usk, it was necessary to build debtors' rooms to satisfy the requirements of change of status.[4] A succession of statutory changes to the law relating to debt culminated in a statute of 1869 which nominally removed the process of imprisonment for civil debt. In fact it never had that result, as many debts were reconfigured as rooted in fraud or contempt of court, thus making the incarcerated debtor *de iure* the nearer equivalent of other persons who lived on property not their own (beggars, vagrants, thieves), rather than simply de facto sharing their accommodation.[5] Whilst it is tempting to see this change in the treatment of debtors as a result of a shifting Victorian attitude towards speculation and financial markets, it is, as has been suggested, probable that the changing rationale of the 'new' prison itself not only had an effect on making its use in civil process look increasingly anomalous in the decades prior to the 1869 measure, but also made the post-1869 use of that anomaly at least technically more defensible. Attitudes towards prison, as well as attitudes towards credit, had changed, and the debtor consequently remains a crucial figure in the process of understanding the process of transition in the Victorian county gaol.

It is clear that in Carmarthen the 1869 Act did not remove debtors from the gaol. In a return of 1868–9 the prison inspector had recorded twenty-two committals for debt in the previous year, while for the year ending September 1877 Governor Stephens recorded eighteen as being in the gaol for that cause. Whilst female debtors were incarcerated on occasion, the majority of Carmarthen's prisoners were male, a factor explicable in terms of legal capacity and social acceptability to pledge credit. When the prison inspector visited in 1851 he found the female debtor's cells and yard occupied by men.[6] Debtors tended to be labelled in accordance with the authority committing them; so records refer to Chancery debtors, Excise debtors[7] and, after the new tribunal was set up in 1846, County Court debtors.[8] By the 1860s it was the County Court which provided most of those imprisoned.[9]

With the abolition of imprisonment for most debts of less than £20 in 1844, those held in Carmarthen thereafter were for considerable, but not great, sums — the highest amount found being £108. 12s. 5d., and most being for less than half that sum.[10] It is probable that this piece of restrictive legislation also played some role in the decision to abandon the borough gaol, which had for some time mostly held prisoners for debt.[11] The social status of the post-1844 debtors was, as might be anticipated from those who could contract such liabilities, rather higher than many of the criminal detainees, as probably was their average age. Included in their number was a solicitor, Charles Vaughan,[12] and a man admitted as the Revd Stephen Evans, over whose clerical status Governor Stephens was later to entertain some doubts.[13] John Williams, incarcerated in 1847, seems to have been sufficiently well connected to have had permission to have visits by his family and servants as well as the use of wine and spirits as ordered by one of the Justices. He was also visited in the gaol by the MP for the borough, David Morris.[14]

It has been noted in chapter 2 that both county and borough gaols before amalgamation had extended to their debtors the privilege of remaining within the Rules, rather than necessarily within the buildings themselves. Nield's investigation at the beginning of the nineteenth century mentions no such anomaly[15] and it is possible that it had been abandoned in the post-Howard period of enthusiasm. That chapter also revealed, however, that the relatively privileged condition of the civil prisoners, whose presence of course was unknown in the central convict prisons which were increasingly setting the agenda for county gaols, produced problems in terms of opportunities for trafficking. It is necessary to consider the experience of incarcerated debtors in rather more detail here.

Though the description 'relatively privileged' is accurate, it must be remembered that life in prison was still unpleasant. In the minutely detailed accounts recording expenditure on tea, coal, potatoes and the like, which were made in 1845 and endorsed 'Mr Samuel Bowser, Carmarthen County Gaol', there are two tiny references to '4 Job 8 & 9', the sentiments of which ('they that plow iniquity, and sow wickedness, reap the same') indicate a mind not calmly reconciled to its fate.[16] Whilst they were excused some of the more onerous aspects of prison life, the debtors were nonetheless not immune from discipline. Westlake intercepted, read and marked two letters from a female debtor, Eliza David, to the governor of Monmouth gaol.[17] The solicitor Charles Vaughan was placed in the refractory cell for drunkenness on New Year's Day 1846, whilst David Thomas was immediately placed there for three hours on his remand to gaol having arrived drunk, and the practice of debtors' drinking with their committing officers on the way to the institution seems to have been an established one.[18]

On the other hand, those who had either the financial or familial support could ameliorate their conditions to an extent. John Williams was not the only individual who received support from outside. Thomas Daniel was nursed by his mother during an illness. He was also allowed wine, which no doubt helped him to cope with the delirium tremens to which he was subject and may have contributed to his decision to remain in the gaol for an extra day after his discharge, having missed the mail coach to Llanelli and being too ill to walk.[19] In March 1847 it seems that three of the debtors were being regularly attended by a female servant or servants to perform such tasks as lighting the fire.[20] Alcohol was prescribed to debtors by the surgeon with sufficient frequency to suggest that the medical requirement was considered easily satisfied in non-criminal cases, the surgeon even producing a pro-forma to be filled in when the need arose.[21] For the truly destitute, however, the county funds had to provide. In 1838, before the imposition of the lower limit of indebtedness meriting incarceration, all the confined debtors were reported to be in receipt of 2s. per week allowance, and the practice continued on occasions thereafter, as is evidenced by the grant of the same sum to John Cure in 1847.[22] The process of granting money directly was, however, disapproved of generally by the prison inspectors and was subsequently replaced by incorporation of debtors into the dietary, the inspector remarking in 1851 (in terms indicative of the changing perception of the imprisoned debtor's character, to which this assimilation to the treatment of other inmates was no doubt connected) that 'County Court and fraudulent debtors' were then receiving the same diet as remand prisoners.[23] There was in addition to this continuing county support for the particularly indigent a special fund for poor prisoners which comprised charitable donations, most of which were provided at Christmas,[24] and which was distributed by the magistrates. The donors, Earl Cawdor, Lord Dynevor, Lady Lucy Foley, the bishop of St David's and the rest, were continuing a long-established tradition of provision of this nature, no doubt an expected paternalist gesture from those whose wealth would insulate them from a more intimate connection with the gaol. This fund was in part distributed in cash and kind at Christmas,[25] but some was retained for more particular applications. In May 1846 James Brabyn was paid 10s. from the fund for his work in constructing 'shutes and coal Boxes' for the prison, and a further 10s. was granted to Thomas Evans for porter 'has he is in a very weak state of health'.[26] The same fund seems to have been used to finance applications for official discharge from custody, with legal representation in appropriate cases. In January 1847 it was ordered that £2 be made available to Cure, Daniel and a third debtor,

David Rees, for attorneys to 'git them throo the Insolvent Court'.[27] It was by this court, originating in a statute of 1813, that most debtors were released from incarceration.[28]

The distribution of donations was a matter which could cause some controversy, with prisoners claiming entitlements in an area where the prison authorities might have preferred the language of discretion. A dispute over the Christmas 1845 bounty was continuing in August of the next year when Vaughan, the debtor solicitor, wrote to the Visiting Justices.[29] Indeed, the entitlements of the debtors, to cohabitation with spouses,[30] to play at quoits,[31] to refuse attendance at chapel,[32] to weekend visits,[33] become an obvious source of contention in the 1840s. As was suggested in the previous chapter, the ability to appeal over the head of the gaoler to a higher authority, and the transition to a system of prisons of increasing uniformity was leading to a more concrete perception of 'prisoners' rights' amongst all inmates. In respect of debtors, the Carmarthenshire evidence suggests that a combination of an articulate subset of prisoners with a very real uncertainty over the position of this 'civil' class, increasingly anomalous in a service where rules and practice were being determined by the convict model, exposed certain weaknesses in the regulations of the county gaol. Local tradition and discretion again look anomalous, yet central direction, in a decade when imprisonment for debt was thought by some to be nearing its end, was not forthcoming. Here is another point of tension in the story of the emergence of the 'modern' prison.

Remand prisoners

In an adjoining yard to the debtors in Carmarthen Gaol were the untried prisoners on remand. In traditional prison historiography, which it has been argued is based rather too firmly on the consideration of punishment for serious crime, debtors and remand prisoners are represented as almost the only inhabitants of pre-nineteenth-century penal institutions. Like the debtors, the remand prisoners also formed a category of inmate whose conditions were less restricted than their convicted fellows, since the presumption of innocence governed their position. Yet again, however, it can be seen that the untried too begin to be assimilated, as time goes on, more closely to the new paradigm of the post-trial prisoner. In Carmarthen, for example, the use of tobacco and the grant of subsistence monies, both remnants of an older model of incarceration, were withdrawn from remand prisoners in the 1840s. Yet it will be seen in this section that the position of this class of prisoner continued to pose questions to authorities for whom the convicted were increasingly the major objects of attention.[34]

Prisoners could be remanded for both felony and misdemeanour,[35] but for this latter class of offence remands to the county gaol would seem not to have been common, though it should be remembered that a night in the cells of one of the increasingly common and regulated police lock-ups preceded many court appearances for drunkenness and assault.

A case in 1847, which ended in proceedings in the Court of Queen's Bench, is fascinating in its exposure both of the possibility of manipulation of remand in custody and of the personal tensions which existed amongst those involved in the administration of justice in Carmarthenshire. The events began when William Griffiths and his son were apprehended on the property of a tramway near Llanelli by McKiernon, the superintendent of the line. McKiernon believed the two to be poachers and had them arrested, but instead of being taken before a local Llanelli magistrate and bailed for a misdemeanour as might be anticipated, Griffiths senior was remanded to the county gaol by J. E. Saunders, a JP of forty years' standing, and sent to Carmarthen in a phaeton. Saunders refused offers of bail (interestingly, the other magistrates who subsequently sat on the committal seemed to think that this was obligatory for a misdemeanour), though Griffiths's family were impoverished by the loss of his income. Allegations surfaced that Saunders had refused the bail because those offering it were tradesmen not farmers, that he did not trust the Llanelli magistrate Rees to refuse bail to Griffiths for anything short of murder and, most seriously, that Saunders was friendly with McKiernon and had received the gift of a turbot from him. Saunders also wrongly claimed that Griffiths's certificate of good conduct on discharge from an earlier sentence of transportation (he had served four years for an earlier theft of cheese) was a forgery, 'sold in the hulks for 6d a-piece'. Griffiths, brought to trial on a charge of offering violence to McKiernon to prevent

apprehension, an offence graver than that of the simple misdemeanour of trespass in pursuit of game, was acquitted. His case
was then taken up by George Thomas, an attorney and coroner.
At one point Thomas was involved in a heated argument with
Westlake at the gaol after he was refused a second copy of
Griffiths's commitment. Thomas threatened to write to the secretary of state about the case, which at some point he did, being
advised to start an action in the Queen's Bench. At the trial of the
action Lord Denman found that no sufficient evidence of corruption had been adduced, but was critical of Saunders's conduct and
refused him costs.[36] For his part, Thomas had been accused of
maintaining the action out of animus against Saunders, who had
previously refused some of the former's claims for expenses as
coroner. Subsequently, letters in the local press accused Thomas
of impropriety in respect of the lists of those to serve on special
juries.[37] The whole affair and the publicity it provoked,
suggesting as it did the kind of personal manipulation of justice
which was supposed to have been consigned to history, must have
caused some embarrassment within the county.

In the following year (though whether this case played any part
in the process I do not know) the law relating to bail and remand
in custody was reformed by Jervis's Act, and bail became compulsory for most misdemeanours.[38] For felony, however, the remand
in custody, though not universal, remained usual. Given a felony
conviction rate of approximately 75 per cent in the period
covered by Carmarthen's *Felons' Register*, the period spent on
remand might be the only time spent in custody by a number of
suspected individuals.[39] One of the questions which will need to
be considered here is the extent to which pre-trial imprisonment
may have been regarded as de facto punishment and, therefore, as
a factor operating in the minds of grand juries faced with the decision as to whether to sanction a trial or of petty juries determining
guilt.

There are some complicating factors. A prisoner could be
remanded for felony to be convicted, ultimately, of misdemeanour. I have suggested that in respect of sexual offences such
a process is by no means unusual.[40] By contrast, if an offender
received a sentence at the top end of the penal tariff his position
became slightly anomalous even after trial. Those condemned to
death had always had a different experience pending the

execution than that of other convicted criminals. But those sentenced to transportation or, after 1853, penal servitude, were also, in a sense, on a sort of 'remand' in their 'home' institution before their transfer to the destination at which the sentence proper would begin. Such prisoners caused a certain amount of confusion to the Carmarthenshire authorities. In 1842 the inspector, Bisset Hawkins, remarked on finding a transport mixed with the remands because he had not been put to hard labour.[41] Seven years later, Governor Stephens asked the Justices how much oakum should be picked by Anne Matthews pending her removal to start a sentence of ten years' transportation.[42] In 1864 the inspector, J. G. Perry, was obliged to clarify the issue as to whether those sentenced to penal servitude could be required to perform hard labour, stating that this was permissible if ordered by the Visiting Justices.[43]

Whether remanded to gaol before or after trial the prisoner had to be accompanied by the appropriate documentary authority, and both Governors Westlake and Stephens were rightly concerned if it were absent.[44] Before 1848 there was also the possibility that prisoners for indictable offences could be examined before trial by a magistrate in an attempt to extract information concerning the offence. Such examinations continued after the Indictable Offences Act of that year, though the questions to be put, in theory at least, were far more restricted.[45] Carmarthen's *Felons' Register* provides a space in which to record such examinations, and practice suggests that second examinations, when under-taken, were generally carried out, at least before the Act, within the gaol itself, the prisoner only being considered 'fully committed' after this second examination. In one case from 1871, however, the 'further examination' of the accused was clearly undertaken outside the gaol. John Murray, a native of Laugharne, charged with unlawfully inflicting grievous bodily harm, was taken from the gaol back to his home village to the bedside of his victim, David Roberts, and 'committed for trial' from there by the magistrates, J. T. Beynon and T. Powell.[46] Although details of the practice of further examination are difficult to establish, in at least one instance there is a suggestion that the prisoner was held on remand for a lesser offence whilst a graver one was investigated. In October 1848 a prisoner held for trial for being a rogue and a vagabond was, after examination, charged with the offence of housebreaking. In other cognate cases (although conceptually distinct as involving convicted prisoners) it seems clear that conviction on summary offences such as vagrancy allowed time for the gathering of further information which could lead to arrest on a serious charge immediately upon discharge. The prisoner could be separated during his sentence for inquiries to be made, and arrested immediately on expiry of the initial sentence.[47] In inquiries into a murder in Brecon in 1848, suspects remanded on suspicion for the offence were held until the Brecon authorities had sent someone to interview them. In subsequent investigations into the same murder, two more individuals held for the same reason were allowed to remain in the gaol for an extra night after they had been exculpated by the Brecon investigators only in the evening and had no money or place to stay.[48]

Remand prisoners were held in the Trebanda in cells on both the ground and first floors. The upper cells, mostly with glazed windows, allowed communal accommodation for these individuals long after the prison inspectors had urged their separation,[49] the single ground-floor cell typically taking individuals who for any reason were felt unsuitable to mix with other prisoners.[50] Despite the decision in *R.* v. *Justices of North Riding of Yorkshire*,[51] which had given the principle an early validity, labour was apparently not enjoined on untried prisoners in Carmarthen at the period in question, Governor Westlake specifically noting that the four remands who helped to dig out the well in the sickness epidemic of the summer of 1846 were volunteers.[52] Although by mid-century they had been added to the dietary, rather than in receipt of money,[53] remand prisoners could still be provided with food by their friends, who were allowed to speak to them, under supervision, through a grille in the door.[54] They were also allowed to wear their own clothes unless these were deemed unwholesome, but the expedient of providing them with a standard prison uniform drew adverse comment from the inspector in 1851, as not distinguishing between convicted and unconvicted prisoners.[55] Indeed, this strict classification of prisoners, an established nostrum throughout the century, was regularly endangered in Carmarthen before the enforced major rebuild of the 1860s. If the correction cells were full, then convicted misdemeanants might find themselves in the remand section of the Trebanda, a practice (like that of their previous mixing with the debtors) which again angered the inspectors.[56] Another problem was that, particularly in the years in which staffing was at minimum levels, it would seem that the untried prisoners were left mainly unsupervised. This, together with the sharing of cells, would lead to the danger of fighting amongst the remands[57] and the relatively high proportion of escapes and attempted escapes, sometimes in combination, from this area of the gaol.[58] The demands of economy, discipline, suspicion and the presumption of innocence were not always easily compatible.

It may be instructive to examine the rather different stories of three particular remand prisoners, all women, to see what they can reveal about the operation of the gaol more generally.

Mary Hughes

Mary Hughes killed her three children, all under six years of age, by hanging them, apparently under the insane delusion that they would starve. She was the prisoner who, in an unusual move, was smuggled into the prison in the early hours of the morning, no doubt to avoid the attentions of Carmarthen's residents, aware of the case through word of mouth and the initially hostile reporting of the local press.[59] Hughes was then a figure of notoriety and interest, and an increase in the number of visits to the gaol by JPs and their guests suggests that a prurient interest in the case was not solely the preserve of the working class.[60] At her trial in July 1847 Mary Hughes was found to be insane and was subsequently removed to an asylum in Devizes. Her period on remand, though clearly in some ways atypical, gives further substance to the claim that, at least at this time, the system of classification could be effectively undermined by the exigencies of real life. For part of her remand, until intervention by one of the Justices, David Davies, she was being held in the single room of the Lower Trebanda, strictly part of the male prisoners' quarters, rather than in the women's prison.[61] She was watched over by fellow prisoners, Jane Jones, Ann Awberry and Mariah Thomas.[62] Whilst the principle of inmate nursing was not in itself objectionable, indeed, had been advocated by no less than Elizabeth Fry,[63] the employment of Awberry and Thomas, whose conduct in the gaol could be far from acceptable, suggests either a bold penal initiative or Hobson's choice. Moreover, at least two of these prisoners had been convicted rather than being on remand themselves, meaning that the rules on silent confinement as well as classification were being breached in their cases.[64]

Phoebe Jones

The case of Phoebe Jones, remanded in 1858, also raises some interesting questions. In his report to the July quarter sessions the surgeon records that 'Phobe [*sic*] Jones committed on a charge of child murder extremely weak when brought to prison having been recently confined. She was at once placed in the infirmary and every attention paid to her and is now quite recovered.' The grand jury found 'No Bill' against her when she appeared in court. It has been explained elsewhere that in cases involving crimes of this nature, indeed, in any offences which might loosely be called of a 'moral' character, successful prosecutions were exceptionally rare. Although it is impossible to penetrate the minds of the jurymen concerned in such cases (or, indeed, in others, particularly where verdicts seem to run counter to the evidence), it may be that the taste of imprisonment experienced before trial was an operative factor in the discharge or acquittal. Thus the remand may have been construed by the jury as being punitive (as, indeed, would be de facto the case when a judge explicitly made allowance for it in passing sentence, as in the case of Margaret Jones in 1850, whose trial was delayed by her weakness) and taken into account in deciding the prisoner's fate. It is clear too from the neonatal offence cases that initial medical inspections were made in the prison,[65] and on at least one occasion apparently the whole committal proceedings took place there.[66] Given the weakness of some of the women in these cases, and their desire to conceal their condition in the outside world, the experience of gaol (in particular the medical and dietary provision) could, albeit in a limited way, even be construed as beneficial.[67]

Anne Matthews

The final case which may be allowed to detain us briefly is that of Anne Matthews. The female remands we have been discussing so far are generally women from the poorer, even the poorest, section of Carmarthenshire society. By contrast, Anne Matthews was a 'respectable' woman, and her trial, which resulted in a sentence of transportation for ten years, attracted considerable attention. It confirms that social differences which existed outside the walls of the gaol were not entirely forgotten within them. Matthews was the daughter of Carmarthen's postmaster and was herself employed by the Post Office at a salary of £40 per year. Her family was known to some of the most influential people in the town, as the appearance of a number of magistrates (including the apparently rehabilitated J. E. Saunders) and churchmen as character witnesses at her trial in March 1849 indicates. She was found guilty on a specimen count of stealing a letter from the mail, evidence being adduced to show that she had removed a large number of items. Her background, together with the eccentricity of behaviour which formed a key element of her defence, no doubt attracted the immense crowd which followed the trial.[68] During her pre-trial remand, and again pending her removal to Millbank, Matthews posed some problems to Governor Stephens. She was brought meals from outside whilst unconvicted and was allowed daily visits from her spiritual advisor, Archdeacon Bevan. There was some initial problem with other visits being not properly authorized. After the trial, Bevan, who had been a character witness, continued to visit, and Matthews was also allowed, on the order of Daniel Prytherch JP (another character witness), the singular privilege of being allowed to take the sacrament in the gaol alongside her sister. On one visit she complained to Bevan that she was ill and had not been properly attended by the surgeon. Stephens declared this a falsehood, but a flurry of medical visits ensued in the next few days, and a bowl of fruit was sent in by order of the surgeon. It has been seen earlier that a question was posed as to the quantity of oakum she was to pick prior to her removal, which took place some seven months after her conviction. It is difficult, when reading the details of Anne Matthews's treatment alongside the entries relating to other prisoners, convicted and unconvicted, to conclude that the ideal of equality before the law had been fully realized within the gaol at this time.[69]

Non-felonious offenders

Margaret Jones, whose case was mentioned in the last section, was acquitted of the murder of her child but convicted of the misdemeanour of concealment of birth. Offences less than felony which resulted in sentences being served in the gaol encompassed conduct ranging from the deeply disturbing (Jones's child had been partially eaten by a pig, from which it was only with difficulty recovered) to the bizarre (malicious damage to a trombone)[70] and the trivial (playing pitch and toss on a Sunday).[71] Important subcategories included various offences which might be grouped around such conduct as poaching and vagrancy, and it has been seen earlier that a gaol sentence could also be imposed to reinforce the disciplinary role of other institutions: many prisoners in Carmarthen's gaol were there for refusing to work in, or damaging the property of, the Union workhouse. It is difficult, then, to say much about the 'typical' prisoner serving a sentence for a minor offence, and in Carmarthen at any rate it is difficult even to produce overall statistical analyses, for the records which would provide most information in this respect are lost.

It is in record-keeping and in the accommodation provided in the gaol that the ancient distinction between felons and other offenders survives longest. The terminology merits a brief excursus, for it is in itself indicative of a changing punitive world. This section was originally to be headed 'misdemeanants', recalling the ancient division of non-treasonable secular offenders which was still formally important (as regards to pre-trial process and, as we have seen, bail) throughout the nineteenth century. The grounds for that nominal distinction had, however, become increasingly unclear, to the extent that by the 1880s the influential criminal jurist Stephen was urging its abolition. Insofar as it had depended on the liability to the death penalty (a distinction blurred as early as the thirteenth century by the recognition that petty larceny was a non-capital felony), the penal revolution of the late eighteenth and early nineteenth centuries, by reducing capital crimes and extending custodial sentences, had rendered the felony/treason distinction less comprehensible. Increasingly, the favoured distinction comes to be drawn in accordance with the mode of trial rather than the form of punishment, and 'summary offences' becomes a standard (if still a conceptually difficult) term for lesser crimes. Prison inspectors incline towards discussion of 'criminal' prisoners generally, and if they do distinguish between categories of offences it tends to be along different lines from the felony/misdemeanour axis, as, for example, in selecting vagrants for particular discussion. Indeed, the paradigm shift which saw local gaols take their lead increasingly from the convict prisons made the experience of minor offenders appear, if anything, less central to the custodial venture – arguments over the influence of religious reform or the progressive stage system had very little meaning in respect of prisoners who might be discharged within a few weeks or even days. In 1865 the nominal difference between the 'gaol' and the 'house of correction' was abolished, completing the de facto assimilation of their functions. At one time felons and debtors, the inhabitants of the 'gaol', were wholly distinct categories from lesser offenders in the prison world. Now, as has been seen, debtors become increasingly incorporated into the punitive rationale, and misdemeanants become characterized as serving shorter terms of, rather than having entirely different varieties of, incarceration than felons, who now remained in prison after as well as before trial.

Minor crime, of course, remained of great importance. It is true, indeed, that the nineteenth century witnessed an explosion in the types of activity (vaccination, education etc.) which were hedged about by criminal sanctions, but foremost amongst the penalty for these 'minor' offences was the fine. To enforce the fine the term of imprisonment remained vital, but it was seen as a derivative rather than a primary punishment. Yet the ideological emphasis of the prison had evolved into one focused primarily on serious crime. At least it finally coincided with the perspective which has since then dazzled most penal historians!

Yet it is probable that Governors Westlake and Stephens and their staff would have been surprised by any idea of the relatively low significance of the minor offender within their gaol. Even bureaucratically the high turnover of short-term prisoners would occupy considerable amounts of time. In 1867 only 20 out of 290 committals were for terms of over three months, in 1870 only 9, with 119 in the latter year serving between fourteen days and a month.[72] Moreover, as this section will demonstrate, the persistent alcoholic prostitute could determine the daily experience of the prison staff much more immediately than could any celebrated felon.

The relative absence of long-term prisoners from the gaol (and, as we have seen in chapter 1, from the courtroom) gives an interesting slant to perceptions of rural Welsh criminality, to which the inspector's words with which this chapter began add a further element of commentary. Welsh criminals were, it seems, of a relatively unadventurous kind, neither violent nor (after Rebecca) 'political', and relatively tractable once they were inside. It is not necessary to accept, as Bisset Hawkins apparently did, the explanation of the borough gaoler that the local population were neither addicted to theft nor indulged much in drink and 'accordingly they do not often get into scrapes'.[73] The official picture need not entirely reflect reality. It comes as something of a surprise, for example, to see an early report stating that few poachers were confined to gaol when they feature so frequently and consistently amongst the summary convictions.[74] Again it is as well to remember that the prison population is the end product of a number of culturally influenced variables, such as the incidence and outcome of prosecution decisions.

Of the specific forms of lesser offence which are regularly mentioned separately it is perhaps vagrancy which merits particular attention, and it was noted, both in chapter 1 and in the discussion of a specific local 'criminology' in the last chapter, that it sometimes receives it. In the absence of comprehensive surviving documentation for Carmarthenshire some conclusions on the subject must remain speculative, though David Jones's impressive study of the problem in Wales generally provides instructive material from elsewhere.[75] It has been seen, then, that vagrancy is the most obviously penal arm of the various legal measures available to deal with the poor. Vagrancy was poverty in the wrong place, dangerous both because it could be a precursor to other crimes and because it involved persons who were strangers and, consequently, potentially outside the web of unofficial local surveillance and therefore meriting a more vigorous official form.[76] It has been noted earlier that in one case a number of 'vagrants' were questioned in gaol concerning a murder in another county, and Jones concludes: 'It is clear that tramps were sometimes taken in on the flimsiest charge, in the hope that something would be proved against them.'[77] It is a plausible hypothesis that an increasing fear of mobile criminality in general in the second half of the century[78] focused attention upon vagrancy as symptomatic of a wider sense of insecurity. It certainly seems to have been the case that periodic increases in the number of poor on the roads could focus local attention upon the problem.[79] Yet it would seem that the county gaol probably received most of its vagrants from in and around its county town, in this respect acting more like a borough than a county institution. It may not have been worthwhile for a policeman or magistrate further afield in the county to send a tramp to Carmarthen, and a night in the police cell or an instruction to move on might have been a more obvious response to the offence.[80] Vagrancy was also, of course, a phenomenon which could challenge the punitive nature of the experience of imprisonment itself, by pressing the issue of 'less-eligibility'. It was part of the appeal of a new, 'graduated' dietary adopted in the gaol at mid-century that it acted as a direct deterrent, it being rather optimistically reported as being 'found very distasteful to the vagrant population, very few commitments for vagrancy having taken place since its adoption'.[81] The severity or otherwise of the punitive response of a county was often perceived as responsible for the moving on of the vagrants and the threats which they represented.[82] In 1848 it was ordered that a small grate and chimney should be placed in a cell to keep vagrants apart from other prisoners, and there is a further reference to dampness in the 'vagrants' cells' in 1867 by a non-official source, suggesting a degree of extra-statutory classification within the gaol.[83]

Ann and Mary Ann Awberry

It may be surprising to suggest that the prisoners who spent the longest period of time in Carmarthen prison in the period under discussion were not felons, but a pair of individuals whose repeated convictions for minor offences, mostly of public disorder, resulted in prolonged occupancy over a period of years. These were women who were taken for crimes associated with vagrancy, but their settled residence in the town did not allow of the expedient of simply moving them on as might be done with vagrants properly so termed. Ann and Mary Ann Awberry[84] both had colourful if tragic connections with the gaol, and their cases merit our attention because they invite reflection on recidivism, on the maintenance of discipline and on the availability of other forms of disposition in a particularly direct way. Ann Awberry was probably the more often convicted. The frequency of her appearances elicited a degree of resigned amusement from the bench. On 10 January 1851, for example, she appeared on a charge of drunkenness, appealing for another trial after her conviction and claiming that 'she would certainly reform and become a better woman in her old age'. The mayor, reflecting that 'it was her first offence, this year, and not a very heinous one', discharged her, only to see her return on the next day and be sentenced to two months.[85] By July, returning to court only two days after being released from gaol, 'The Mayor said this was only the 14th time [presumably in that year] of Ann's committal but Mr Alderman Morris said it was nearly the 114th time'.[86] She was recorded as still working as a prostitute at the age of sixty nearly a decade later.[87] But Mary Ann Awberry, often incarcerated at the same time as her namesake, was also a very frequent inmate, at one time being brought to the gaol at ten o'clock at night without any warrant or committal, almost as though it was her expected residence.[88] The women were unusual but not unique, being only the most persistent of an underclass of persistent female delinquency which included Mary Ann Thomas ('a nymph and one commonly called and known as "Nanny Awberry the second"')[89] and (for it would appear that this was a different woman) Mariah Thomas.

Both Ann and Mary Ann Awberry at different times spent considerable periods in the prison infirmary, and both too were familiar with the refractory cell. The former facts lead us to speculate on the general health problems which those who lived on the streets and in the common lodging houses would bring into the prisons. This is a matter which we will address in more detail in chapter 6. As to the issue of conduct, then the women seem to fit a stereotype noted in other nineteenth-century institutions. This maintained that women could prove to be more disruptive and destructive prisoners than men. Mary Ann Awberry in particular marked her numerous sentences with a string of assaults, acts of damage and outbursts of abuse which must have stretched both the temper and resources of those staffing the prison and had an impact on the conditions of imprisonment of their fellow prisoners. Westlake, in one of the moments of candour which characterize his expansive record-keeping, remarks at one point of Mary Ann: 'The prisoner his a most vile creature.'[90] A couple of examples will give an indication of the way in which the routines of regime, staffing and accommodation could all be upset by a single non-cooperative individual. On 9 July 1846

Westlake remarked of the prisoner who had been readmitted on the previous day: 'Mary Ann Awberry refused to pick oakum and Barrackaded her door so has to prevent any one to enter by placing her Bed stead at the Back of the door which I ordered the door to be burst open and put two other females in the room with her to sleep.' On the next day,

> Mary Ann Awberry put in to the refractory cell for refusing to pick oakum when ordered by me & throwing a chamber untensil & a Jug at my head & destroying the county property. Inconsequence of her mutines conduct I was obliged to put her in Irons which I reported the case to Dl Prytherch Esq.[91]

Three weeks later we read:

> Mary A Awbery put in the refractory cell at 1 oclock, PM for mutionnes conduct at 3 oclock I was obliged to put her in Irons and at 6 oclock I visited her with the female Turnkey and I ordered the Irons to be taken of if she would go to bed quiet which she defied me or any of the officers which I Kept the Irons on and reported the circumstance to Dl Prytherch Esqr at 7PM her conduct up to 9 oclock PM was very bad.

On the next day, 'I ordered the female Turnkey to take her Irons of in sodoing she took old of the Tin jug and thro it at me & then her allowance of bread also which I ordered her to be put in Irons a gain.' The following day, 'I forgave mary ann awbery of the refractory cell she having promised not to Violate the rules of the prison any more', but, later on the same day, 'I was obliged to put Maryan Awbery in the upper Trebanda in consequence of her Bad behaviour to wards the other female prisoners'.[92]

These instances of misconduct, and they could be multiplied many times in the sentences of this class of female street offenders,[93] reveal much about the reality of daily life in Carmarthen gaol. Rules and systems and the routine so important in maintaining a functional regime were challenged fundamentally by the sheer intransigence of the difficult prisoner. But the 'difficult' prisoner seems to have been a not unusual presence in the local prison.

The habitual criminal

A consideration of the cases of Mary Ann Awberry and other repeat offenders of her type necessarily leads to the discussion of the problems associated with habitual offenders generally. It is undoubtedly the case that after mid-century the twin issues of the identification of, and appropriate punishment for, recidivists assumed a major place in the concerns of the administration of the maturing prison 'system'. As the prison succeeded in assuming a central role in the punishment of criminals, so too did the evidence of its failure (whether conceived of in terms of rehabilitative or deterrent ideology) become an issue of vital importance in its administration. Much of the rhetoric of the second half of the century became directed towards the existence of a 'criminal class', marked by its persistence in crime, and the ways which might be employed to defeat it. It is, when stated starkly, a quite surprising proposition and one which had a profound effect on the way that criminality came to be understood. Those who did not respond 'correctly' to the experience of incarceration became identified as a different sort of human being from those who did. This premise shows, as much as anything, the importance which the prison had achieved in shaping a Victorian view of the world. While the discourse may be understood, by contemporaries and historians alike, as part of wider cultural transitions – a reformulation of ideas of moral responsibility, the result of 'scientific' taxonomy or Darwinian theory, the impact of a media-fuelled 'moral panic' – it is easy to forget that the entry point to the process lies in the concern over reconviction rates. The 'habitual', before he or she becomes anything else, surfaces as a failure of the criminal justice system. There is much in this process that needs unpacking before we can consider the Carmarthenshire evidence relating to that issue.

It is tempting to see the concern over the habitual offender as starting with the decline of transportation. Radzinowicz and Hood, whose analysis admittedly develops with rather more subtlety, begin their discussion of the topic thus: 'As long as transportation provided the means of flushing large numbers of criminals to the antipodes, there was no urgency about considering how to control them at home.'[94] There is undoubtedly some substance in this claim, and the impact of the release of 'ticket-of-

leave men' from convict prisons into the anonymity of London or
Portsmouth rather than the anonymity of distant Australia is of
crucial importance in understanding some of the legislative measures which attempted to deal with the problem of habitual
offenders. Yet people had been discharged from the hulks, and
from Millbank, for many years before the Penal Servitude Acts,
albeit in smaller numbers. Moreover, recidivism was a local
problem before it ever became a national one. Offensive drunks,
persistent prostitutes and regular vagrants were not new
phenomena in the nineteenth century. Although we know that
many of those transported had committed offences, normally
against property, of a relatively trivial kind after previous convictions,[95] it would be an error to believe that the majority of minor
repeat offenders had ever been so disposed of.

As much as changes in the penal sanction were responsible for
the creation of unease concerning the existence of a criminal class
in the second half of the century, so were the factors which, as
was seen in the Introduction, promoted those changes or were the
wider consequences of them. Whilst Nanny Awberry remained
Nanny Awberry in Carmarthen gaol, she became a member of a
class when that gaol became a member of a system. The habitual
drunkard/vagrant/robber is identified as a member of that species
when identity becomes determined, at least in part, by the criminal justice system rather than by the broader social community.[96]
National trends and problems were identified only when the
concerns came to be addressed from a national perspective. And,
whilst Foucault is right to point to the self-reinforcing acquisition
of expertise by the collection of data within the institution, it is
clear that, in one sense, this results in less being known about the
offender rather than more, for specific criminological knowledge
takes over from more general knowledge – of family, background,
non-offending characteristics – which was available to those
whose knowledge of crime and its perpetrators was local rather
than national.

Categorization at this criminological level is, then, a process
which depends, paradoxically, upon anonymity. That anonymity,
and hence that susceptibility to 'asocial' categorization, is nour-
ished by the aggregation and social separation of the 'masses' in
the city. As Matthew Davenport Hill pointed out in 1852, 'in
small towns there must be a sort of natural police, of a very

wholesome kind, operating upon the conduct of every individual ... But in a large town, he lives, as it were, in absolute obscurity.' Reflecting upon the wealthier classes' propensity to move out of the town centres, Hill adds:

> Now this was not formerly so; it is a habit which has, practically speaking, grown up within the last half century. The result of the old habit was that rich and poor lived in proximity; and the superior classes exercised that species of silent but very efficient control over their neighbours.[97]

The drive towards criminological categorization is connected to personal mobility within the country as a whole, for this moves people easily beyond the locus of wider social knowledge. And it is added to by the production of statistics, which we have noted as an important factor in the nineteenth-century penological revolution, which replace social biographies by subheadings. By the time that Henry Mayhew, a great champion of, and taxonomist of, the class of 'habituals', introduced personalities to his readers, he was operating from a very different paradigm from that which could still prevail in a Welsh village. He was 'fleshing out' a statistical phenomenon and introducing criminals to a section of society who had no real experience of them as individuals.[98]

It is to these rather more fundamental changes rather than to particular legislative measures, or even the upsurge of concern caused by the well-explored 'garrotting panic' of 1862, that we should look to explain the increasing unease about habitual criminals after mid-century. But, although it has been argued that Carmarthenshire was still, in many ways, a society which in itself was not a manifestation of the new paradigm, it was not, of course, insulated from the concerns which that new paradigm both reflected and promoted. Readers of the *Carmarthen Journal* were aware of both the practice and the terminology of 'garrotting' a whole decade before the robbery of Hugh Pilkington MP sparked a renewed metropolitan-based media campaign around it.[99] And Carmarthen gaol was attuned to the discourse surrounding the habitual offender and the difficulty of his detection.

It is clear that Governor Stephens had a sensitivity to the problems of recidivism which was, as we have seen, shared by the new breed of prison chaplain who served under him, but which was not marked in the time of Governor Westlake. In Stephens this sensitivity manifested itself in a number of changes in his record-keeping from the late 1850s. An increased attention to the changeability of identity, evidenced by his noting the aliases used by those in his gaol, and also to the dangers of relying on the words of the prisoners themselves, evidenced by the use of words like 'says' or 'supposed' in recording information such as place of birth or last residence or previous criminal record, display clearly an awareness of the fact that the particular sentence being served by the particular offender is now not the only concern of the governor of a county gaol. George Stephens's use of photography in his register from the first half of 1858 onwards, though not unparalleled, was an indication not only of the perception of the problem but also of a belief in the capacity of science to overcome it. The Habitual Criminals Act of 1869, indirectly, and its successor, the Prevention of Crimes Act 1871, directly, subsequently incorporated the technique of photography into the battle against the 'criminal class'. In October 1870 the Carmarthenshire bench granted its governor £10 for his expenses in buying and using the camera and the 'glass house' he had erected in which to employ it. The real importance of these developments lies in the network of associations upon which they are predicated, for here we see the movement towards the identification of a 'national' criminal within a national penal system. Whilst we have generally seen Carmarthenshire as lagging behind in the apparently inexorable drive towards centralization, it should be noted that, in this respect at any rate, Governor Stephens seems to have acted as a pioneer.[100]

The argument being advanced here, that the issue of recidivism is intimately and necessarily connected, as both cause and effect, with the development of a national criminal justice system based firmly upon the dominance of incarceration as a penal measure, is important in a number of ways. On a personal level it was, as has been seen, the necessity of conveying repeat offenders to other penal establishments which gave local governors their most immediate and physical exposure to conditions and regimes elsewhere.[101] The need to 'prove a conviction' against an accused in another county could likewise reveal to men like William Williams the operation of the system outside their own home town and their role in that wider system.[102] Criminals too could compare conditions with those they had experienced in other gaols and could themselves play an active role in the drive towards assimilation of those conditions. It was suggested earlier that it seems no coincidence that those prisoners most willing to provide challenges to the authority of Governor Westlake and his Visiting Justices over matters such as diet or haircuts were men with previous custodial experience elsewhere.[103] And, of course, the climate of concern over habituals could lead to important effects on both policing and prosecution policy, which in themselves could fuel the very concern upon which they were based.[104]

There is little evidence in the Carmarthenshire records of 'dogging', the formal police supervision of habituals introduced by the 1869 Act, although the chief constable was aware of the legislation and had outlined the procedures to be taken under it in his orders to the force.[105] Not all were so careful, as is made clear by the record of a conviction before Edward Jones JP, suggestive as much in the presumed nature of the legislation as in its own legal imprecision, of one John Roberts for resisting a police constable 'in the execution of his duty under the Vagrant and Habitual Criminals Act'.[106] The 1871 Act similarly made little direct impact, appearing as the source of the authority under which a police constable was operating when assaulted in 1872[107] but being used, apparently, in only one case to determine a sentence.[108] Yet it is undoubtedly true that the concern which underlay the measures was reflected in the behaviour of the local police.[109] As with the prisons, so too with the constabulary, the perceived danger of a class of domestic predators increased the flow of information. The paperwork concerning a ticket-of-leave man had to be explained to a colleague by Sergeant Thomas in 1865,[110] but thereafter the concentration on recidivism seems to develop. Convictions for repeated drunkenness[111] and for being a 'suspected person' under the Vagrancy Acts[112] are a notable feature of the court records of the 1870s. The traditional haunts of pickpockets, local fairs,[113] were policed with an apparent new vigour by police drawn from throughout the county on the lookout for old hands. In 1870 Sarah Howell, 'an habitual thief', was followed around Llanelli Market,[114] whilst two years later two women taken as members of a pickpocket gang at the same market had their lodgings in Swansea searched for evidence of professional criminality.[115] Whilst the figures are too small and too inconsistent[116] to allow of any real statistical analysis, the impression of a determination to identify and prosecute (rather than simply move on)[117] the suspected 'hardened' offender seems clear. This in its turn might be expected to have resulted in an impact on the number and nature of those incarcerated in the prison, and a tendency to feed the contemporary perception of the existence of a recalcitrant class of criminals and the institution as their natural location, albeit one which was destined to fail with them. The evidence from Carmarthenshire is, however, again unclear, for an analysis of the *Felons' Register* seems to suggest that amongst serious offenders previous custodial experience remained fairly constant from the 1840s to the 1870s. The fear of an underclass of 'old hands' seems to have affected the county, but on no particularly sound basis. It may be that the evidence elsewhere is similarly unsupportive. In the history of crime and punishment, perception is invariably a more important motor for change than 'simple' fact.

Children

If the habitual offender marked one end of a criminal career then the child represented the other, and as the century wore on the prison came to be regarded as an unsuitable location for the young. That a number of factors were responsible for this change – developing concerns about the aetiology of crime, an extension of educational provision, crusading journalism and an increasingly constructed Victorian conception of the innocence of childhood, to name but a few – is undeniable, but the perception of the nature of incarceration itself should also be counted amongst them. As we have seen in the discussion of debtors above, the dynamic of prison, which after mid-century increasingly sought a uniform, deterrent regime, was ill-fitted for the non-standard case. Whilst it is certainly possible to see the crisper focus of carceral provision as the consequence of a greater degree of specialist treatment (for the mad, drunk or diseased as well as the young), there is a point too in seeing it as a cause of that fragmentation. The whole development of nineteenth-century imprisonment, away from the unanalysed and therefore plastic local experience, but also away from the failed ideology of reformation of the early 'specialists', was carving out its key constituency in positive terms perhaps as much as maudlin Dickensian portrayals of betrayed childhood might do so negatively.

Yet when we examine the experiences of children and juveniles within the penal system in Carmarthenshire in the third quarter of the nineteenth century we are reminded yet again of the dangers of overstatement in many narratives of the history of that system. Those, whether 'Whigs' or 'revisionists', who speak of the prison eclipsing older notions of punishment of the body, must ignore or marginalize the legislative initiatives on whipping juvenile offenders of the late 1840s. Those who discuss the 'specialist institutionalisation' of the new reformatory schools must presumably ignore or marginalize not only the whipped but also those who continue to be incarcerated in the 'adult' prison.[118] Those who look only at the pronouncements of central government will see neither the 'misinterpretation' of legislative provisions by local benches, nor the steady flow, controlled only by discretion, into the prison of children innocent of any offence. The experience of those of tender years deserves rather more careful analysis.

It is necessary at the outset to define the category to be discussed here. In respect of those prosecuted for criminal offences the class extends from those at the earliest boundary of criminal responsibility to those considered adult. The lower limit is decided on an individual basis, the latter becomes settled by statute at sixteen.[119] Yet even the youngest to be prosecuted for felony in Carmarthenshire, the nine-year-old Evan Lloyd, acquitted of murder in 1844, was employed (as a 'labourer'), as were the two ten-year-olds who were the youngest of those receiving punishment who appear in the *Felons' Register*.[120] This fact alerts us to the ambiguity of Victorian experience of childhood amongst the poor, where the workplace, as well as the prison, was a site where young and old might mix, albeit that this promiscuity was increasingly contested in both places.[121]

Other ambiguities were also apparent in the experience of criminal children. To what extent should the state intervene in a domestic economy of punishment? Insofar as a reluctance to involve the criminal law might be manifested by unwillingness on the part of Carmarthenshire juries to convict, it may be suggested that the extension of summary jurisdiction was an important factor in the success of any policy of increased intervention in juvenile criminality.[122] Yet we have seen earlier, and will see again shortly, that magistrates themselves might have views on the appropriate punishment of children which did not always correspond to the law.[123] Moreover the law itself, with its uneasy balance between corporal punishment and reformatory regime, spoke eloquently of a lack of unanimity in the response favoured by the legislator.[124]

The gaol itself was certainly under attack as a suitable location for juveniles. Yet the statute of 1847 which prescribed whipping for thieves aged under fourteen 'instead of or in addition to imprisonment' demonstrates a certain lack of singularity of purpose, which is compounded by its declared desire to remedy the evil of protracted periods on remand.[125] The measure was employed for the first time in Carmarthenshire in August 1847 against a borough prisoner, John Morgan.[126] In February 1848, eleven-year-old Thomas Davies was sentenced to one month's hard labour and two dozen stripes with a birch rod for theft. Notwithstanding its evident (and repeated) failure in Davies's case, corporal punishment continued to be used throughout the period against some juvenile offenders, although the criteria of selection for the penalty remain elusive.[127] The crudity of the penalty may well have encouraged magistrates to use it without too much regard for the legal technicalities, for the records show unlawful variations on the sentence. Ten-year-old Emma Samuel was ordered the punishment in 1868 by a Llandovery bench which seemed to develop an enthusiasm for it,[128] notwithstanding a statutory limitation to boys. In 1873 Evan Evans was ordered to be privately whipped 'by his father',[129] with no indication that the latter was a constable, as required by the legislation for those so punished outside the gaol. The latter case may be evidence of a reluctance to oust parental responsibility, as, in a rather different way, may the otherwise surprising instances of fines being used against juvenile thieves.[130]

Parental responsibility was certainly compromised in the other significant development in juvenile justice in this period. The reformatory school idea, like that of the corporal punishment legislation, was based on the premise that gaols and houses of correction were insufficient for the 'educational and corrective treatment of young children', although paradoxically the statutes required a minimum of fourteen days' incarceration before transfer to the more specialist institution.[131] It was a provision of which Carmarthen's chaplain had cause to complain. In 1878 Aaron Roberts reported that

> An experience of over fifteen years in prison polity, convinces me that the treatment of juvenile offenders requires considerable modification. Where punishment is considered as necessary and previous to the reformatory, would it not be better to birch the culprit and send him direct from court to reformatory or industrial school, and not to prison? From fourteen days to a month is too short a time for a prison chaplain's attention to be attended with permanent results. Such incarceration also gives a poor child a very mistaken idea of prison discipline, he being too young for hard labour, and only seeing adult prisoners in the pleasant part of the prison — the Chapel.[132]

Even before the legislative framework for reformatory schools was introduced in 1854 the *Carmarthen Journal* had caught the changing mood, observing after the trial of fourteen-year-old John Higgs in 1847:

> The prisoner is a mere child but from his behaviour in the Dock it is feared that he is old in crime, not appearing to feel the situation he was placed in, although he perfectly understood the nature of his offence. It is much to be regretted that there is not some Institution established where boys of such tender age might be placed, and not to be left exposed to the pernicious influence of a gaol.[133]

Provision of reformatory schools was slow throughout Wales, however, and it was not until 1858 that the Carmarthenshire bench announced its intention to enter into an agreement with the 'Directors or Managers of any Certified Reformatory School or Schools' to accommodate the county's juveniles.[134] Thomas King, a fifteen-year-old convicted of theft, became the first to be transferred, having initially served three months with hard labour within the gaol. Thomas Williams, the chaplain, was delighted by the new approach to errant juveniles:

> One to my great happiness has been sent to such a school this year, and another, who is now in prison, I am glad to say, is now to be sent. She has been convicted several times of theft, although only twelve years of age, and now in prison does evil, merely for the love of mischief.[135]

King was sent to the 'Howdre Ganol' Reformatory near Neath in Glamorganshire to which boys continued to be sent into the

1870s, whilst girls apparently went to no less celebrated a destination than Mary Carpenter's Red Lodge in Bristol.[136] In 1867 the governor reported to quarter sessions that 'the Reformatory' would not take juveniles sentenced to terms of under four years, citing the case of a girl sentenced to two who had been refused admission. A proposal to sentence thereafter to four years with the intention of early release was popular, but rejected as an intervention in the bench's independence in sentencing. It was resolved to write to the Home Secretary on the issue.[137] The reformatory sentences, taken as a whole, were generally for three years, with some of the maximum of five years. Terms of several years' duration, when set against the triviality of the offences for which they were imposed (such as the fourteen days' hard labour to be followed by three years in Howdre Ganol for John Evans and Daniel McCarthy for 'attempting to steal strawberries'),[138] seem unduly harsh, yet such sentences were intended to benefit those to whom they were given. Again it is hard to know on what particular grounds the reformatory school sentence, as opposed to other dispositions available in the cases of juveniles, was awarded within the county.[139] Analyses in terms of previous convictions or place of residence are inconclusive. The sentencing at different times of the brother and sister Sarah and John Evans, whose father had a criminal record, and that of David Noyes whose brother too was an offender, perhaps suggests that family background, if known, might be material in the court's decision.[140]

If the reformatory system was progressive in intention, its philosophy came at a cost. The 1853 Committee which had recommended the use of specialist establishments had proposed that the system be funded partly by local and partly by central finance, a compromise indicative of a more general sharing of responsibility for offender provision at mid-century. It had also, mindful of the dangers of rewarding inadequate upbringing, suggested the recovery of the costs of detention from the parents where appropriate. Provisions to allow this had appeared in the 1854 and 1857 Acts, and the matter was the subject of consideration by the ever-vigilant Birmingham Grand Jury in 1861.[141] No evidence has come to light of parental contribution being levied in Carmarthenshire, and the costs of reformatory provision continued to rise. After modest beginnings the annual expenditure had reached £12. 8s. 7d. by 1869 and £45. 11s. 8d.

by 1877.[142] A county like Carmarthenshire which had no local establishment was faced with the expenses not only of maintenance but also of transportation of offenders; the transfer of Elizabeth Williams in 1867, for example, had apparently cost £9. 1s. 10d.[143] An attempt to pass this latter expense on to the Treasury drew a rebuff to the county's magistrates and local responsibility was subsequently confirmed by a circular.[144] For a county already obliged to spend considerable sums of money on the refurbishment of its gaol, the further expense of provision for those for whom that gaol was now considered inappropriate may well have featured in consideration of the nationalization proposals in the 1870s.

The particular specialist carceral disposition which seems to have been regarded as the most serious for juveniles was infrequently applied by the county. Only three of Carmarthenshire's offenders were, it seems, sent to the juvenile penitentiary which had been established in 1838 at Parkhurst and which closed in 1864. The first, William Smith, originally from Northumberland, whose surname and profession ('bellhanger', a description which seems to have been favoured by itinerant criminals) can hardly have inspired confidence, had already received a sentence of one month's imprisonment and thirty-nine lashes, the highest total recorded in Carmarthen, just before his return to gaol in May 1858. Another, Francis Smith, was an escapee from Stoke Prior Reformatory School and had previously absconded from a similar establishment at Hammersmith. A local boy, Daniel Thomas, seems to have been sacrificed for the sake of consistency, having been convicted of the same offence, housebreaking, at the same quarter sessions as Francis Smith.[145]

The general story to be gathered from the discussion above seems clear. Although the nature of the appropriate penalty for juveniles (corporal punishment, the reformatory, the penitentiary) was open to argument, it is often assumed that the guiding principle to be applied, namely diversion from the local prison, seems at least to be uncontroversial. Yet a study of Carmarthenshire's records reveals that, again, this received truth seems less than clearly established. Until the 1870s, juvenile offenders in Carmarthenshire continued to be sentenced to imprisonment as a sanction in its own right, not simply as a precursor to an alternative disposition. Fifteen-year-olds were regularly sentenced to hard-labour terms like the adult offenders they so nearly resembled, but younger criminals too might suffer the same fate, though the labour involved might be, but not invariably, downgraded to activities such as picking oakum.[146] Even in the last decade of the county gaol, criminal juveniles, despite the talk of diversion, and despite the refinement of regime around the standard of the adult male, continued to occupy a place in its history.

Other children too, though they had committed no offence, found themselves in the institution. I have discussed in some detail elsewhere the instances of children being born in prison to women inmates, such as Jane Bowen (pictured in plate 6) or those infants who were brought in by their mothers upon committal.[147] Whilst the numbers are not vast,[148] the practice deserves rather more notice in prison histories than it has attracted to date. The custom of allowing women prisoners to keep young children with them whilst they saw out their sentences continued to be regulated by local discretion rather than bureaucratic rule, as apparently did the inevitable compromises which their presence demanded of regimes of labour, silence and subsequently separation within the prison. The Victorian ideal of uniform and consistent discipline yet again was obliged to accommodate itself to the inevitable variety of the circumstances of the prisoners with which it was confronted. Within the Home Office such cases, and the very real issues of regularity, responsibility and penal and social philosophy which they raised, might be largely ignored. That was an option, however, which was unavailable to Governors Westlake and Stephens.

Military prisoners

The presence of members of the armed forces, almost invariably soldiers, within the county gaol at first sight deserves little comment. Soldiers, like members of other trades – puddlers, labourers and the like – appear before quarter sessions accused of theft and receive custodial sentences. A note by the governor to the effect that an individual might be detained after the expiry of his original sentence for desertion would in such cases appear to be the only distinguishing feature of their custodial experience. But in addition there were a number of prisoners condemned for offences by military courts using military procedures, and awarded sentences outside the range of those available to civilians. McConville reveals that such a class formed a small, but rising proportion of the prison population in the jurisdiction as a whole, 2 per cent of all committals in 1857, 3.2 per cent in 1877.[149] Whilst some of those sentenced by courts martial in Carmarthenshire (and for a time apparently from Pembrokeshire)[150] may have committed offences which were in essence the same as those under general criminal law,[151] other breaches of the disciplinary code issued under the annual Mutiny Acts, such as insubordination or 'making frivolous charges',[152] had no direct equivalent. Desertion was the most frequently encountered offence, and we have noticed in the previous chapter that Chaplain Williams had cause to voice his concern over this category of prisoner in the years following the Crimean War.[153]

There were reasons why these military prisoners were disruptive of the routine which was both necessary and desirable in a local prison. Some of the courts martial were held within Carmarthen gaol itself,[154] which at least gave advanced warning that a custodial sentence might be imposed, but other prisoners seem to have been delivered from their barracks with little or no previous notice.[155] In October 1845 Westlake reported a disagreement between himself and Captain Arkwright of the 6th Dragoons over the custody of soldiers convicted of drunkenness, whom Westlake believed should have been taken to the (then still distinct) borough gaol.[156] While in the gaol the soldiers under a normal custodial sentence were generally treated much the same as other prisoners, their hair cut on admission,[157] working on the wheel alongside others,[158] even being put to overlook prisoners who needed special supervision.[159] Although routine inspections as to fitness to labour seem to have been undertaken by the gaol surgeon,[160] there were times when soldiers were taken out to be examined by military doctors.[161] Their spiritual needs prima facie would involve no particular provision, but the fact that many of the army were recruited far from where they were stationed, including many from Ireland, meant that they significantly increased the proportion of Catholic prisoners within the population. It was noted earlier that of the deserters in the gaol in 1859 seventeen were Catholic, the same number Anglican and only two Nonconformist.[162]

Other military prisoners, however, might pose rather more acute problems to the local institution. In addition to determinate prison sentences (exceptional only in being often expressed, even in longer terms, in days),[163] some deserters seem to have been detained for an indefinite period, their release awaiting an order from the Secretary for War.[164] But some, including those over whom Westlake had his argument with Captain Arkwright, were sentenced to solitary confinement. As has been shown earlier, before the rebuilding necessitated by the 1865 Prison Act Carmarthen had, save for its punishment cells, no provision for separate confinement. Where, as happened in February 1848, five soldiers arrived on one day, specifically sentenced to isolation, the pressure on accommodation might be acute.[165] In such cases, too, special labour requirements would be needed since the wheel provided an insufficient degree of segregation.[166] Richard Tarfey was sentenced by a court martial in 1844 to a bizarre six-month sentence, alternate months being assigned to solitary confinement and hard labour.[167] Though the Cathcart Committee on Military Prisons in 1844 had 'waived all idea' of the universal application of principles of separation to military sentences,[168] the evidence from Carmarthenshire suggests that it was routinely ordered, notwithstanding the capabilities of the receiving civil institution. As experience of civil and military incarceration were brought closer together at mid-century in the figure and philosophy of Joshua Jebb,[169] the practice of solitary confinement thus insinuated into an otherwise 'associated' county gaol, together with the blurring of the county boundaries which the demand for military detention had created, looks less like a temporary distraction for the local authorities, and more like a foretaste of the future. It may be noted that when the gaol was inspected in 1877 prior to its transfer to central government control, the man deputed by the Prison Inspectorate to perform the task was an officer of the Royal Engineers.[170]

Conclusion

This chapter has shown the diversity of classes and, at another level, of individuals which formed the population of the Victorian local gaol. The inevitable variety at the individual level presented problems of management which tested the application of the rules of the prison, as will be seen in the next chapter. It is one of the major contentions of this book that an exaggerated sense of the 'mechanical' ideology of discipline – whether conceived of as aimed at deterrence or reformation – drove penal policy (as it has also distorted prison historiography) for many years. If only the correct 'formula' could be applied, then prisoners, increasingly seen as symptoms of a national problem rather than elements of a local community, would respond in a largely uniform fashion. The 'nationalization' of crime and punishment, though it resulted in the collection of much information about individuals, paradoxically was not particularly interested in them *qua* individuals. It was a perspective which could never be entirely shared by the staff of small local prisons, for whom the daily negotiation of the carceral experience necessarily involved more personal and more discretionary engagement.

At the level of classification too we have seen a recasting of the role of the prison in the nineteenth century. The model of the adult, (predominantly) male convict which underpinned the penitentiaries and later the convict prisons was such an influential new paradigm that the experience of debtors and remands, whose presence had been (literally) the defining feature of the county gaol for centuries, was restructured to bring their experience closer to it. It has been suggested that the subsequent specialist treatment (insofar as it did exist, and it is clear that this was a limited provision) for such groups as the young offender or, as we will see, the insane, was premised on this dominant paradigm rather than one of diversity of provision. This may seem to be a distinction without a difference. It could be argued that it matters little whether we see the later nineteenth-century specialization of institutional provision as marking a firmer delineation of the model of imprisonment or a rather clearer ideological engagement with those seen as unsuitable for it. Of course, the two go together. But we should not, in our desire to construct elaborate theories of the latter, ignore the cruder exclusionary impetus of the former.

In any event it will have become clear from this narrative of the variety of Carmarthen's prisoners, that an investigation of the apparently simple concept of the prison regime may be rather more complicated than at first appears. It is this point which must now be considered.

~ 5 ~

Labour and Discipline

The preceding chapter has revealed an important truth which must irritate the historian in the search for the triumph of the idea of uniformity, no less than it did those nineteenth-century policy-makers who so ardently pursued it. The variety of those incarcerated within the local gaol means that it becomes misleading to seek to identify 'the regime' as practised within the institution. Different categories of prisoner, male and female, convicted or on remand, felons or debtors, resulted in a number of different regimes operating within that institution. The availability of the punishment cell and the infirmary further complicates the picture, whilst in a small, understaffed gaol like Carmarthen we have seen that daily exigencies might result in a degree of movement across the boundaries of official categorization. Even such an apparently absolute principle as the operation of the 'silent system' of discipline has been shown to be undermined by the presence in gaol of dependent children or the incapacity of the officers fully to enforce it. Within the prison, then, there were a variety of regimes which were negotiated daily by the staff, and on occasion by the prisoners. In the discussion which follows it will be necessary to look at two central, but variable, components which featured within the experience of many, though not all, of Carmarthen's prisoners. It need hardly be said that their application to individual prisoners will be found to be on occasion far more problematic, far more dependent upon discretion, than the apparent certainties of rule and doctrine might suggest. But both components, that of labour and of the enforcement of discipline within the prison, are of importance not only because of the part they played in its practical daily administration, but also because they relate directly to the very nature of experience of incarceration as a penal sanction. The everyday life of the prisoner must hang somewhere, on average, rather worse than an outside existence, which might involve an individual in onerous work for little reward, and rather better than was to be expected if he refused to cooperate in that disadvantage, where, that is, he broke the prison rules. Staff and prisoners both knew that what the latter were obliged to do when serving their time, and the ways in which they were compelled to do it, were crucial determinants of the very nature of the carceral experience.

Labour

Despite a handful of entries in the *Felons' Register* which suggest the contrary, it has been seen that remand prisoners generally were not obliged to engage in labour within the prison, though the option was open to them, whilst debtors' conditions were similarly unconstrained.[1] The majority of those sentenced in Carmarthenshire for felony, however, and presumably also for misdemeanour (though the records for these have been lost), had 'hard labour' as an integral component of their sentence. There were occasional problems in discovering whether or not the sentence required the component. William Powell was sentenced, rather strangely and against a backdrop of some controversy over the jury's behaviour, to a term of six months by Wightman J at assize in 1847, three days of which in each month were to be spent in solitary confinement. The governor was unsure as to whether hard labour was also required, and the quarter sessions and the assize clerk, both having been consulted, disagreed on the question.[2]

For men, though not for women, 'hard labour' usually meant the treadwheel, installed in 1833. It has been noted earlier that the operation of the wheel, at least at one time, was advertised to those outside the prison in a fashion which suggests that the 'theatricality' of punishment did not disappear entirely with the 'Bloody Code'. But, though the mechanical operation of the wheel was then visible outside the prison, those labouring on it were not. Indeed, in the first visit to the gaol by an inspector, the ability of those working within the wheel to see and be seen even by those within the gaol was a matter for criticism, and led to the installation of blinds to the front of the wheelhouse as well as compartments within it.[3]

The wheel was placed in the heart of the gaol, close to the governor's house. Originally the wheel would employ eight individuals, though later it seems to have had sixteen compartments, suggesting a response not only to the increasing central drive towards separation but also to a perceived need for greater capacity.[4] Presumably the original compartments, which seem to be the ones considered large enough for the blind prisoner John Wilson to walk about in, and to allow (it may be deduced from an incident in which prisoners were punished for kicking each other whilst working) men to work side by side, were divided, for the wheel as a whole does not seem to have been extended.[5] After the rebuilding of the prison nineteen could be accommodated.[6] Employment on the wheel (the formulation preferred by Westlake; Stephens favoured 'in' the wheel), however, was conducted, as elsewhere, by only half of the party at any one time, the two groups alternating between spells on the wheel and resting at the foot of it. A journalist visiting the gaol in 1867 reported that the spells were of five minutes' duration, but that after that time those on the wheel were 'perspiring freely and some gasping for breath'. Those resting had the opportunity to read books provided for them, as well as contemplating the scriptural passages displayed on the walls of the wheelhouse.[7] At some point thereafter, no doubt again in response to an increasingly penal ideology emanating from central government after mid-century, the volumes were taken away and the waiting shift were employed in picking oakum.[8]

Work on the wheel was certainly strenuous. The original intention appears to have been that the labour should be used, for the tender for its construction specified the provision of 'one pair of stones', presumably for grinding grain.[9] Yet apart from the period spent turning the pewter model it was for long periods unproductive, only apparently in the 1870s was it used to raise water from the well, a change possibly introduced more to ensure uniformity of labour (previously, selected prisoners had performed this task with a hand pump) than efficiency. For this task two-thirds of the wheel had to be full.[10] The hours of labour were dictated by daylight, ranging from seven in December and January to ten for the majority of the year. The first stint was conducted before breakfast. The treads of the wheel were 7½ in. apart, and the total ascent per day was reckoned at 18,000 ft in summer, of which, as explained, each labouring prisoner was personally engaged in half. By 1876 each prisoner's daily requirement had been increased to 9,500 ft.[11] Although such figures suggest mathematical precision, indeed, were produced precisely in order to suggest it, there is room for some scepticism. Carmarthen's wheel boasted no device like Mance's 'ergometer', being used elsewhere to measure the work performed by prisoners. Instead, the figures were produced 'by a minute survey of the revolutions of the wheel', a phrase which suggests a degree of attention which the general ethos of the prison cautions us may have been overstated.[12] The wheel was not operated on Sundays, nor on the major holidays of Christmas Day, New Year or Good Friday. Other interruptions were less predictable. In January 1846 the wheel was stopped for an hour as a mark of respect while the turnkey's wife, who had resided in the gaol, was buried.[13] When cholera hit Carmarthen in 1849 the Visiting Justices ordered that labour be suspended for a day of 'prayer and humiliation', the apparent success of which was marked by another holiday on account of 'general thanksgiving' a month later.[14] A longer suspension ordered in February 1846, at a time when the diet and regime were under general consideration, is not readily explicable.[15]

Two further reasons for repeated, though irregular, cessations merit further comment. There were several occasions on which there were insufficient prisoners to operate the wheel, particularly when those sentenced to hard labour were diminished in numbers by injury or illness, or by use of the punishment cells.[16] Again it becomes clear that the mechanical uniformity of regime which the treadwheel seemed to promise was not easily guaranteed within a small local institution. Moreover, the wheel was prone to mechanical problems, necessitating both its routine maintenance and more specific intervention in cases of breakdown.[17] Some of the failures seem to have been the result of deliberate sabotage by the prisoners. On 1 December 1845 Westlake noted: 'The wheel did not work be fore Breakfast Inconsequence of it having stone be tween the cogs of the wheel which throw other parts out of it place.'[18] In May 1849 William Thomas was caught attempting to put a stone under the spindle of the wheel,[19] another indication that the prisoner, as has already been noted, cannot always be relied upon to play the role of mere passive recipient of discipline.

Other acts of resistance were predictable. Once the silence rule had been introduced, the problem of talking on the wheel became a disciplinary problem. Occasionally, too, prisoners would simply refuse to work on the wheel. In one instance involving soldiers it is possible that the refusal was based on a claim to legitimate exemption on grounds of their status,[20] whilst, as has been noted, attempts to evade labour on grounds of illness were not uncommon. Prisoners are also punished for insufficient application to the task, or 'sculking' as it was known.[21] It is not clear exactly what was being done in such cases; possibly there were methods of keeping the feet off the treads entirely, or possibly it referred to the practice of standing forward on the treads so that body weight, rather than muscle power, provided the motion. This latter activity could result in injury as the prisoner's leg was caught by the descending tread. A dispute as to the notorious Charles Hunt's refusal to show his shin to the surgeon may have originated in such an injury, which was sufficiently common to have earned the treadwheel its slang name ('the shinscraper') amongst inmates.[22] Instances of such routine rule-breaching must have been difficult to detect, with one officer at the wheel watching both the active and resting prisoners. Occasional outbreaks of violence in the wheelhouse indicate more serious lapses in discipline. There were two fights in the wheelhouse within a month in the summer of 1849, in one of which a sixteen-year-old, John Coupland, pulled another prisoner off the wheel.[23]

An alternative form of hard labour was stonebreaking. When formal categorization was employed, stonebreaking, used of course within the workhouse as well as the prison, was ranked alongside oakum picking as 'second class' labour.[24] Such tasks were undertaken by male offenders who were for some reason were exempt from the wheel. So, for example, in February 1847 the seventy-six-year-old Lewis Lewis, convicted of illegally fishing in the Tywi, was certified by the surgeon as unfit for the wheel, though fit to break stones or pick oakum. He was also, exceptionally, allowed tobacco 'as he fancies he cannot exist without it'.[25] The stones were broken in a yard next to the wheelhouse, originally in the open, but subsequently in sheds, built, like the box apparently used to grade the size of the broken stone, by the prisoners themselves.[26] Segregation in the yard appears to be connected with the rebuilding of the 1870s. The hours for this 'second class' labour were slightly shorter than those spent by prisoners on the wheel, but fixed quantities of stone were required; daily targets in 1868–9 were recorded as ½ yd of hard stone, or ¾ of the softer variety.[27] The stone was, an inspector noted a few years later, 'broken smaller than is usually done' and was, particularly the harder variety, the source of most obvious profit to the gaol.[28] Demand was limited, however, and the county sometimes itself utilized the labour, as when in 1847 30 tons of stone were sent to the gaol by the surveyor to be broken for use on the turnpike road. This commission apparently resulted in the employment even of those who would normally have been at the wheel.[29]

Less profitable still was another form of hard labour which was undertaken by men unfit for more demanding tasks and used as the principal form with women prisoners. This was oakum picking. Old ship's rope was purchased on the open market and picked into its constituent fibres before being sold on to be used for caulking the seams in wooden ships. Clearly the expansion of an institutionalized national workforce together with changes in maritime construction meant that oakum picking was economically of limited importance to the gaol. In 1846 Westlake was buying rope from the 'Trawling Company' at 8s. 4d. a hundredweight, and two years later he was writing to Liverpool to obtain it.[30] In 1850 the oakum was selling for 17s. 6d. a hundredweight, or about twice its cost.[31] In 1862 the year's total profit on the oakum was less than 11s.[32] Yet oakum had considerable advantages as a form of labour. It could be given to a range of inmates (juveniles, the ruptured, women with children with them) and required no dedicated equipment. Its utility as a residual form of labour is evidenced by Westlake's comment in May 1846 that he had taken two prisoners, John Evans and John Howells, off the wheel to pick oakum 'has they where taken medicen'.[33] Whilst the men, until separation was enforced, generally picked oakum in association in the Upper Trebanda,[34] it could be done by women in the female prison, or by soldiers sentenced to solitary confinement in their cells. It required no particular skill and, based on the requirement of picking a set quantity per day, it was largely self-policing: the task was either finished or it was not. Setting the quantity might lead to some dispute, as it did in the cases of Mary Ann Awberry or Anne Matthews, both in their own ways anomalous characters,[35] but once set the prisoner could be left to get on with it. It would seem that prisoners frequently were. The staffing arrangements reviewed in chapter 3 suggest no permanent monitoring of the oakum room, and the suspicion must be that silence was not enforced there. A reference to undisclosed 'improper conduct to a fellow prisoner' in the oakum room is suggestive of other forms of wrongdoing.[36] It is possibly the only reference to inmate sexual impropriety in all the many Carmarthenshire records reviewed here, though equally possibly it refers to nothing of the kind. Occasionally prisoners would attempt to hide or destroy the rope to be picked; in one case Benjamin Howells threw about 2 lb of it down the privy.[37] In another instance a prisoner, Jones, was sent to the refractory cell for supplying spun yarn to a colleague, Davies, who two days later was inspected by the surgeon for an injury to his finger. Such injuries were typical of oakum work, and it is possible that Jones had been trying to ease the burden on Davies by supplying him with an easier means of meeting his quota.[38]

One of the striking features revealed by a study of the records of the daily operation of the gaol in the late 1840s and early 1850s is the quantity and diversity of the work undertaken by the prisoners which was devoted to the upkeep of the institution itself. From the point of view of those charged with running the gaol the economic benefits of using the convict labour force was obvious: in 1862, unspecified 'work for the county' proved almost ten times as profitable as oakum picking.[39] There was an advantage too for the governor, for whom the range of necessary labour, ranging from light cleaning to heavy manual labour, allowed a fit to be made to the strength and skills of particular inmates. Routine maintenance as well as significant construction work meant that the fabric of the buildings employed many prisoners – erecting a chimney, brick-facing the chapel and house of correction, flagging the floor of the infirmary, painting the ironwork, caulking the wheelhouse and other such tasks – as well as the major building project necessitated by the 1865 Act.[40] The insides of the gaol were limewashed, the inspector reporting in 1840 that this took place two or three times each year, although the governor's records suggest that the repainting of the chapel (closure of which, since it interfered with the routine of worship and instruction, was specifically noted) at any rate was repeated only after two years, although this would have been a relatively lightly used area.[41] Privies and drains needed to be flushed out and ash-pits emptied.[42] Routine cleaning of the prison buildings was necessary, the prison inspector noting in 1868 that such 'service' was reserved 'for those who have behaved well' as well as those incapacitated from, or not sentenced to hard labour.[43] Other exigencies involved particular interventions: clearing the yards of snow in the winter[44] and, as will be seen, in an outbreak of illness in the summer of 1848, deepening the well and baling out the water.[45]

Prisoners were also involved in providing their own necessaries. Uniforms, not only the larger items but also things like stocks and stockings, were both made and repaired within the gaol.[46] Men and women were both involved in these tasks, though women were generally responsible for washing,[47] and the washhouse was located within the female prison. It was occasionally necessary to buy in clothing from outside,[48] presumably if there was insufficient expertise amongst the inmates, but generally the raw materials were brought in to be made up by the inmates. Thomas Franklin, by trade a railway navvy, imprisoned for assault with intent to murder, complained to the prison inspector in 1865 that he was kept in his cell working at tailoring and asked to be transferred to the treadwheel. The request came when the inspector was concerned that the cells had not been certified for separate confinement, and was acceded to.[49] In the following year the governor asked quarter sessions to authorize expenditure on a sewing machine, declaring this to be necessary because the female prisoners were generally 'helpless creatures'.[50] Not only the clothing but also the footwear was being manufactured by prisoners, certainly into the 1850s, as wood and leather were transformed into clogs. By this stage the wearing of clogs was unusual within prisons, as the inspector reported, and they were not popular with all the prisoners, though their attractions to a cost-conscious county were obvious. 'One of the greatest objections to their use', observed Perry,

> is that of causing corns and callosities to the feet in people unaccustomed to them, but they are also objectionable from wearing out the stockings more than shoes of leather, and also from impairing the gait of the wearer, which to working husbandmen is a serious injury.[51]

But stockings could be made and repaired within the gaol more easily and cheaply than leather shoes. As we have noted elsewhere, the pressure for uniformity of prison practice – in this case relating to what prisoners wore – was one which could have financial repercussions for local authorities.

Other work produced items for use within the gaol. Riddles, mops and wooden spoons were made, and mattresses stuffed.[52] A reference to 'making tins' (presumably the mess tins from which prisoners ate) in October 1849 suggests a degree of expertise beyond the norm, and is probably connected to the presence in the gaol at that time of a Northumbrian coppersmith, Robert Shaw, who on discharge was given the sum of 10s. for his 'work in the gaol'.[53] It is perhaps inadvisable to look too hard for the relationship of any such work to the hard labour to which Shaw had been sentenced. His incarceration seems to have presented an opportunity which was considered too good to miss. Other employment decisions seem similarly to have been driven by pragmatism rather than principle, but not also to such positive ends. The kitchen was traditionally a favoured location for prisoners, both as warm and as providing opportunities to take extra food. Both women and men could be employed (though almost certainly with no mixing between the sexes), sometimes possibly in pairs,[54] and without supervision after basic instruction from the governor.[55] At first sight, then, it seems strange to find the notoriously troublesome Charles Hunt cooking (and apparently still complaining about the quality of the food!) in March 1847.[56] But Inspector Perry, after finding John Vickerman (whose bold attempt at escape has been discussed earlier) working as a cook, noted in 1851 that the 'greatest offenders' often filled this role on account of their experience.[57] As we have seen in other contexts, alternative candidates might be limited, particularly in a small institution.

Regime and discipline

The difficulties which inhere in the relationship between the regime to which the individual prisoner was subjected and the disciplinary means of ensuring compliance with it have been hinted at earlier. The regulations of the prison will specify appropriate behaviour and thereby necessitate punishment for that which is inappropriate. Moreover, the severity of the regime applicable to the conforming prisoner will necessarily play a role in determining the nature of the punitive sanction. The paradox of deterring individuals in circumstances which were already supposed to be deterrent, of punishing those already being punished, is an interesting one. In an age of penal transition it is one which needed some adjustment.

Seen from this perspective, the national debate concerning the respective merits of the 'silent system' or of separate confinement casts interesting shadows. Clearly the introduction of a rule of silence into a gaol in which it had not been used before was likely to increase the number of cases of rule-breach which called for punishment. Moreover, since it is a rule easy to breach and, in an understaffed institution at any rate, almost impossible to enforce absolutely, it may necessitate a degree of tolerance and/or the danger of arbitrary enforcement. On the other hand, physical separation will cut down the risk of communication (as also of violence and sexual contact), but it simultaneously removes, or diminishes, isolation as a disciplinary sanction in itself within the prison. This latter was amongst the objections which the anti-separationist inspector, Bisset Hawkins, had voiced in his report for 1837–8 at a time when his colleagues of the opposite persuasion were gaining the ascendancy in the wider debate over regime.[58]

Hawkins had found neither system operating on his first visit to Carmarthen. 'Silence has not hitherto been enjoined', he recorded; 'The discipline of this prison has been rather lax.'[59] Indeed, the 1835 Select Committee on Gaols had revealed that within Wales only Cardiganshire claimed to operate the policy. That committee had found evidence that such laxity was dangerous in the evidence it took from a twenty-year-old prisoner in Millbank, who had found his way there via Carmarthen and the *Discovery* hulk, following a conviction for sacrilege (in this case, stealing church plate). The anonymous informant, in reality one David Jones, had told of the 'reprehensible' conversations to which he had been exposed in Carmarthen, 'sometimes cursing and swearing and occasionally obscene stories', before concluding that he 'Prefers infinitely the Silence and Discipline observed in the Penitentiary to the unrestrained Communication and License permitted at Carmarthen Gaol as he is positive it is enough to ruin any young man'.[60] Jones probably had no idea that his (for the committee) conveniently positive evidence as to the value of silence would reach his former custodians. But it is clear that it did so. Hawkins, on inspecting Carmarthen, was told by the governor that 'There is much in that statement that is completely untrue', and that upon the reliability of the testimony of its author, since reconvicted, 'no reliance can be placed'.[61] In 1840 Hawkins reported a change of policy, or at least a change in what he was being told about it: 'Silence is said to be moderately well observed: there are not many cases of punishment for breach of it. The prisoners are very tractable.'[62] In fact, as we know, Westlake was complaining of his inability to enforce the silent system, which he seems to consider a novelty five years later, when the Home Secretary, Sir James Graham, had enjoined it alongside other practices.[63] Westlake's uncertainty over the enforcement of the rule is perhaps evident in some of his journal entries at around this time. He specifically cites the turnkey as a witness to one infringement,[64] whilst in other entries, such as the punishment of John Smith for refusing to be quiet after demonstrating 'highly Insubordinate conduct',[65] or of David Jones 'for neglecting to work the wheel in is turn and calling George Gilbert a blind eye has he had lost a eye',[66] it is not clear to what extent Westlake believes he is punishing the failure to maintain silence as an offence distinct from the initial indiscipline or simply as an aggravating circumstance of it. The qualification (as well as the gender specificity) contained in his 'General Order' to turnkeys, issued in March 1846, is also instructive: 'every man and boy in the House of Correction and Gaol to have a number and to be referred to by it and the silent system be adopted as far as practicable.'[67] Notwithstanding the difficulties, silence was, in theory, the most evident expression of centrally directed penological theory in Carmarthen until the cellular rebuild of the 1870s. The extent to which its existence may have ratcheted up the severity of penalties for other offences remains a matter for speculation. There were, of course, a number of other disciplinary offences to be dealt with, many of which have been encountered earlier. They included the possession or trafficking of prohibited items, attempts to escape, damaging prison property, refusal to work or other forms of resistance to authority (of which 'insubordination' was a lesser offence than 'mutinous conduct') and violence used against either fellow prisoners or the staff.

In some cases of possession of unauthorized material it would seem that simple confiscation was the sole response. So we have seen that John Wilson's discovery with an illicit lump of cheese seems not to have led to any measure beyond its removal.[68] In cases where the item could not be linked to an individual, that was indeed the only feasible response. It is probable that the gaoler did know who was responsible for the irregularity discovered by the inspector on his first visit, indeed, may have been himself unperturbed by it. 'In the day-room of the tread-wheel felons', reported Bisset Hawkins, 'I found "The Devil on Two Sticks" in English; it was immediately removed.'[69] Other forms of 'indirect' punishment might include the failure to consider a prisoner for a position of privilege, or their removal from that position if it had been conferred. We have noted earlier, however, that the exigencies of a small gaol might involve even notorious individuals in such roles.

For graver offences punishment was generally imposed through a combination of restriction of diet, confinement to the punishment cell, and, in the most extreme cases, restraint in irons. Dietary punishment administered on its own was at the lower end of the tariff, but was not without difficulty. As will be seen in the next chapter, the poverty of the normal diet, and in particular that of short-term prisoners, was itself regarded as part of the 'less-eligibility' requirement of the carceral experience. Reduction of rations might risk the health of the inmates and had to be circumscribed accordingly. On occasion food might be removed altogether, as when the governor records in August 1848 that a prisoner was 'deprived of supper for disobedience of the Turnkey'.[70] Such deprivation seems to be limited to single meals. More usually there was a reduction of diet. Later in the same month, for example, a female prisoner was assigned to receive two meals of bread and water on the day following her offences of 'quarrelling and riotous Conduct'.[71]

Mostly, however, the restriction of diet was imposed in combination with a remand to the 'refractory cell'. The food allowance seems to have taken the form of 1 lb of bread per day and 1 quart of water, as opposed to the 1½ lb of bread and servings of gruel which comprised the ordinary minimum.[72] In normal cases remands to the refractory cell were made at the discretion of the governor, but only for a maximum of three days.[73] It was probably the dietary component which was responsible for this restriction, and also for the daily inspection of prisoners in the refractory cells by the surgeon or his assistant.[74] Longer remands were possible but only on the governor's application to the Visiting Justices, although surviving records disclose only one such example, a seven-day period being served by the recalcitrant Mary Ann Awberry.[75] There was no minimum period of confinement. Awberry herself was sent on one occasion for ten minutes, before being released because of her susceptibility to fits at the time.[76] In January 1847 David Thomas was sent to punishment 'over the dinner hour' with no gruel, and punishments of a few hours' duration seem to have been common.[77] It is probable that most such short punishment periods were decided in advance, and seem to have been related to differential levels of guilt, even in respect of the same incident. So in December 1848 Sarah Morris and Mary Jones, who had been 'quarrelling and fighting', received five and two hours respectively.[78] In other cases, though, prisoners seem to have been released, particularly from longer spells in isolation, not at a predetermined time but, rather, when they had shown themselves amenable to discipline. As has been seen in chapter 3, Westlake, and possibly to a lesser extent Stephens, seem to have placed importance on the practice of 'forgiving' prisoners and releasing them from the refractory cell in return for promises of good behaviour in future, an indication of the existence of a reformatory ideology operating at this intra-systemic level. On 8 May 1846 two soldiers were released from the refractory cell to which they had been sent for 'refusing and neglecting to work the wheel' at 6 o'clock, having 'begged to be forgiven'. On the following day one of them, Hegan, was again found to be 'Sculking' by Westlake and sent to the cell at 3 p.m. Westlake records: 'the prisoner sent for me at 7 PM & asked me to forgive him which I told him I could not think of releasing him has it was only yesterday that I forgave him for Refusing to work the wheel.' Hegan was finally released, having given a further promise as to his future conduct, after spending forty-three hours in the cell.[79]

It is easier to recover the incidence of punishment than it is to reconstruct its exact nature. The term 'refractory cell' has been used so far, but references in the records also mention the 'solitary', 'dark' and 'underground' cells. The first term seems to refer to the same punishment as the 'refractory', but its relation to the others is less clear. The prison inspector, writing in 1838, recommended the abolition of 'rarely employed' underground cells and the construction of a 'dark cell'. In 1840 such a cell had been fitted up.[80] By 1845 the Visiting Justices had ordered prisoners to work on repairing the 'solitary cells', of which there seem to have been, by then, four.[81] In 1851 Perry described two 'dark cells' then currently in use as being 'beneath the basement' of the house of correction. These were 7 ft 3 in. square and 7 ft in. height, with no warmth or ventilation and iron plates fixed to the walls for beds. 'I cannot but regard this severity of punishment as unjustifiable and dangerous to health, perhaps even to life', reported Perry, before going on to warn that the bed brackets could also be used as weapons, as had happened in the past. A separate 'refractory cell' was recorded as on the ground floor of the building, though the usage of the *Gaoler's Journal* does not apparently distinguish the locations when recording punishments.[82] The offending bed brackets, which had, indeed, been used in anger, had apparently been removed from the 'punishment cells' (if these are, indeed, the same) by 1867, when prisoners were described as sleeping on 'a raised platform' with one blanket.[83] Whichever of these 'refractory cells' were being used in the 1840s and 1850s it seems clear that they were unheated. In March 1846 James Francis was 'forgiven' by Westlake from the refractory cell in which he had spent a night 'Inconsequence of the weather being so cold and freezing'.[84] On the other hand, in warm weather punishment could seem a rather better alternative than continuing with hard labour. This latter point, acknowledged by the governor in a hot spell in August 1846,[85] could effectively diminish the penality of the measure in the very circumstances in which control of the prison was most difficult. The report of a single day in the summer of 1849 gives an impression of the fractious nature of the institution when temperatures rose: 'Upon going into the cell of Wm Thomas at 6 AM Today', wrote Stephens,

> I found he had torn his shirt sleeve off and a strip from his waistcoat and John Copeland I found had also torn both the sleeves off his shirt wilfully for which I deprived them both of their breakfasts and 'Copeland' I also placed in the refrac cell for refusing to work. I afterwards went into the Trebando with the turnkey 'Rees' to investigate a complaint made against John Ward a Transport and while doing so

Wm Brown another Transport was very insolent and abusive and laid hold of me and rose his fist to strike and I then placed him in the refractory cell with irons on one leg — I at bed time directed the Turnkey to send him to his bed and when doing so he became exceedingly obstreperous and I then placed him in the refractory cell for the night.[86]

When the chapel was rebuilt in 1859 two new refractory cells, measuring 6 ft × 11 ft 9 in. × 10 ft, were designed to be constructed beneath the main structure, though apparently not built.[87]

The reference to irons above is indicative of the most extreme form of internal punishment which the governor ordered within the gaol. Irons came in a variety of forms, handcuffs (which could be applied 'behind' in serious cases), leg irons and, in the case of the uncontrollable inmate, chains to secure them to the wall.[88] They were usually reserved for prisoners who were violent or otherwise grossly resistant to authority. A prisoner who struggled when ordered to the refractory cell or misbehaved whilst in it might expect to be ironed. William Brown, just mentioned, was in irons for an hour on a previous occasion, having been placed in the refractory cell and then kicking the door and making a noise.[89] A month earlier, William Thomas, again mentioned in the report above, found himself punished for bad language and threats

and while in the cell tore off a portion of Iron plate from the door. I then placed him in Handcuffs and then was to begining other mischief I placed the traveling chains on his legs and fastened his hands to them and kept him in the refractory cell for the night without his supper.[90]

Chains were also used on women prisoners. Some of the occasions upon which Mary Ann Awberry was ironed have been mentioned earlier,[91] but though a frequent offender she was not the only one to be so constrained. On 18 July 1847 Mariah Thomas was placed in the refractory cell 'for exposing her self and threatening to tare the Matron cap of her head, her conduct in the cell was most Violent and breaking a mess tin'. On the next day she was 'in irons for refusing to wash clothes and breaking another mess tin and telling the Governor she did not care a dam for him or the matron'.[92]

Awberry and Thomas challenged the system of penal discipline both immediately in the behaviour in which they engaged, and more fundamentally in the sense that ideas of regime, upon which other superstructures of reform or deterrence might be erected, were based on the unspoken assumption of the prisoner as a homogenous recipient of discipline. So too the use of labour as an integral part of penal ideology was more fraught with uncertainty in reality, when brought up against issues of eligibility and capacity, than it ever was when voiced as a principle. The local prison, filled with its miscellany of classes and of individuals and consistently understaffed, was a less than perfect channel for the ideology of the adult, male convict prison (itself inevitably compromised even in those institutions by the exigencies of real life). Moreover, the world outside the prison walls provided a scale against which the penal experience was to be measured. The experiences of 'free' labour, their conditions at work and in the alternatives to it, indirectly set standards for the prison population, and there was no guarantee that such standards would not, did not, change. It is sometimes tempting to see the debates about the carceral regime which were so important in the nineteenth century simply as struggles for dominance of particular 'philosophical' models. In fact the prison was engaged in a rather more elemental struggle. It was trying to locate its own experience against that of the (changing) wider world, and it was struggling to reconcile the generalities of doctrine and rule with the particularities of locality and individuality. It is sometimes surprising that the optimism and confidence with which the tasks were approached survived as long as they did.

Diet and Health

The matters to be explored within this chapter may seem to concern interesting but incidental details of the nineteenth-century penal experience. It is to be hoped, however, that the preceding discussion will have alerted the reader to the fact that they represent rather more fundamental concerns than that. The diet available to prisoners had to be carefully pitched to arrive somewhere between state-sponsored starvation on the one hand and the demands of 'less-eligibility' (not only to mark the distinction from the often precarious life of the free labourer but also from those seeking institutional relief from poverty) on the other.[1] We have seen too that food as a weapon was also to be used to secure obedience to the regime of the prison, a practice which seems to have been tacitly exempted from Sir James Graham's celebrated announcement in 1843 concerning diet in general, that it 'ought not to be made an instrument of punishment'.[2] Such distinction on the basis of conduct necessitated a gradation of allowance, and other such gradations might be needed to deal with different categories (men and women, sick and well, labouring and non-labouring) of prisoner. The discovery of proper levels of sustenance, often against a background of almost total scientific ignorance,[3] was one of the more difficult incidental issues thrown up by the occupation of the centre of the penal stage by imprisonment rather than bodily punishment in the nineteenth century. Put crudely, the heartiness or otherwise of the condemned man's breakfast had hitherto been a matter of proverbial, but not of penological interest.

However, it is not simply the case that the quality and quantity of food produced difficulties to be overcome. The desire for uniformity has been a theme throughout this discussion. Yet to impose uniformity of diet throughout a national prison population would be a great step, indeed, one regarded as too great to be feasible for most of the century. If there was no uniformity of diet in an increasingly mobile age, ran the logic of some, then crime

could not be tracked down and expunged but merely chased from
county to county as criminals sought out the most liberal institutions. But dietaries were locally funded. Not only were there
political objections to a retreat from such 'subsidiarity' but
economic ones too, for some areas were simply richer than others.
Nor was food without cultural connotations either. We do not
have to remind ourselves of the divergent British popular national
signifiers of roast beef, oats, potatoes and toasted cheese respectively to recognize that the formation of a 'national' diet was both
the result of, and the motor for, significant social change. In this
context the centrality of such non-indigenous foodstuffs as
'Indian meal' and cocoa in the debates over prison diet have,
perhaps, an added significance in their capacity to transcend more
local differences. Whatever the truth of such speculations, it is
undoubtedly true that food is important; and probably nowhere
more so than in prison.

Health too was of more than individual concern in the development of the prison. It was not simply that contagion had been a
potent physical force in the early years of the new penality and
continued to be a metaphorical one in the development of newer
models of regime. The importance of a decision as to a prisoner's
health, a decision which of course depended on variant and
fallible human judgement, was also, as we have seen, related to
eligibility for diet, for labour and for isolation. These key determinants of the prison experience and the related question as to who,
prisoner or prison official, controlled that experience, came into
sharp focus over the issue of health. Even more than this, though,
mental illness in particular blurred the clear line between bad
and good, and cast doubt over the ideologies of deterrence and
reform intended to negotiate the boundary between the two.
Theoreticians of our own day have often chosen to stress the links
between prison, hospital and asylum in the development of institutionalization in the nineteenth century, and it was seen in
chapter 1 that such links at a local level were personal as well as
functional. But we miss the point if we see the development of
these institutions as simply the progress of an all-pervading
ideology of institutionalization or confinement. The Victorians
were more concerned with the distinctions between the institutions than with the almost inevitable similarities of bureaucracy
and buildings which so exercise commentators now. Such

distinctions proceeded ultimately from assessments of the differences between individuals which could be incredibly difficult to determine. Moreover, chapter 4 has shown how the development of the prison as the nineteenth century progressed increasingly centred on the adult, criminal prisoner rather than, say, the debtor or the child. A case can be made for a more sophisticated scientific grasp of human deficiency behind a programme of 'diversion' from gaol into other institutions for those considered vulnerable (the child) or degenerate (the drunk) or disordered (the mad) rather than properly criminal.[4] But we should not forget that institutions have their own self-definitions and their own momentum. The development of an ideal of a uniform, goal-determined prison regime may be as important as a reason for the greater diversity of scientific classification of deviance and abnormality rather than simply as a consequence of it. These issues need to be considered within this chapter.

The dietary

One of the least noticed consequences of the withdrawal of punishment from public display into the relative privacy of the institution was the scope that that process gave for the operation of public imagination in the construction of a version of the penal regime. This construct could then feature within debate, irrespective of any relation to the reality of lived experience.[5] The 'less-eligibility' argument which raged throughout the nineteenth century was sustained by layers of ignorance in the very middle-class commentators who contributed most to it: ignorance of the reality of the diet of the free labourer (did the London tailor really survive on cups of tea?)[6] and ignorance of the reality of prison provisions. Whilst the hardness of the labour expected within the gaol could be to an extent validated by the display of rotation of a pewter figure above the line of the walls, the gastronomic reality of 'stirabout' was less susceptible to dramatic representation. Prison also revealed a further ignorance, perhaps an even more disturbing one as expert opinion increasingly claimed a superiority over its popular counterpart: the ignorance of science. It was simply not known how much or little food a prisoner required or what it was in potatoes which combated scurvy. In discovering minimal nutritional requirements the prison became a laboratory. When Dr Edward Smith, who had admittedly had the decency to perform the initial experiments upon himself, testified to the Carnarvon Committee in 1863 as to the number of grains of carbon and nitrogen which the prison diet required, he was at least trying to move the debate beyond the retrospective principle of nutritional regime, which determined the sufficiency of diet only by reference to the illness and mortality which followed it. Even so he could be ignored.[7]

Local variation in dietaries was a cause of concern to the Home Office throughout the period covered by this book. In 1842 Sir James Graham had commissioned an inquiry into the subject, and in the following January he urged the adoption of the graduated tables by county benches. The political and economic climate of the decade, and in particular the Irish catastrophe, kept issues of 'less-eligibility' and of criminality close to the surface of concern. Yet Graham knew that he could only cajole rather than compel, and the dietaries were far from generally adopted. Quite apart from local markets and local tastes, the daily allowance of food for prisoners represented an immediate focus for debate on the extent of local funding for penal provision. It is not surprising that the Carnarvon Committee, that great champion of uniformity, revisited the issue of variation in 1863, and in November of that year a specialist commission was invited by Sir George Grey, the Home Secretary, to investigate the diet question in the localities. Their revised tables appealed to both the sense of economy and the prevailing disposition towards tougher treatment which marked the time. Even so, as Grey conceded in the debates on the 1865 Prison Act, they had not been universally adopted, and he had concluded that to hope for a realization of such a result was unrealistic.[8]

If the focus is shifted to the level of the local institution itself it is possible to view the same tension of political authority from the other side, and to see how the uncertainty which it created was exploited by the prisoner. To catalogue every change in the Carmarthenshire dietary would be tedious, but it may be noted that it was a subject which was revisited on a number of occasions within the period covered by this book. When first inspected in the late 1830s the allowance seems, in comparison with later practice, a generous one. Convicted men, women and boys all received 1½ lb of bread and three pints of gruel per day (excepting Saturdays for gruel), with 12 oz of meat and 1½ lb of potatoes on Sundays and Thursdays. On all other days two pints of soup were provided, with 3 oz of cheese on Tuesdays and Fridays. Non-convicted prisoners (debtors and remands) made their own arrangements or were granted a 2s. weekly allowance. The inspector suggested a rather different diet, with no meat in it, and graduated in accordance with whether the sentence was one of hard labour or not.[9] Nonetheless local tradition held fast, at least for a time. The 'Graham' dietaries, much more restricted (particularly in regard to meat) and more rigorously graduated according to the nature of the sentence, were declared to have been adopted by 1844,[10] but the extent of compliance in practice is unclear. What is clear is that Home Office intervention seems to have prompted a review of local provision and an uncertainty over authority to enforce the results of that review. In December 1845 the governor of Carmarthen sent to Cardiff gaol to discover the allowance granted there, and its cost.[11] In April 1846 a new dietary, which included no meat, was approved by the local Justices, but it seems not to have been implemented, Westlake having already purchased meat and then the Justices apparently losing their nerve as the new dietary had not received the secretary of state's approval.[12] Certainly meat was still being served in July, when a dispute as to whether it was to be weighed with or without bone showed a greater punctiliousness on the part of prisoners over their rations, and a consequent need for greater precision in regulation. In December 1849, however, a change of dietary was approved by the local authorities and Stephens displayed the new tables prominently within the prison. While not as finely graduated as the Graham models, the new diet clearly distinguished between male and female, hard labour and 'common gaol', and long- and short-term offenders (which latter were now on bread and gruel in the No. 1 diet for those serving no more than fourteen days). Meat had indeed disappeared, apart from the 3 oz (without bone) which, with 2 oz of oatmeal, 1 oz of rice, vegetables and herbs, found its way into the quart of soup allowed twice a week to long-term, hard-labour prisoners. Interestingly, when the inspector visited in September 1850 he noted that the alteration in diet had still not been sanctioned by the secretary of state.[13]

There was a further change in provisions in 1853,[14] when Jebb's doctrine of 'hard bed and hard fare' was working its way down from the national convict establishments, and later the national debate which crystallized around the Carnarvon Committee and its aftermath reached out into west Wales. The principle of starting all prisoners on the minimum diet, notwithstanding their total sentence, was introduced. The inspector noted that the cost of food per prisoner was 2s. 9½d. in 1866 (it had stood at 3s. ¾d. in 1857), but this began to creep up, and in 1869 and again in 1871 it was reported that the quantity of bread in the dietary had been reduced.[15] It would have been difficult, in the last decade before nationalization, to support Sir James Graham's argument to the effect that diet was not used as an instrument of punishment.

To set the dietary was one matter, to administer it was another. As elsewhere, we should be cautious of assuming that the mechanical routine of the diet table was completely inflexible. Provisions were bought from local contractors and depended on local markets.[16] In the ill-fated summer and autumn of 1846 Westlake, only weeks after proudly announcing that he had served new potatoes for the first time that year, was reporting that those available were 'scarce and bad' and was replacing them with boiled rice and 'suit dumplins'.[17] Moreover, changes in penal thought changed the way in which the meals were prepared and served. Originally, food for the convicted prisoners was prepared in the governor's own kitchen, whilst remand prisoners cooked the food (which they had bought themselves) within the day rooms. Both practices carried a little of the savour of the pre-Howard gaol and both were to disappear. By mid-century, meals were prepared by one or two selected prisoners in a cookhouse located next to the Trebanda, and remands, if not provided with food by friends, had been added to the dietary.[18] Meals continued to be eaten in association in the day rooms until the post-Carnarvon crackdown, when they were taken individually in cells.[19]

One of the reasons for the rise of the separate system was, of course, its capacity to overcome by architecture the possibility of combinations amongst the prisoners, combinations which could be formed, *inter alia*, around issues of food. Food was not simply a matter of vital interest for the prisoner, it was one of the few

recognized entitlements, rather than obligations, within the institutions. As such its quality and quantity were matters which were
frequently raised by inmates as matters of contention with the
officers of the gaol. It was not unusual for members of the staff,
and particularly the surgeon, to be called upon to pronounce on
the quality of the fare, and portions were weighed and measured
in response to complaints. In no case is there evidence that those
who tasted the food failed to support the governor, though it
perhaps strains credibility to hear one of the Justices, Captain
Phillips, declare that the bread, baked within the prison from
'seconds' flour and deliberately not served fresh, was 'nearly as
good as that eaten in his own family'.[20] It was a high-risk strategy
for a prisoner to refuse a meal, to send it back, or, as Mary Ann
Awberry did on one occasion, to throw it out of the window.[21]
Yet it appears that on at least some occasions a challenge to the
diet would be used as part of a campaign to annoy and disrupt the
authority of the prison staff, as when employed by Charles Hunt
and James Hargrave, sometimes in association with others, in
their incarceration in 1846–7. The uncertainty of the responsibility for diet, shared as it was between local and central
authorities, could also be exploited by prisoners appealing
directly to the prison inspector or the Home Secretary.[22] That
some disputes were genuine is undoubted (Hunt seems to have
extracted the building of a new bread oven from his arguments),
but that some were engineered seems not entirely improbable.
The reasons that the bread was not served fresh, the reporter from
the *Carmarthen Journal* was told in 1867, were that it gained
weight in standing, and also so that prisoners could not 'pulp it
and claim it is dough'.[23]

The battle over entitlement to provisions was often waged in
other ways, and, as we have seen, the crucial figure in the dispute
was the surgeon. Dr Smith complained to the Carnarvon
Committee in 1863 that allocation of extra diet to prisoners
deemed to be unfit was an issue which gravely undermined any
hope of uniformity.[24] Yet in truth there was no escape from the
problem. The surgeon could, on medical grounds, alter both the
quantity and content of the diet. Extra items – tobacco,[25] beer,[26]
fruit[27] – could also be added to the approved allowance if the
surgeon determined, or could be persuaded to determine them
necessary. The routine nature of such grants is evidenced in

Carmarthen by not only the substantive evidence of the records but also their form, for pre-printed certificates are found, leaving only the specific entitlement to be filled in. It was because of the importance of decisions as to health in respect of the key penal constituents of labour and diet that the attempts by prisoners to influence them were so significant. Not only did these matters intrude into the daily life of the institution and might directly affect its atmosphere, for they were productive of disputes amongst staff and grievances amongst prisoners, but they are also of profound theoretical significance. They reveal yet again the latent futility of the Victorian idea that prisons could be run upon mechanical principles.

Health

The experience of incarceration provides information on some of the types of illness and injury of which prisoners complained whilst undergoing imprisonment. Yet because prisoners were inspected upon reception to the gaol, the records of institutions also give an insight into the medical complaints from which they suffered before that time. It is true that Carmarthen's domestic records contain no list of 'Distinguishing Marks' in the form that other such records, such as those issued in the 1870s in the attempt to identify and control habitual criminals, did. These lists, alongside the descriptions of tattoos, frequently reveal striking evidence of individual medical histories with their not infrequent mentions of scarring and missing body parts. Photographic practice elsewhere, which often shows prisoners holding up their hands to the camera, also indicates the frequency with which agricultural and industrial life in the nineteenth century was attended by the risk of loss of fingers.[28] Other medical details, such as nutritional deficiencies, are undoubtedly hidden within the bald statistical information which is recorded in Carmarthenshire; the average adult height of prisoners of around 5 ft 1 in. for females and around 5 ft 5 in. for males is clearly suggestive in this respect. Yet other details are more immediately forthcoming.

Despite the early complaints about the lack of proper reception cells it does seem to have been routine practice to bathe and inspect Carmarthen's prisoners upon admission.[29] The presence of a specialist room, the 'itch ward', is itself indicative of perhaps the most common condition from which prisoners were suffering on admission, and the governor's journals indicate that it was very frequently occupied. Scabies (the infestation with the parasite *acarus* or *sarcoptes scabiei*) required treatment for the patient and the removal of the mites from infected clothing, or the destruction of the latter. Occasionally, whole groups of prisoners admitted together were found to be suffering from the condition, and for many remand prisoners, who would otherwise keep their own clothing, it was this which led to the first contact with prison uniform. Instances of itch regularly reached into double figures for each quarter in the 1870s and the highest quarterly total of sufferers, 27 in January 1870, represents more than a third of the total number of prisoners admitted in that period.[30]

Perhaps a more surprising finding is the frequency to which reference is found within the prison population to susceptibility to fits, though the condition and its causes are not explored in any detail in the records. It may be that in some cases it developed only after incarceration and also may have been a symptom which, if regularly witnessed, could be feigned by healthy prisoners. Yet there is no doubt that in some cases the condition was in existence and known before the term of imprisonment began. A prisoner called Davies, admitted in March 1847, came with a note from the surgeon of the workhouse which was explicit both as to the cause of the seizures (epilepsy) and their treatment: 'should he be seized in Gaol attend to the undoing of his neck-cloth should it require slackening and leave him under quilt where seized until he comes to himself.'[31] In May and June 1846 Mary Ann Awberry was suffering up to three fits a day, and had also had them at night. Westlake ordered another inmate, Sarah Mathias (a felony prisoner serving a nine-month hard-labour sentence, again showing how medical exigencies could cut across the requirements of classification – Awberry of course was a misdemeanant – and silence), to 'sit up for the Night to mind her', giving candles to Mathias for that purpose.[32] Ruptures and venereal disease were other conditions not infrequently encountered. Given its significance in the social history of nineteenth-century Wales it is surprising to find that 'consumption' is not more evident in the records. Certainly it had to be reported in the case of Michael Anderson, who died and was buried in the prison cemetery in 1858. Anderson, a twenty-one-year-old Irish tailor, was recorded as suffering from the disease on admission and was employed only 'lightly' and 'occasionally' despite a six-month hard-labour sentence at assize for burglary. The reference to labour is intriguing, for the surgeon's records suggest that Anderson was 'scarcely able to leave his bed' from the time of his pre-trial remand. It is possible that, if only in his records, the governor was unwilling to be seen to have failed to implement the sentence of the court.[33] Other cases of 'inflammation' of the chest or lungs, which killed one prisoner and severely affected another, may well refer to tubercular illness.[34]

Certain other pathologies also call for special mention. It was not only in circumstances of mental disorder, to be discussed shortly, that the medical state of the prisoner was directly connected to the offence which had led to the incarceration. The position of women who were remanded, though rarely convicted, for crimes relating to neonatal infants has been adverted to earlier. Such cases reveal an overall blurring of penological functions which again cautions us against over-rigorous application of theoretical boundaries.[35] Moreover, the gaol surgeon could find himself in such cases not only operating as the defendant's medical attendant but also as a witness at the trial. These were messy affairs, blurring the lines between shame and guilt, pathology and wickedness, punishment and welfare, not only on the day in court, but also throughout entire periods of the women's incarceration.

Similar difficulties for an institution increasingly taking its disciplinary paradigm from the central figure of the adult male convict emerge from consideration of the position of young children admitted to the gaol with their mothers. Such cases have been noted earlier, and not the least important thing about them is their almost complete invisibility at the level of government policy or regulation. Yet children were not only brought into gaol, they were also born there, although only a handful of cases have been found. The delivery was presumably supervised by the surgeon (for there are no records of the use of a midwife in Carmarthen), and the baptism conducted by the gaol chaplain. One debtor's wife seems to have been allowed by magistrates to give birth in the prison because her husband was there. Another instance was narrowly avoided in 1846 when Mary Davies, convicted of refusing to maintain two children, was released; 'the prisoner was very large in the family way when discharged which the surgeon of the Gaol gave me orders to obtain a cart to convey her to Llanelly Union which I did so & paid 2/6 for her conveyance'.[36] Not all the results of prison pregnancy were happy ones. In 1857, twenty-two-year-old Maria Williams was recorded as 'confined of a stillborn child in gaol'.[37] Mary Bryant had been delivered of twin boys in 1852, but one of them died. The inquest heard that this was due to natural causes, the mother being unable to feed sufficiently as a result of having an ulcerous condition of the breast. This also necessitated sending the surviving child out of prison to a nurse.[38]

Deaths in prison were, as has been seen, events to be avoided, even at the cost of a failure to prosecute after initial remand or discharge before the end of the custodial sentence. Where they did occur they were followed by inquests. There are no records of suicide within the gaol at Carmarthen during the period studied, although a 'recent' attempt using a razor was noted in 1838, and two other attempts, one apparently 'pretended', were recorded in 1840.[39] Causes of death found by inquest jurors were found to be 'natural', such as the 'disease of the heart' which struck down George Adams shortly after his confinement began (see plate 7), or the 'inflammation of the chest' which claimed sixty-seven-year-old Jenkin Jones.[40] In one case, however, there was criticism by the coroner's jury. John Jones, described as 'very ill', had been removed to gaol by cart by bailiffs for 'contempt of the county court judge' in a process which drew condemnation from the jury.[41] In another instance, rumours of improper treatment had apparently circulated following the death of a prisoner in 1841. He had been struck in an altercation with the then governor's son, but no impropriety was found after investigation by the Visiting Justices. Whatever the truth of the events, this case, together with a later allegation of mistreatment following a death in the Carmarthen lunatic asylum, are reminders yet again that the creation of the 'closed institution' inevitably simultaneously creates the possibility of a narrative of abuse.

Carmarthen's gaol had been described at its first inspection as 'very healthy', although the failure of the surgeon to keep full records of the diseases encountered and the treatments prescribed renders any such judgement impressionistic.[42] After 1865 his quarterly reports to sessions do give terse details of numbers suffering from a number of more or less precise complaints. Whilst it is possible to discover some details of medical complaints and procedures, the limitations of the record evidence are as important a part of the story of prison disease as are the recoverable details. Like the issue of institutional abuse, institutional disease was not a thing which local authorities were keen to advertise.

Cholera was a significant disease inside the gaol and out. In the previous chapter it was noted that an outbreak of the disease in town in 1849 had resulted in the almost medieval ritual of a day of 'humiliation' being observed within the gaol as outside.[43] In his report for 1851 the prison inspector noted that the disease had been prevalent in the town, but only one case had been found in the gaol. His comment in the same report that the only bath was almost useless, that the drains were defective and the water closets 'offensive' might render this information surprising, but crucially the source of drinking water was the self-contained well within the gaol.[44] A few years later, when cholera was again prevalent elsewhere, the gaol was again spared the ravages of the unnamed 'fever' which had affected 400 people, including two of the three surgeons in town, in one month alone.[45] At the same time as the science of epidemiology was experiencing its celebrated early success with the removal of the Broad Street pump handle in London (in the cholera epidemic which notably had failed to take hold in a neighbouring workhouse which had its own well),[46] the evidence of Carmarthen's gaol was pointing to a similar aetiology. By the time of a mention of a case of 'English Cholera' in the prison in 1871 the mention of a 'dangerous' cesspool within the gaol may well indicate a more informed acceptance of scientific research.[47]

Yet events within the gaol in the summer of 1846, though the evidence is (deliberately?) less transparent than it might be, confirm that the linking of disease with deficiencies in the water supply in the 1850s was well established when 'miasma' was still the dominant causal model. Quite apart from this, Westlake's observations on the outbreak of illness merit some attention, for they show how difficult the management of an institution with limited resources and personnel could be at a time of crisis. In late May 1846 a number of prisoners are reported as being on the sick report, or in receipt of extra diet or medicines, and for the next few weeks the problems seem to have got worse. Whether all prisoners were suffering from the same condition is unclear, as is any possible relation of their conditions to the vacillation over the reduced diet which was taking place at the same time. The symptoms too are elusive, though the fact that the surgeon ordered a 'night chair' to be constructed for the infirmary, and in the end the Justices ordered two to be made, is perhaps suggestive. Both Mary Ann Awberry and Francis Jones were also recorded as having repeated fits, although this may be unconnected. After the general reports of May, information becomes a little fuller, generally a sign of the governor's discomfort. A debtor, Thomas Evans, was reported as 'in a very weak state of health' on 31 May, and on 2 June another prisoner, John Evans, was removed to the infirmary. David Joshua, serving two years for forgery and himself recently unwell, was detailed to spend the night with him 'in case he should be taken worst'. After a number of visits from the assistant surgeon and from Thomas Jones MD (one of the Justices), this John Evans was discharged in the mail coach to Llandeilo on grounds of ill health on 5 June. By this time, however, yet another Evans, Henry, was in the infirmary. The assistant surgeon ordered him to be bathed, and Westlake took this as a signal for wider action. 'I ordered the wheel to stop at 3 oclock PM for the prisoners to Bathe themselves in the Bath in the Infirmary.' The next few days saw more activity: another visit by a medically qualified JP, Henry Lawrence, Mary Ann Awberry removed to the infirmary with an attendant to watch her at night, and another prisoner named Davies removed from the wheel ill. On 10 June volunteer remand prisoners began deepening the well, which was subsequently baled out. The itch ward, to which new prisoners were also being admitted, was ordered to be fumigated. On 16 June, illness necessitated that a military prisoner was taken before an army surgeon. On 18 June Frances Jones was ordered to the infirmary where her feet were bathed with hot water and hot bricks applied to them; she was joined on the following day by the rest of the female prisoners. Later, as normality had apparently begun to reassert itself, on 21 July Hannah Harries, already ill for some time, was removed to the infirmary where she apparently remained for six weeks until her discharge, after which the infirmary was washed by two female prisoners.[48]

A few general points are noticeable during this crisis. Not only was the prison response to illness afforced by specialist intervention by the visiting Magistrates, it was also crucially dependent on the cooperation of the prisoners themselves. Regulations concerning classification and accommodation were quickly ignored as a matter of expediency, and the early discharge of John Evans was apparently secured with little delay or formality.[49] Whatever the promise of mechanical discipline emanating from Pentonville at this period, it was clear that regimes, particularly at times of trouble, were still liable to be negotiated in the local prison.

Apart from an outbreak of 'sore eyes' which necessitated mass treatment, another (connected?) parasite problem which necessitated the purchase of two dozen 'small tooth combs'[50] and the instances of diarrhoea which recur in the medical reports, there would seem to have been no other disease which troubled the prison as a whole in the period studied. Illnesses tended to be individual ones and, though overall costs of medication survive in gaol accounts, details of treatment remain largely elusive. It seems clear that extra diet, accompanied by removal to the infirmary in more serious cases, was often the first response to illness. More specific measures (such as the warming of feet noted earlier, a practice designed to precipitate 'crisis' in a disease) would seem to have been largely conventional. The unfortunate Henry Evans, whose later illness has already been noted, had had a 'blister' applied to his chest as part of the treatment for one illness. Despite, or perhaps because of, his ill health he was noted as a model prisoner, learning English and reading Matthew Chapter 3 from the Bible on the morning of his discharge.[51] Evans's experience, in regard not only to education but also to medical treatment, again raises obliquely the issue of 'less-eligibility'. This spectre surfaces again with the possibility of a prisoner remaining beyond the expiry of the sentence to recover from illness — a sort of mirror image of the practice of early release on grounds of ill health. Instances are infrequent, but are not unheard of. It might be thought that, since discharged prisoners who were ill would often simply have to resort to the workhouse, the option of remaining in gaol would be restricted to those who were local, for whom the physical and economic consequences of such a transfer would be less marked. Yet John Ainger, 'detained' for an extra day beyond his sentence in 1867, was a silk worker from Hackney, though he subsequently turned up in Haverfordwest,[52] whilst the local John Morris 'refused to stay longer', despite the 'very critical state' of his health occasioned by an 'inflammation of the lungs', at the expiry of his sentence.[53] Some were certainly still ill at discharge. John Jenkins, originally from Kent but last resident in Merthyr, seems not to have been offered the chance to stay, but at least had his passage to Swansea paid and a sum of money given to him.[54] James Hayes, a highway robber originally from Ireland, had spent eight of his twelve-months sentence confined to bed in the infirmary. He was discharged 'nearly cured'.[55]

Apart from the illnesses suffered there were also cases of injury sustained by prisoners whilst in the gaol. It is not known how many, if any, of the ruptures which prevented men from working on the treadwheel had in fact been caused by it, but the possibility of the wheel causing injury to the shin or, indeed, of finger injury caused by oakum picking, was considered in the last chapter. Other injuries could be more dramatic and, indeed, more serious. In July 1849 Thomas Davies, attempting to secure a ladder, 'overbalanced himself' when the rope broke, fell 14 ft 'and very much injured himself' (the defensive use of the transitive verbs by the governor is interesting).[56] In September of the same year William Dixon, serving a six-month sentence for theft, was severely cut on the head when the well handle struck him.[57]

In considering the role of the surgeon, the investigation of instances where illness was thought to be feigned was considered. Whilst sources from other prisons show how sophisticated, and indeed how distressing, were the means employed by prisoners to create the impression or actuality of physical disease or injury, Carmarthen's records provide few such details. In 1873, however, Dr Rowlands does allow himself a rather triumphant note. 'One case only requires special notice', he reported to the July quarter sessions,

> that of Thomas Howarth who on admission complained of chest affection and spitting of blood. It was soon discerned that he was a Malingerer, the blood coming from wounds produced by himself. After the discovery was made he soon got well and he is now doing his work properly.

Nonetheless the ploy achieved a modest success, though its limitation is rather consciously noted in the surgeon's next report,

where he observed that extra rations had been prescribed 'for
debility caused by bleeding himself secretly daily, for the purpose
of simulating disease in order to obtain extra diet on a liberal
scale'.[58]

Mental illness

For those intent on feigning illness the simulation of mental
disorder might be a more attractive option. If it failed to result in a
discharge without trial, as it had in the case of Eugene Buckley
whose behaviour had raised suspicion in some,[59] then it might at
least result in a transfer to an asylum, the conditions of which
were considered superior to those found in the prison. Indeed,
James Davies, appearing before Carmarthen's magistrates on a
charge of being drunk and disorderly, pointed to his head and
declared: 'I am not right there, and the drop of beer I drank made
me worse.' He said that he wished to return to the asylum at
Briton Ferry, declaring it the 'best shop he had ever been to, as
there was plenty of grub there, and the inmates enjoyed the life of
gentlemen'. He did not get his wish, the case being dismissed.[60]

Despite the distinction drawn within this chapter it should be
noted that the difference between physical and mental disorder
was yet another matter of judgement, both by 'experts' in general
and individual practitioners in particular, rather than a simple
rigid dichotomy. The fits which resulted from epilepsy have been
noted in the preceding section, yet it should be noted that an
'epileptic ward' was proposed for the Joint Counties Lunatic
Asylum in 1874.[61] In 1877 the surgeon reported on Samuel
Evans, whose sanity had been doubted by the committing magistrate: 'The man's mental condition has been carefully looked into;
he appears to be of sound mind but a little stupid from deaf-
ness.'[62] It is perhaps interesting to modern sensibilities that a
prisoner like Mary Ann Awberry, not only susceptible to fits but
also apparently incapable of any prolonged existence outside the
institution or of good behaviour within it, seems never to have
been regarded as anything other than morally reprehensible. The
effects of alcohol, which certainly played a part in Awberry's
history, are seldom specifically addressed, though its social
consequences were being discussed in the wider society of

Carmarthenshire and beyond. One debtor, Thomas Daniel, whose case was considered earlier, was described as suffering from 'delirium tremens' in 1847, as was another prisoner in 1871, and 'Alcoholism' does appear as a diagnosis in a report by the surgeon in 1873, presumably in reference to the unnamed prisoner who is recorded as having received extra diet 'for debility, caused by exposure and intemperance'.[63] Distinguishing between physical illness, mental disorder and moral weakness was not necessarily a simple task, nor one in which criteria corresponding to our own sensibilities were applied.

A diagnosis of insanity could be arrived at at any point in the period of incarceration. In some cases prisoners taken on remand were considered to be insane. Some were never brought to trial. Llewellyn Edwards was not prosecuted for the murder of his brother but removed eleven days after his remand to 'Bethlem Lunatic Asylum, St George's Fields, London' by order of the secretary of state.[64] No such order for removal is recorded in the case of David Jenkins, transferred to the newly opened asylum in Carmarthen in 1867, only four days after his remand. Jenkins, whose puzzled, 'fresh, fair' face underneath its bowler hat is one of the more enduring images from the *Felons' Register* (see plate 8), had a True Bill returned against him for stabbing at the quarter sessions but was never tried.[65] The judge in the case of the child-killer Mary Hughes perhaps surprisingly instructed the grand jury to find no True Bill at her trial, but the finding of insanity seems to have been made instead by the trial jury. She was returned to gaol for almost a year before being removed to an asylum at Devizes, after initial exchanges with Briton Ferry failed to secure a place for her there.[66] David Jenkins (not the same man mentioned above) was acquitted of stealing clothes at assize but returned to gaol, presumably with the intention of removal elsewhere. After two months, however, he was released 'by an order of Her Majesty, having been previously certified not insane'.[67]

Other prisoners became, or were classified as, insane only once their sentence had begun. It is not clear in all cases what process was employed in transfer to an asylum, for not all cases explicitly record the intervention of the Home Office, though that does not necessarily indicate that it was not involved.[68] In one case we know that the prisoner succumbed to mental illness after release, the governor noting on the record of Edward Williams that 'after

leaving the prison about 3 months he became insane and was sent
to Briton Ferry Lunatic Asylum where about Jan 1866 he was
murdered by another lunatic'.[69]

It has been noted previously that information gathered by officers of the gaol when involved in the custody of remand prisoners
might be used at their trial or, indeed (in the cases of Buckley and
of the 'hysterical' Frances Anne Jones which were considered in
chapter 3), may have been influential in the decision not to
continue the prosecution. At the trial of Mary Hughes in 1847
evidence was given to the assize jury not only by Surgeon
Rowlands, who declared her not to be of sound mind, but also by
Thomas Jones, the gaol chaplain, and by Governor Westlake. In
such circumstances it may have been considered wise to invoke
this non-medical opinion, for despite increasing claims made for
specialist evidence within the legal system as a whole it would
seem that 'robust' Carmarthenshire juries were not always ready
to surrender a social judgment to a medical one.[70]

Even to the medical practitioner the issue of diagnosis might
involve fine distinctions. Findings that a prisoner was 'mentally
weak', 'nervous' or 'imbecilic' seem not to have satisfied the test
of insanity.[71] In 1874 the surgeon recorded a case of 'Mental
Alienation, a troublesome case as the patient was at one time so
violent as to render constraint necessary, but the case was not
such as to justify a certificate of Lunacy'.[72] The potential of an
unstable prisoner to disrupt the routine and order of the gaol had
long been recognized. David Lewis, committed for an assault in
September 1845, seems to have been immediately regarded as
insane upon admission, and Westlake was obliged to use both a
straitjacket and irons on him on the first day. The prisoner
assigned to stay with Lewis at night was, unusually, a military
offender, David Morgan, a deserter from the 75th Regiment.
After Morgan's release (to proceed to Ireland with the 37th
Regiment) it seems possible that Alexander Gregory was put with
Lewis. Again this would have been an interesting decision, for
Gregory's behaviour in gaol was described as 'very bad' and it is
conceivable that the task was regarded as an irksome one.[73] It
proved to be so, for Gregory was assaulted by Lewis. Lewis's case
also sheds light on the issue of financial responsibility for the
maintenance of the disordered. The Visiting Justices seem to have
decided in October 1845 that since he was insane the burden of

his upkeep properly lay with the Poor Law authorities rather than the prison, and Westlake went to the relieving officer of Llandefeilog to claim 4s. 1d. for a week's maintenance. The relieving officer, understandably, refused to accept responsibility for what appears at this stage still to have been a criminal remand. After examination of the prisoner not only by the surgeon but also by three medically qualified JPs, Lewis was eventually taken by Westlake to Mr Leech's Asylum in Briton Ferry.[74]

Once prisoners had been transferred to another institution they disappear from the gaol records. The fate of some is traceable in other sources, such as John Williams, declared to be 'convalescent' in the Joint Counties Asylum to which he had been removed from the prison, after a remand for horse theft in 1873.[75] Perhaps it was an expectation that he would see her again that led Governor Stephens to record the discharge 'as cured' of Sarah Jones from the Joint Counties Asylum. A recidivist, who had even served a term of penal servitude, Jones had been removed from gaol initially to Briton Ferry and was transferred to the Carmarthen asylum once it had opened.[76] Like the news of the death of Edward Williams, murdered at Briton Ferry, the case shows the transfer not only of inmates but also of information within the institutional nexus.

Conclusion

This growth in the nineteenth century of an institutional network within which the prison was located is one of the more important developments which this chapter has noted. The apparently binary oppositions, between sane and mad, well and ill, bad and damaged, have been revealed as matters of complex judgement in which the actions of both surgeon and prisoner play a part. It has been suggested that, on a national level, the institutional developments which are associated with these decisions (the construction of specialist repositories for the immature, the drunk, the prostitute and the insane) may be read not simply as a recognition of the limitations of the prison. The diversion of those who do not 'properly' belong in prison may be a result, in part at any rate, of a clearer perception of those who do. This may seem to be a distinction without a difference, but the point is simply that the archetypal criminal around whose form the prison is closing is as much a positive construction as a negative one. Prison was not, within the period surveyed here, the institutional 'dustbin' it was to become. If such an institution did exist at this time it was the workhouse, where minor criminality, illness, deprivation and dysfunction rubbed shoulders daily. But prison was trying to demarcate its constituency, to hone its punitive models.

It is clear too that issues of diet and of health have implications directly for these models. 'Less-eligibility', the very concept that made an experience punitive, was being measured in the loaves that were baked and the scabies mites which were killed. Yet adequacy of diet and fitness to labour were not matters susceptible of scientific evaluation, or at any rate if they were (as Dr Smith urged), then such evaluation was not uniformly accepted. Nor were these matters upon which the authorities alone, though they might protest otherwise, had a monopoly of information. The apparently inflexible regime of the prison dietary should not blind us to the fact that what a particular prisoner found on his plate might depend on the interplay of a number of forces: central and local government, the surgeon and, of course, the prisoner himself.

Conclusion

After nationalization Carmarthen prison continued to operate, although latterly as a male prison only, until its closure was ordered in September 1924. It is no part of this book to investigate that final period, but a few observations may be in order in relation to the last rites of the institution. The memorandum notifying the grounds for discontinuance begins with an explanation of criteria considered in making the decision, these being the 'position as regards other prisons and their size'. The railway connection to Swansea was adverted to as bearing on the issue. Moreover, the memorandum goes on to state that 'Carmarthen is not a good Prison for carrying out the modern treatment of prisoners. It is a small place with no industrial possibilities ... So far as the treatment of prisoners is concerned the closing of such Prisons is a step in the right direction.'[1] Reconsideration was urged by the MP J. Hinds, who was assured that the town's status as an assize venue would be unaffected. The Home Office, in pursuance of section 34 of the 1877 Act, offered the property to the county council, as representing the former prison authority, for £3,249. 12s. In 1937 the council contracted for its demolition, though belated efforts were made to rescue the Nash portico. Council offices now stand on the site.[2]

The documents, like the building, may be profitably deconstructed. The reasons for the nationalization of the gaols in 1877 were: the desire to create a penal 'system', with establishments linked to each other rather than to the community in which they were located, operating with a regime which was standard across that system and responsive to 'specialist' government direction, the whole supported by arguments from economic efficiency; the same reasons were given for the closure of Carmarthen's prison two generations later. Local prestige was still an issue for local representatives, but the decision rested with the Home Office. Bureaucracy, with a hint of what will later be known as 'heritage', was designated to occupy the site standing over the town, rather than penality, which has become a matter of national shame rather than of local pride. What have the preceding chapters told us about the transitions which are invoked in these considerations?

By placing the events of an individual prison and the experiences and interactions of particular staff and prisoners at the centre of the narrative it becomes possible to see the events of the 'penal revolution' from a rather different perspective than that offered by much modern historiography. What becomes evident is not merely a 'top down' projection of central government power, nor even a reaction to or modification of that projection at a local level. The formulation of penal policy was, similarly, not simply the programme of a new breed of experts, whose preferred views vied for dominance as the system developed in efficiency and sophistication as the nineteenth century wore on. Nor was it merely a progressive idea doomed to founder on ancient parochial intransigence. Rather, the development of penal policy in the nineteenth century has to be seen in terms of an initial construction, by trial and error, of what it was possible to imagine, followed by the attempt to apply that imagination. The idea of the drive for uniformity has been a key determinant of the discussion. But it is wrong to see this as a concept which emerges fully formed, to be applied or resisted as a matter of political choice or in the interests of different power groups within the nation. Imagining 'uniformity', like imagining 'the nation', was itself a developing process rather than an event. Similarly, governance by rule (whether of an individual institution or a system of institutions) rather than by discretion may be a good slogan, but ultimately it represents a philosophical impossibility: no rule-maker can foresee every individual occurrence, nor could language contain the possibilities if that foresight were possible. So the construction of every new rule inevitably involves the construction of a new uncertainty, the response to which – another new rule (with new uncertainty) or not – itself depends upon the exercise of discretion and is again uncertain. It is because of this deeper underlying problematic that the experience of a particular prison can be properly illustrative of essential tensions in the construction (by nineteenth-century participants and by twenty-first-century historians) of penological models. The occurrence of a particular event which exposes the conceptual limitations of uniformity or the softness at the edges of any formulation of rule, and the response which any actor or actors may make to it, are matters of inevitable particularity. Nowhere else did a man exactly like Henry Westlake have to decide whether a man exactly like John Wilson was obliged to undertake labour in a prison exactly like Carmarthen. That is not the level at which I seek to consider the 'typicality' of events in the matters discussed in earlier chapters. Yet the essential particularity of events, the essential problems of formulation and application of rules, and the way that imagination and experience combine and recombine to address or overlook the inevitable tensions thereby produced – these are matters which make the discussion important beyond a narrative of local history.

The reader may well feel cheated at this point. Even if the highlighting of the limitations of rules and the experiential contingencies of producing guiding concepts were to be regarded as ideas worthy of mention, it might be objected that they comprise observations so banal as to merit at most a footnote reference in other rather grander theoretical discussions. Whilst it is submitted that an appreciation of the centrality of this perspective can serve essentially to recast our reading of penal history, the reader may want to know what, in less abstract terms, this study adds to our understanding of Victorian penal history.

The first point to make is an obvious one, but it is no less important for that. There does, indeed, seem to have been a significant reorientation of penal practice in England and Wales (and also in Ireland and Scotland, though those jurisdictions have their own historians to tell those stories) in the period spanning the late eighteenth to the late nineteenth centuries. The story has been routinely oversimplified (by ignoring continuities, by concentrating excessively on the history of serious crime, by mistaking policy for practice and in other important ways), but it will do no great harm still to think in terms of a 'revolution' in penality. From Howard to nationalization, prison changed. It changed in establishing securely its centrality within the range of punitive dispositions. It changed in the potential imagined for it and the type of individual whose treatment is regarded as paradigmatic within it. It changes the orientation of its essential connections, from local communities of decision-makers and local milieus of decision, to networks of other institutions and central governmental (and other 'specialist') influence. The account of Carmarthenshire's experience given here – the Nash 'Enlightenment rebuild', the treadwheel, inspectors, silence, separation – seems unproblematically to fit into this inevitable progression. Whoever we choose to see as the instigators of the changes (and as was seen in the Introduction the candidates proffered include the reformers, the capitalists and various abstract nouns), the changes happened, and they happened in rural Wales as well as in other places.

Yet the extent to which the 'revolution' was experienced as such by those involved within it was, of course, limited. The smooth trajectory seen in hindsight is experienced by contemporaries as a series of relatively distinct and particular events, each one contingent upon possibilities created or excluded by previous ones. Security, diet, cost and routine are the types of immediate issues around which changes were argued and resolved within the individual institution. Issues which may seem more important to historians, questions of regime, for example, or of penal philosophy, are generally subservient to questions of what was physically or economically possible, of what could be got away with. The ideal of uniformity constantly beat against the reality of inevitable contingency. Rules constantly collided with the discretion with which they must inevitably be applied. Despite appearances, the changes in the nineteenth-century penal experience came about by a process which more resembles evolution than creationism. Of course, big things happened: the 1877 Prison Act is one of those big things. But to understand it we need to see how its possibilities were formed.

Moreover, one of the insights which a microscosmic institutional study reveals is the nexus of interconnection involved in charting these possibilities. Accounts, for example, which take the status of 'prisoner' as unproblematic will perceive penal change as only contingently related, if at all, to other important issues – changes in the law of evidence, the growth of summary jurisdiction, the creation of national rather than regional social norms – rather than intimately entangled with them. The penal revolution of the nineteenth century was part of a wider realignment of attitudes to crime, its detection and its trial. Accounts which assume that the only role of the prisoner is as the (generally passive) recipient of discipline not only ignore the underlying bilateralism which inheres in carceral control but also miss the role which prisoners could play in shifting the nature of that control. It has been suggested that it is not only the existence of the Prison Inspectorate or the increasing intervention of the Home Office which could push for change of regime, but prisoners who were willing to assert claims to those bodies, prisoners like Charles Hunt and James Hargrave who could challenge local autonomy. Yet neither were local authorities, only the hapless victims of a change of constitutional balance. The building of Carmarthen's unsegregated prison infirmary or Cardiganshire's simple neglect of the 1865 Prison Act are eloquent late testimonies to the vigour, and, just as important, the torpor of localism. More routinely issues of funding, of staff, building and food meant that nineteenth-century penal experience remained much less an application of the panopticism of Bentham, the theology of Crawford and Russell, or the disciplinarianism of Jebb than our desire for clean lines of development would have us believe.

It might be objected that it is narrow parochialism which informs this version of the story. The big things were happening elsewhere. That the young people of west Wales may be wearing high street versions of high fashion rather than haute couture does not mean that one is not an imitative, but rather cheaper and more practical version of the other (though it may mean that a history of fashion which ignored the former would be, paradoxically, an impoverished history). But that is not the point I am making. Millbank, Pentonville, Portland were important institutions in the history of imprisonment. They were not, however, designed as models for county gaols. Penitentiaries and, when their ideology began to waver, the less specifically designated convict prisons, moved incarceration to the centre of the penological spectrum. Because they handled serious criminals and because serious criminality catches the attention of historians no less than it does newspaper editors, the suggestion seems to be that they simply set the agenda for local prisons. Whilst the importance of ideas developed in such institutions needs to be acknowledged, and whilst the relationship between the two undoubtedly becomes closer as 1877 approaches, the story is a rather more complex one.

Throughout the nineteenth century county institutions held debtors, remand prisoners, misdemeanants and felons serving short-term sentences. For none of these classes, for a variety of reasons, were regimes designed for serious or persistent felons serving long terms after conviction suitable. It must be remembered that the whole point of these convict institutions was that the prisoners under sentence in them had been specifically removed from their local prisons. The evidence of Carmarthen's *Felons' Register* (which does not include debtors, military prisoners, or those remanded or convicted of misdemeanour) shows that only approximately 5 per cent of those who are recorded went on to receive a sentence of transportation (which at the relevant time, of course, did not necessarily mean removal from the jurisdiction) or of penal servitude.[3] Such men, and the majority *were* men, are by definition extraordinary, yet their experience has distorted much of the academic debate about the history of imprisonment.

Paradoxically, the collapse of the traditional distinction between the county gaol and the house of correction, a process sealed by statute in 1865, is important in allowing local institutions to override ancient boundaries between types of prisoner.[4] In a sense it both marked and sealed a shift in focus on the part of the local institutions towards the model of punitive imprisonment. We have seen in chapter 4 that this may have been responsible for a realignment of the perception of debtors to fit more comfortably into this new paradigm. We saw there too that this movement, and the apparently diametrically opposed process of 'decarceration' to specialist institutions for the young or drunk or mad, may well have been prompted by developments within the institution as much as, and possibly rather more than, outside it. But, though there were centrally administered punitive establishments operating at the same time as local ones were adopting a more consistently punitive ethos, this does not mean that the relationship between the two was simple, or that influence passed only from the centre outwards. We must remember too that a shift in emphasis or focus does not remove the debtors, the remand prisoners, even the children, or the differences – philosophical as well as simply traditional – between such classes and the adult convicted. It was, in short, simply not the case that Carmarthen was supposed to be like Pentonville. That would have been absurd. But increasingly it was important that Carmarthen was like Cardigan and Caernarfon and, importantly, like Cambridge too. As was seen in chapter 1, this reconceptualization of crime and punishment as national phenomena was not a process without difficulties.

Moreover, in the 'feedback loop' which influenced and changed thoughts on and practice within the field of law enforcement, experience in the localities was of great significance throughout the nineteenth century. It has been seen that concern over mobility of and identity of criminals is evidenced in the sceptical record-keeping and the evocative photographs of Governor Stephens for some time before it found expression in legislation like the Habitual Criminals Act 1869. This feature alerts us to another question which shows the impossibility of isolating simple lines of influence in the creation of the institutional dynamic. Records create a form of reality as much as reality creates records. Issues of identity become problematic when someone is charged with recording them. Yet the records created, what they reveal and what they conceal, impact upon the perception of reality which may influence future decisions. This is not some postmodern trickery. The rather different records which Governor Stephens leaves from those of his neurotic predecessor Henry Westlake suggest a more formal, less personal, more bureaucratic version of the prison experience. But was the prison shaping the bureaucracy, or vice versa? And was the change (of record, of practice, or of both) a product of personality, of local initiative, of central government expectation or of some wider temporal mentality? It is not simply that such questions in themselves test the limitations of our evidence. They may warn against unhelpful oppositions (as explaining 'old' and 'new' practice) in what is in reality a complex amalgam. Similar questions can be asked of the development of the quasi-criminological reflections of the two later prison chaplains discussed in chapter 3. Are these fresh interests or freshly recorded ones? The products of individual initiative, the expectations of others, or the things which are felt properly to fill reports?

Even when it seems clear that changes have, indeed, been introduced, the temptation to look to obvious sources may need to be checked. Vectors of influence into local institutions might be indirect. We have seen, for example, that it was not through the influence of any 'separationist' prison inspector that solitary confinement first became a feature of Carmarthen prison experience, but through the sentences of courts martial on soldiers garrisoned within the principality. In respect of the connections with other institutions such as the workhouse or the lunatic asylum, or other initiatives such as public health reform, it is notable that the existence of a numerically limited class of local gentry who fulfilled a variety of official roles necessarily placed different specialist provision in a rather homogeneous de facto philosophical context. If we concentrate only on ideologies or cultures of confinement we may miss important patterns of more immediate influence.

It has been suggested that it was at base the drive for uniformity championed by a cadre of 'experts', and enabled by an increasingly confident and bureaucratically capable Home Office, which led to the legislation of 1877. Local authorities, by then accustomed to the erosion of an older constitutional balance which social and technological change had rendered unsustainable, eventually succumbed, tempted by perceived economic advantages. Yet the positivism which sought to impose this uniformity, which elevated rule over discretion and certainty over flexibility, ultimately sought to achieve the unattainable. This survey has shown that the nineteenth-century gaol was a site of complex, sometimes contested, human interactions. On this proposition, if on nothing else, Henry Westlake and Mary Ann Awberry might have found themselves in agreement.

Notes

Abbreviations used in the notes

CarmJ   *The Carmarthen Journal*
CRO   Carmarthen Record Office
FR   *Felon's Register*
GJ   *Gaoler's Journal*
QS   Quarter Sessions

Full references to official publications are given in the Bibliography.

Notes to Introduction

[1] David Davies (Dai'r Cantwr) was transported from Carmarthen for his part in the Rebecca Riots. William Spurrell's didactic note on his verse deserves quotation. 'When in gaol under sentence he wrote a "Lament" of which the first verse is given here, as a specimen of the concatenation of sounds of which the Welsh language is capable. Let the reader observe the complicated alliteration and rhyme, to which attention is called below in Italics.

"Drych i fyd wyf i fod:	*f, f, f*
Collais glod all'swn gael.	*ll s g l, ll s g l*
Tost yw'r nod – dyrnod wael –	*r n d, r n d, fod, glod, nod, dyrnod*
I'w gafael ddaeth â mi.	*gael, wael, gafael*
Yn fy i'enctyd drygfyd ddaeth:	*i'enctyd, drygfyd*
Yn lle rhyddid, caethfyd maith	*rhyddid, caethfyd*
Chwanegwyd er fy ngofid.	*chwanegwyd, gofid, alltud*
Alltud wyf ar ddechreu'm taith.	*ddaeth, maeth, taith*
Ca'm danfon o fy ngwlad –	*d n f, f ng d*
Ty fy nhad, er codiad tirion,	*ngwlad, nhad, codiad*
I blyth y duon gôr –	*tirion, duon, gron*
Dros y môr, o'm goror gron.	*g r, g r, gôr, môr, goror*
O'r fath ddryghin i mi ddaeth!	*th dd, dd th*
Alltud hir – gyr hyn fi'n gaeth	*h r g, r h g*
Dros ugain o flynyddo'dd.	*flynyddo 'dd, modd*
Tost yw'r modd, cystudd maith."	*st m dd, st dd m, daeth, gaeth, maith*

'Notwithstanding the intricacies of the metre, the lines will bear close translation without violence to the sense, which is not in them sacrificed to a mere re-echoing of vowels and consonants;–

"I am to be a spectacle to the world
I have lost the reputation I might have obtained.
Severe is the stroke – the sad buffet –
To the reach of which I am brought.
In my youth adversity came:
Instead of liberty, long captivity
Has added to my grief.
I am an exile at the beginning of my course.
I shall be sent from my country –
From my father's house, notwithstanding tender bringing-up,
To the midst of the black hordes –
Over the sea, from my fair confines.
Oh what distress (literally bad weather) has overtaken me!
Long banishment – this will drive me bound
For twenty years.
Hard is the measure, long affliction."'

W. Spurrell, *Carmarthen and its Neighbourhood* (2nd edn, Carmarthen, 1879), pp. 150–1. Thomas Evans (Thomas Glyncothi) is also reputed to have written his Welsh Dictionary of 1817 in Carmarthen gaol.

2   The first edition of Henry Mayhew's *London Labour and the London Poor* was published in 1851 and the three-volume edition in 1861. Mayhew and John Binney's *The Criminal Prisons of London* was published in 1862.

3   Charles Dickens's *Great Expectations* dates from 1861, *The Legacy of Cain* from 1888, Marcus Clarke's *His Natural Life* was finished in 1872, Charles Reade's *It Is Never Too Late To Mend* (informed by the Birmingham Borough Gaol Scandal) in 1856, Tom Taylor's *The Ticket-of-Leave Man* is from 1862, W. P. Frith's *The Race for Wealth* was painted in 1880. For the latter see R. W. Ireland, 'The policeman and the rail: crime and punishment in the paintings of W. P. Frith', *Art Antiquity and Law*, 4 (1997), at 381.

4   The magnetic attraction of the National Archives may play a part in the orientation of study towards serious crime. For the records see C. Emsley, *Crime and Society in England 1750–1900* (3rd edn, Harlow, 1996), pp. 21ff.

5   J. M. Beattie, *Crime and the Courts in England 1660–1800* (Oxford, 1986), Introduction.

6   J. Davies, *A History of Wales* (London, 1994), p. 371.

7   See, for example, the discussion and references in W. D. Hines (ed.), *English Legal History: A Bibliography and Guide to the*

Literature (New York, 1990), pp. 91–5; Emsley, *Crime and Society*, Introduction.

[8] The theoretical understanding of punishment which informs this discussion is elaborated in detail in C. Harding and R. W. Ireland, *Punishment: Rhetoric, Rule and Practice* (London, 1989).

[9] *FR*, nos 919, 1033.

[10] *FR*, no. 1036.

[11] *Prison Inspectors' Sixteenth Report* (1851).

[12] See *GJ* at those dates.

[13] See the cross-examination of Margaret Evans, 20 July 1878, by the defendant Rose Haney: 'No I did not curse you but you called me an old Devil. I did not call you an old bugger. You called me an old thief.' Evans seems to have acted as an interpreter when Haney was confronted by the prosecutrix in this case, Elizabeth Jones, who could not understand English. *QS* Box 26.

[14] He also used the name Charles MacKintosh; *FR*, no. 126.

[15] S. F. C. Milsom, *Historical Foundations of the Common Law* (1st edn, London, 1969), p. xiv.

[16] I speak here with some personal experience, see P. Carlen, *British Journal of Criminology*, 26 (1986), 417–18. We were very young in those days.

[17] Though 'Whiggist' analysis more generally still has an influence, see the exposure of, and engagement with, 'presentist' analysis in S. Kilcommins, 'Impressment and its genealogical claims in respect of Community Service Orders in England and Wales', *Irish Jurist*, 34 (1999), 223–55. See also, for an engagement with 'revisionist' theory, the same author's 'Context and contingency in the historical penal process: the revision of revisionism using the Twelve Judges' Notebooks as one tool of analysis', *Holdsworth Law Review*, 19 (1998), 1–54.

[18] For these schools, see Rawlings in Hines (ed.), *English Legal History*, pp. 62ff.

[19] The starting point for an analysis of class bias in the legal system remains the classic essay by Douglas Hay, 'Property, authority and the criminal law', in D. Hay, P. Linebaugh, J. G. Rule, E. P. Thompson and C. Winslow, *Albion's Fatal Tree* (London, 1975), pp. 17–63. The debate thereby engendered and the literature it produced is discussed by Rawlings in Hines (ed.), *English Legal History*, pp. 67ff.

[20] For a discussion, see D. Garland, *Punishment and Modern Society* (Oxford, 1990), ch. 4.

[21] 'The law of England from the earliest times has recognized three classes of persons at the least, as liable to imprisonment, the debtor,

the accused criminal and the convict', anon., 'Prisons and penitentiaries', in *The Quarterly Review* 30 (London, 1824), 404–40 at
p. 405.

22 See R. W. Ireland, 'Theory and practice within the medieval English
prison', *American Journal of Legal History* 31 (1987), 56–67.

23 M. Foucault, *Discipline and Punish: The Birth of the Prison* (originally published as *Surveiller et Punir: Naissance de la prison* in
1975), (London, 1979 edn, A. Sheridan trans.), p. 82.

24 Garland, *Punishment and Modern Society*, p. 152.

25 Ibid., ch. 7.

26 W. I. Miller, *The Anatomy of Disgust* (Cambridge, Mass., 1997),
p. 170. Note also the comment of Robert Wiener, *Journal of British
Studies* 26 (1987), 87 n. 6: 'Michel Foucault ... for all his irritating
imprecision and overreaching raised profound questions.'

27 See G. Burchell, C. Gordon and P. Miller (eds), *The Foucault Effect:
Studies in Governmentality* (Chicago, 1991), p. 81.

28 L. Zedner, *Women, Crime and Custody in Victorian England*
(Oxford, 1991), *passim*: the quotation is from p. 97. See also
M. DeLacy, *Prison Reform in Lancashire 1700–1850* (Manchester,
1986), *passim*. This author concludes her analysis by observing, in
respect of the contending historiographical 'schools', 'The radical
case may assume an overly conspiratorial élite, but the traditional
account is naïve in assuming a universal benevolence' (p. 227).

29 M. Ignatieff, 'State, civil society and total institutions: a critique of
recent social histories of punishment', in D. Sugarman (ed.),
Legality, Ideology and the State (London, 1983), p. 191.

30 Compare the analysis of Norbert Elias, *The Society of Individuals*
(London, 1991 edn).

31 See R. W. Ireland, 'Howard and the paparazzi: painting penal
reform in the eighteenth century', *Art Antiquity and Law*, 4 (1999),
55.

32 Beattie, *Crime and the Courts*, p. 568.

33 Ibid., ch. 10.

34 See Harding and Ireland, *Punishment*, ch. 10.

35 See D. McCloskey, '1780–1860: a survey', in R. Floud and
D. McCloskey (eds), *The Economic History of Britain since 1700*
(Cambridge, 2nd edn, 1994), at p. 243; but see also P. Lindert,
'Unequal living standards', ibid., p. 357.

36 V. Gattrell, *The Hanging Tree: Execution and the English People
1770–1868* (Oxford, 1994), p. 25. Note too, in relation to the
earlier discussion as to the combination of wider social forces and
particular circumstances, the analysis in P. Handler, 'Forging the
agenda: the 1819 Select Committee on the Criminal Laws revisited',
Journal of Legal History, 25 (2004), 249–68.

[37] The opposite contention, namely that the factory was the handmaid to the prison, primarily a disciplinary rather than a technological innovation, though important, is not one which can be investigated here. See the discussion in B. Godfrey, 'Factory discipline and "theft": the impact of the factory on workplace appropriation in mid- to late nineteenth-century Yorkshire', *British Journal of Criminology*, 39 (1999), 56–71.

[38] The expressions are from David Pye, quoted in A. Briggs, *Victorian Things* (London, 1990), p. 23.

[39] Quoted in M. Freeman, *Railways and the Victorian Imagination* (New Haven, 1999), p. 66.

[40] For an analysis of the development of the factory see M. Berg, 'Factories, workshops and industrial organisation', in Floud and McCloskey, *Economic History of Britain*, p. 123.

[41] For discussion of population and of 'urban job pull' see R. Schofield, 'British population change, 1700–1871', and J. Williamson, 'Coping with city growth', both in R. Floud and D. McCloskey (eds), *Economic History of Britain*, pp. 60, 332.

[42] W. Cobbett, *Rural Rides* (1830); see the introduction to the G. Woodcock edition (Harmondsworth, 1985 edn), p. 13.

[43] For the railways and their impact see Freeman, *Railways* (n. 39 above), in particular chapters 1 and 2. The concept of 'relational space' is discussed at p. 78. Freeman (p. 27) regards the canals and turnpikes as not 'revolutionary' developments in transport. Yet whilst the railways were the most comprehensively disruptive of the established mentality the impact of the earlier developments merits attention. Cobbett (*op. cit.*, *supra*, n. 42, pp. 12, 19) hated railways, canals and turnpikes alike, the latter apparently because of their web of connection to London and urban dominance. In Carmarthenshire it is difficult to overestimate the role of the turnpike as disrupting old patterns and old freedoms; it certainly provoked a 'revolutionary' response, see this volume, pp. 61.

[44] Malthus's *An Essay on the Principle of Population* dates from 1798, in response to some of Godwin's radical views: see the Introduction to the edition by D. Winch (Cambridge, 1992). Malthus had read his Howard (ibid., p. 328 n. 8), as indeed had Godwin; see his novel *Caleb Williams* (1794: ed. M. Hindle, Harmondsworth, 1988, p. 188, note).

[45] See, for example, the discussion in Emsley, *Crime and Society*, ch. 4. Note that it is no part of the argument here that crime was a result of urbanization.

[46] Emsley, *Crime and Society*, p. 26. The whole of Emsley's discussion in his chapter 2 repays attention.

47 *First Report of the Commissioners Appointed to Inquire as to the Best Means of Establishing an Efficient Constabulary Force in the Counties of England and Wales* (1839) [169] xix, p. 2.

48 Emsley, *Crime and Society*, p. 36.

49 Beattie, *Crime and the Courts*, p. 463.

50 Ibid., p. 464.

51 S. Roberts, *Order and Dispute* (Harmondsworth, 1979), p. 88. I believe that the last recorded use of another shaming punishment, the ducking stool, was in the small borders town of Leominster in 1809.

52 *Seventh Report of the Criminal Law Commissioners* (1843), p. 112, quoted in L. Radzinowicz and R. Hood, *The Emergence of Penal Policy in Victorian and Edwardian England* (Oxford, 1990), p. 700.

53 Gattrell, *Hanging Tree*, p. 16.

54 *Seventh Report of the Criminal Law Commissioners* (1843), p. 112, quoted in Radzinowicz and Hood, *Emergence of Penal Policy*, p. 700.

55 See also Emsley, *Crime and Society*, pp. 101–3.

56 S. D'Cruze, 'Sex, violence and local courts: working-class respectability in a mid-nineteenth-century town', *British Journal of Criminology*, 39 (1999), 39–55.

57 Note in this context the invocation of the shame community of co-workers in Charles Dickens's *Hard Times*. Slackbridge, the Union representative, proposes on hearing of the allegation of theft against the ostracized non-Union weaver '. . . that this meeting does Resolve: That Stephen Blackpool, weaver, . . . having been already solemnly disowned by the community of Coketown Hands, the same are free from the shame of his misdeeds, and cannot as a class be reproached with his dishonest actions!' (ed. K. Flint, Penguin, Harmondsworth 1995, p. 249)

58 P. Linebaugh, *The London Hanged* (London, 1991), *passim*, esp. ch. 3.

59 Ibid., pp. 74ff.

60 See J. Walvin, *Leisure and Society 1830–1950* (London, 1978), p. 27; R. W. Ireland, '"An increasing mass of heathens in the bosom of a Christian land": the railway and crime in the nineteenth century', *Continuity and Change*, 12 (1997), 68.

61 For the figures see Radzinowicz and Hood, *Emergence of Penal Policy* (Oxford, 1990), p. 468.

62 Ibid., p. 482.

63 For a synopsis of the evidence see the *Report From The Select Committee on Transportation 1837–1838* (in 669), xxii, pp. 310–13.

64 Quoted from the *Paper on Secondary Punishment* by D. D. Heath, appendix 10 to the *Report From The Select Committee on Transportation 1837–1838* (in 518), xix, p. 259.
65 See C. Reade, *It Is Never Too Late To Mend* (1856: London, 1892 edn), p. 43.
66 *CarmJ*, 26 March 1851.
67 For the criticisms see Radzinowicz and Hood, *Emergence of Penal Policy*, pp. 474–85. For contrasting fictional representations compare Wilkie Collins's *A Rogue's Life* (1856) and Marcus Clarke's *His Natural Life* (1874).
68 *FR*, no. 615; see also no. 1081, James Upton 'supposed previously transported'. It is of course possible that the reference is simply to those who received the sentence of transportation but who served their time without going abroad. The juryman's question concerning James Lewis may well be such a case, though his sentence to seven years was only given two years previously, I share the foreman's confusion despite the newspaper's imputation of stupidity (*CarmJ*, 10 January 1851).The fear, of course, whether the offender actually goes beyond the seas or, as is increasingly likely, does not, remains the same.
69 See the entertaining account in R. Osborne, *The Floating Egg* (London, 1998), ch. 8. Arthur Griffiths, writing at the end of the nineteenth century, observed: 'As a shrewd Frenchman has put it, the world is round, and the farther you remove your exile, the nearer at last he reaches the starting-point' (*Secrets of the Prison House* [London, 1894], vol. 1, pp. 4–5).
70 For an example of a notable opponent of trends in prison reform see Thomas Carlyle's essay 'Model Prisons' of 1850, which follows his earlier criticism of the New Poor Law in 'Chartism'. For both see *Selected Writings* (ed. A. Shelston, Harmondsworth, 1971).
71 Dickens in *Hard Times* pursues the theme of the depersonalization of the subject, and of the methodology of social control in a powerful critique. The whole work demands attention from this perspective – the invocation of the mechanical parallel is not merely a modern metaphor. Dickens criticizes too the drive to uniformity and the mechanical, statistical approach to crime and punishment:

> The jail might have been the infirmary, the infirmary might have been the jail, the town-hall might have been either, or both, or anything else, for anything that appeared to the contrary in the graces of their construction. Fact, fact, fact, everywhere in the material aspect of the town; fact, fact, fact everywhere in the immaterial. (Penguin ed. [see n. 57 above], p. 29)

And in the same polemic (p. 30):

> Then, came the experienced chaplain of the jail, with more tabular statements, outdoing all the previous tabular statements, and showing that the

same people would resort to low haunts, hidden from the public eye, where they heard low singing and saw low dancing, and mayhap joined in it; and where A. B., aged twenty-four next birthday, and committed for eighteen months' solitary, had himself said (not that he had ever shown himself particularly worthy of belief) his ruin began, as he was perfectly sure and confident that otherwise he would have been a tip-top moral specimen.

Clay of Preston took the reference to be to him (ibid., note 7), though I think that he was merely emblematic of what Dickens perceived as a wider constituency.

72 See in this respect the important influence of Norbert Elias in the area of the internalization of constraint, in particular the relationship between '*homo clausus*' and solitary confinement as discussed in H. Franke, 'The rise and decline of solitary confinement: socio-historical explanations of long-term penal changes', *British Journal of Criminology*, 32 (1992), 125–43 at 136–7, and the discussion by B. Vaughan, 'The civilizing process and the Janus-face of modern punishment', *Theoretical Criminology*, 4 (2000), 71–91.

73 See the *First Report of the Commissioners on the Constabulary* (1839), pp. 15, 13.

74 Ibid., pp. 66–7.

75 Memorandum of 25 December 1845, reproduced in H. J. Hanham, *The Nineteenth-Century Constitution: Documents and Commentary* (London, 1969), p. 305.

76 John Austin's *The Province of Jurisprudence Determined* was published in 1832, working from Benthamite ideas. Henry Maine's *Ancient Law* was published in 1861. For more subtle evaluations of the influence, doctrines and limitations of these thinkers see M. Lobban, *The Common Law and English Jurisprudence 1760–1850* (Oxford, 1991); R. Cocks, *Sir Henry Maine: A Study in Victorian Jurisprudence* (Cambridge, 1988).

77 See chapter 1 in this volume.

78 For the origins of borough gaols see Harding et al., *Imprisonment*, pp. 19–20.

79 W. J. Forsythe, *A System of Discipline* (Exeter, 1983), pp. 51–2.

80 K. Wrightson 'Two concepts of order: justices, constables and jurymen in seventeenth-century England', in J. Brewer and J. Styles (eds), *An Ungovernable People: The English and their Laws in the 17th and 18th Centuries* (London, 1979), p. 24. The same author observes elsewhere, in relation to small communities in the period he discusses: 'What really mattered at this level was the maintenance of specific, local, personal relationships. In that task the attempt to enforce conformity to an impersonal standard of legally defined order could be thoroughly counter productive.'(*English Society 1580–1680* (London, 1982), p. 159.)

81 P. King, *Crime, Justice and Discretion in England 1740–1820* (Oxford, 2000).

82 M. Loughlin, *Legality and Locality: The Role of Law in Central–Local Government Relations* (Oxford, 1996), p. 39.

83 Ibid.

84 K. Hoppen, *The Mid-Victorian Generation* (Oxford, 1998), p. 110.

85 M. Garrett, 'The end of the Napoleonic Wars saw a rise in the crime rate which peaked in the 1830s; was the Poor Law Amendment Act of 1834 a penal measure in disguise?' (unpublished M.Phil. thesis, University of Wales Aberystwyth, 1999), 114ff.

86 Y. Williams, 'An examination of some of the Lunacy Laws of the eighteenth and nineteenth centuries' (unpublished M.Phil. thesis, University of Wales Aberystwyth, 2001).

87 Mr Podsnap in Charles Dickens's *Our Mutual Friend* (1864–5), quoted in Hoppen, *Mid-Victorian Generation* p. 104.

88 Hoppen, *Mid-Victorian Generation*, p. 106.

89 Ibid., p. 114.

90 Loughlin, *Legality and Locality*, p. 43.

91 R. Colley, 'The clown's mistress: income tax evasion in mid-Victorian Britain' (unpublished Ph.D. thesis, University of Wales Aberystwyth, 1998). See also the same author's 'The Arabian bird: a study of income tax evasion in mid-Victorian Britain', *British Tax Review* (2001), 207.

92 S. McConville, *English Local Prisons 1860–1900: Next Only to Death* (London, 1995), ch. 5.

93 See H. Hanham, *The Nineteenth-Century Constitution*, p. 314ff.

94 Hoppen, *Mid-Victorian Generation*, pp. 111–12.

95 See for discussion Garland, *Punishment in Modern Society*, pp. 148–9.

96 Quoted in J. E. Thomas, *The English Prison Officer since 1850* (London, 1972), p. 48.

97 See M. Wiener, *Reconstructing the Criminal* (Cambridge, 1990), especially chs 6 and 7.

98 S. and B. Webb, *English Prisons under Local Government* (London, 1922), p. 204. The phrase has since then become widely adopted, cf. McConville, *English Local Prisons*, p. 9.

99 For 'railway time', see J. Simmons, *The Victorian Railway* (London, 1991), pp. 345–7. For football, note the foundation of the Football Association and the debate about rules in 1863 (the same year as the Carnarvon Committee). Note also the role of the Royal Engineers in the process. See F. Hodgson, *Only The Goalkeeper to Beat* (Basingstoke, 1999), pp. 30ff.

100 R. W. Ireland, 'The felon and the angel copier: criminal identity and

the promise of photography in Victorian England and Wales', in L. Knafla (ed.), *Policing and War in Europe* (Westport, 2002), p. 53.

[101] For Bentham's plan for this device, published in 1830, see Ignatieff, *Just Measure of Pain*, p. 75. The satirical flirtation with the idea of mechanical policemen and magistrates is also particularly interesting in this context; see Charles Dickens's 'The Automaton Police' of 1837, reprinted in P. Haining (ed.), *Hunted Down: The Detective Stories of Charles Dickens* (London, 1996), p. 56. See, on the same theme (though rather later in date), the cartoons reproduced in *Mr Punch in Wig and Gown* (London, n.d.), pp. 113, 175. Note too in this respect Babbage's pioneering work on the 'Difference Engine' in the 1830s, the calculator being designed to transcend human fallibility in mathematics. For mechanization of the artistic process, see M. Budd, *The Sculpture Machine* (New York, 1997), p. 1. A spectacularly obscene suggestion for the application of machinery is considered in an anonymous nineteenth-century manuscript at CRO D/Ll/2661.

[102] Hoppen, *Mid-Victorian Generation*, p. 98.

[103] Sir Walter Crofton, 'The Irish system of prison discipline', in *Transactions of the National Congress on Penitentiary and Reformatory Discipline*, ed. E. C. Wines (Albany, 1871), p. 71.

[104] This volume, p. 139, and see R. W. Ireland, 'Eugene Buckley and the diagnosis of insanity in the early Victorian prison', *Llafur*, 6 (1993), 5.

[105] For Awberry and this question, see this volume, pp. 171. For Phillips, see Ireland, 'The felon and the angel copier', p. 54.

[106] Compare D. Garland, *The Culture of Control* (Oxford, 2001), p. 25: 'It needs to be remembered that the emergence of structural phenomena such as rationalities, mentalities, and strategies is, in the first place, the outcome of problem-solving activity on the part of situated actors and agencies. There is no magical, automatic process of functional adjustment and system adaptation that exists apart from this. Analyses that rely on such notions omit the real human stuff of disposition, choice and action – the stuff of which society and history are actually made.'

[107] A prosecution for running an unlicensed lodging house in Carmarthenshire revealed twenty-one people sleeping in a single room: *CarmJ*, 9 April 1851.

[108] D. J. V. Jones, *Crime in Nineteenth-Century Wales* (Cardiff, 1992).

[109] K. O. Morgan, 'Divided we stand', *History Today*, 49/5 (1999), 24–6 at 25.

[110] *The Times*, 14 September 1866, quoted in Hoppen, *Mid-Victorian Generation*, p. 516.

111 See R. W. Ireland, '"A Second Ireland?" Crime and popular culture in nineteenth-century Wales', in R. McMahon (ed.), *Crime, Law and Popular Culture in Europe since 1500* (Cullompton, 2007).

112 J. Davies, *A History of Wales*, p. 397.

113 FR, nos 333 (David Davies, 1850), 378 (James Watkins, 1851), 1130 (Thomas Thomas, 1866), 1133 (Thomas Davies, 1865 [clearly there is something odd in the record-keeping here: the entries are supposed to be recorded chronologically]) and 1357 (Daniel Griffiths, 1870). But note the case of the soldier convicted of this offence (see this volume, p. 278, n. 151), who does not appear in the register.

114 *Surgeon's Report*, July 1850, QS Box 6. His statement from July 1858 in the same box describes the same condition occurring 'as is generally the case during the summer months'.

115 This volume, pp. 135, 160.

116 See *Report of the Commissioners appointed to inquire into the Condition and Treatment of the Prisoners confined in Birmingham Borough Prison*, 1854 [1809], xxxi.1. Note that Thomas, *English Prison Officer*, praises the inspector for his work in this case, p. 18. I think that Charles Dickens in his 'prison novel', *Little Dorrit* (published in 1857, though set thirty years earlier), hints at a general point satirically when discussing segregation in the Marshalsea: 'the smugglers habitually consorted with the debtors (who received them with open arms), except at certain constitutional moments when somebody came from some Office, to go through some form of over-looking something, which neither he nor anybody else knew anything about' (ed. S. Wall and H. Small, Harmondsworth, 1998, p. 68).

117 McConville, *English Local Prisons*, pp. 104–5: 'He [Carnarvon] treated his inquiry like a theatrical production: he wrote the script, designed the sets, chose the players and directed their delivery and ... his was the only show in town.'

118 Forsythe, *System of Discipline*, p. 64: 'By 1850 the nature of the record was wholly different. Where previously accounts of problems or incidents were detailed and often discursive, after 1850 they were short and brusque ... It was as though an impersonal, efficient, severe penal system had eroded and eliminated the idiosyncratic flexibility of individual members of staff whose thoughts and endeavours were so fully revealed in earlier records.'

119 GJ, 20 December 1845. In all quotations from this and other manu-script sources original spelling, grammar and punctuation have been maintained.

120 The surgeon's book was apparently kept at his home. By contrast

the governor diligently made returns under the 1839 Prison Act (2 and 3 Vict., ch. 56, section 10) long after the need to do so was removed by statute. The return for 1869 is endorsed with a note that records the redundancy of the form, citing 21 and 22 Vict., ch. 56 (clearly a slip, as the 1858 Act is ch. 67): QS Box 11.

[121] R. Davies, *Secret Sins: Sex, Violence and Society in Carmarthenshire 1870–1920* (Cardiff, 1996), p. 239.

Notes to Chapter 1

[1] Statute of Rhuddlan (1284) 12 Edward I, Stat. 27 Hen.VIII (1536).

[2] Quoted in G. Parry, *A Guide to the Records of Great Sessions in Wales* (Aberystwyth, 1995), p. xxxvi.

[3] Ibid., pp. xxxvii and xxxviii. The last sitting of the Great Sessions in Carmarthenshire was under Goulburn J in September 1830: see W. Spurrell, *Carmarthen and its Neighbourhood* (2nd edn, Carmarthen, 1879), p. 144.

[4] It is interesting to note that modern criminologists typically address themselves to questions of why the criminal law is *not* involved rather than why it is – an assumption of normativity, which is in itself not necessarily a 'natural' or an 'acultural' position.

[5] So Thomas Phillips in his response to the Blue Books sought to exclude the 'immigrant' communities of south-east Wales from the idealized, more law-abiding areas of 'Wales Proper'; see the discussion by P. O'Leary, *Immigration and Integration: The Irish in Wales 1798–1922* (Cardiff, 2000), p. 165ff. It might be argued that the concentration upon Carmarthenshire in the discussion in this volume feeds the same myth. It is no part of my argument, however, that the information considered here in any way 'properly', or in many of its features necessarily 'uniquely' Welsh. It is the complexity of modelling the process, rather than its chauvinistic simplification, which is intended to be the point of the account found here.

[6] 1841 census figure.

[7] For the figures see the census analyses in Dot Jones, *Statistical Evidence Relating to the Welsh Language 1801–1911* (Cardiff, 1998), pp. 18, 25–6.

[8] Ibid., p. 223.

[9] R. Davies, 'Language and community', in G. Jenkins (ed.), *Language and Community in the Nineteenth Century* (Cardiff, 1998), p. 102. The *Landsker* is the linguistic dividing line to be found in Pembrokeshire. Davies's analysis explores important issues of social class, employment and temporal change on the language. See also the same author's *Secret Sins* (Cardiff, 1996), ch. 1.

[10] Dot Jones, *Statistical Evidence Relating to the Welsh Language 1801–1911* (Cardiff, 1998), pp. 212, 223.

[11] For a masterly overview of nineteenth-century Welsh history see Davies, *History*, chs 7 and 8.

[12] H. Richard, *Letters on the Social and Political Condition of Wales*, pp. 22–3, as quoted in C. Turner, 'The Nonconformist response', in T. Herbert and G. E. Jones (eds), *People and Protest: Wales 1815–1880* (Cardiff, 1988), p. 84.

[13] See *Report of the Commissioners of Inquiry for South Wales* (1844), p. 103 (evidence of Revd Eleazar Evans of Llangranog).

[14] See J. Davies, *History*, pp. 419ff.; M. Ellis Jones, 'The Confusion of Babel', in G. Jenkins (ed.), *The Welsh Language and its Social Domains 1801–1911* (Cardiff, 2000), pp. 609–10. Tithe riots continued through the 1880s and 1890s, see D. J. V. Jones, *Crime in Nineteenth-Century Wales* (Cardiff, 1992), p. 98.

[15] For the settlement of a brawl through the chapel, the parties being 'wise enough to keep clear of the court of law', see D. J. Williams, *The Old Farmhouse*, trans. W. Williams (Carmarthen, 1987 edn), pp. 84–5.

[16] Spurrell, *Carmarthen*, pp. 144–5.

[17] *Report of The Commissioners on Municipal Corporations* (1835), vol. 3, p. 213.

[18] For the history of the formation and operation of the force see P. Molloy, *A Shilling for Carmarthen* (Llandysul, 1991).

[19] *First Report of the Commissioners on the Constabulary* (1839), p. 42.

[20] Ibid., p. 45.

[21] Ibid., p. 44.

[22] The literature is considerable, but a classic treatment is E. P. Thompson, 'Rough Music', in his *Customs in Common* (London, 1991), pp. 467–538. The last example discussed by William Andrews in his suggestively titled *Bygone Punishments* (London, 1899, at p. 305) comes from north Wales in 1887.

[23] See M. Ingram, 'Juridical folklore in England illustrated by Rough Music', in C. Brooks and M. Lobban (eds), *Communities and Courts in Britain 1150–1900* (London, 1997), ch. 5.

[24] D. Jones, *Crime*, p. 19.

[25] R. Jones, 'Popular culture, policing and the disappearance of the Ceffyl Pren in Cardiganshire c.1837–1850', *Ceredigion*, 11 (1998), 19–39 at 27.

[26] Ibid. p. 30. For a conviction in Pembrokeshire, before the assize, see *Seren Gomer* (1840), p. 123. For another conviction before the same court see *Seren Gomer* (1856), p. 187, which includes a description of the carrying of the victim, an elderly but inconstant husband.

27 For the Riots see D. Jones, *Rebecca's Children* (Oxford, 1989); D. Jones, 'Rebecca, crime and policing: a turning point in nineteenth-century attitudes', (1990) *Transactions of the Honourable Society of Cymmrodorion* (1990), 99–115; P. Molloy, *And They Blessed Rebecca* (Llandysul,1983); D. Williams, *The Rebecca Riots* (Cardiff, 1955); D. Howell, 'The Rebecca Riots', in Herbert and Jones, *People and Protest.*

28 'And they blessed Rebekah, and said unto her, Thou art our sister, be thou the mother of thousands of millions, and let thy seed possess the gates of those which hate them' (Genesis 24: 60). For another fascinating use of scriptural quotations, see the petition from Llandevilog, *Report of the Commissioners of Inquiry for South Wales* (1844), p. 112.

29 See Spurrell, *Carmarthen*, p. 149, for the attack. For the apathy see M. Garrett, 'Was the Poor Law Amendment Act of 1834 a penal measure in disguise?' (unpublished M.Phil. thesis, University of Wales, 1999).

30 Quoted in Jones, 'Popular culture', 21.

31 Thompson, *Customs in Common*, p. 522. In its assessment of the time-span of the proceedings, and also perhaps of the universality of a popular voice, the sentiment may be overstated.

32 Quoted in Jones, 'Rebecca, crime and policing', 105. For the Irish analogy see R. W. Ireland, '"A second Ireland"? Crime and popular culture in nineteenth-century Wales', in R. McMahon (ed.), *Crime, Law and Popular Culture in Europe since 1500* (Cullompton, 2006).

33 For the police, see S. Palmer, *Police and Protest in England and Ireland 1780–1850* (Cambridge, 1988).

34 Spurrell, *Carmarthen*, p. 150.

35 Compare, for example, R. Storch, "The plague of blue locusts: police reforms and popular resistance in northern England 1850–80', *Journal of Social History* (1976), 481.

36 D. Edwards, *Reminiscences* (Shrewsbury, 1914), p. 8.

37 Quoted in G. Williams, 'The disenchantment of the world: innovation, crisis and change in Cardiganshire c.1880–1910', *Ceredigion*, 9 (1983), 303–21 at 313. The statement is from 1894. See also the reaction of the borough of Kidwelly to the encroachment on its traditional independence in respect of policing, this volume, p. 249, n. 27.

38 This volume, pp. 72–3, and see R. Wiener, *Journal of British Studies*, 26 (1987), 83–96 at 88.

39 For an extended analysis of the debates concerning language and the law at this period see M. Ellis Jones, 'The confusion of Babel?', p. 587.

40 Quoted in Herbert and Jones, *People and Protest*, pp. 133–4.
41 *Report of the Commissioners of Inquiry for South Wales* (1844), p. 32.
42 Ibid., p. 33.
43 Ibid., p. 34.
44 For 'bundling' see, for example, T. Gwyn Jones, *Welsh Folklore and Custom* (London, 1930), pp. 187–8.
45 *Report of Commissioners of Inquiry for South Wales* (1844), p. 30.
46 See 4 and 5 Will. IV, ch. 76, sections 69, 71, 72. For the link with infanticide see the comments made to Thomas Campbell Foster, *The Times*, 3 July 1843, quoted in Molloy, *And They Blessed Rebecca*, pp. 146–8. Not everyone agreed, of course; see the comments, for example, of the Revd R. B. Jones of Narberth, *Report of the Commissioners on South Wales*, p. 103.
47 See 7 and 8 Vict., ch. 101. For a much fuller analysis of the new Poor Law in Wales, see D. J. V. Jones, *Rebecca's Children: A Study of Rural Society, Crime and Protest* (Oxford, 1989), ch. 3.
48 *Report of the Commissioners for South Wales*, p. 36.
49 For a summary of the events, see J. Davies, *History*, pp. 390ff. The events are known as 'Brad y Llyfrau Gleisiau', 'The Treachery of the Blue Books'.
50 *Reports of the Commissioners on the State of Education in Wales* (1847), pp. 56–7.
51 Ibid., p. 90.
52 T. Phillips, *Wales: The Language, Social Condition, Moral Character and Religious Opinions of the People, Considered in their Relation to Education* (London, 1849), especially ch. IV, and see also *Seren Gomer*, 1853, pp. 83ff.
53 *Seren Gomer*, 1849, p. 256, and cf. 1850, pp. 29 and 63, which latter asserts infanticide to be common in England.
54 *Seren Gomer*, 1848, pp. 45–7.
55 See, for example, K. Williams, *Textbook on Criminology* (Oxford, 5th edn, 2004), ch. 4.
56 To this extent my analysis differs in emphasis from the analysis of Ellis Jones ('Confusion of Babel', p. 595), who argues that 'the legal system was of central importance to the lower orders'. Whilst not, of course, denying the importance of law (even when it is not invoked, the threat of the law is a potent backdrop to other settlement techniques), it remains – here I speak of the criminal law – one of a range of possible responses, the invocation of which depends upon a variety of strategic decisions.
57 D. Parry-Jones, *Welsh Country Upbringing* (London, 2nd edn, 1949), p. 98. For a similar idea of divine retribution see the

gravestone of Eleanor Williams of the parish of Llangyfelach which contains the lines: 'With marks upon her person she was found dead in a well by Llwyngenno farmhouse, then in the occupation of Thomas Thomas, on the morning of Sunday, December 9th 1832. Although the savage murderer may escape for a season the detection of Man, yet doubtless God hath left his mark upon him forever. VENGEANCE IS MINE SETH [*sic*] THE LORD I WILL REPAY.' For the murder, see the *Cambrian*, 29 December 1832.

58 R. W. Ireland, 'Perhaps my mother murdered me', in C. Brooks and M. Lobban (eds), *Communities and Courts in Britain 1150–1900* (London, 1997), pp. 240 ff.

59 D. Parry-Jones, *Welsh Country Upbringing* (London, 2nd edn, 1949), p. 134.

60 P. King, *Crime, Justice and Discretion in England 1740–1820* (Oxford, 2000), p. 26. Despite its different temporal and geographical focus the whole of King's chapter 2 deserves attention in this context.

61 See *CarmJ*, 13 August 1851.

62 *CarmJ*, 26 December 1851, 31 December 1852. The practice remained resistant to suppression; see *CarmJ*, 1 January 1869.

63 *CarmJ*, 26 July 1851.

64 Spurrell, *Carmarthen*, p. 156.

65 E. P. Thompson, *Customs in Common* (London, 1993), pp. 490–1. For an interesting late eighteenth-century English case in which the victim of 'rough music' affected not to know the significance of the event, see J. Coates, *The Diary of a Country Schoolmaster* (Barnard Castle, 1980 edn), pp. 68–9. I am grateful to Diane Watt for this reference.

66 *CarmJ*, precise date mislaid!

67 *CarmJ*, 5 August 1853. See also the prosecution of Thomas Williams and three others reported in *CarmJ*, 3 December 1852.

68 *The Welshman*, 4 April 1851; for the assize, see *CarmJ*, 21 March 1851.

69 *The Welshman*, 4 April 1851.

70 See Ireland, 'A second Ireland', for a discussion.

71 See G. Hughes (ed.), *A Llanelli Chronicle* (Llanelli, 1984), pp. 47–9.

72 See R. W. Ireland, 'Putting oneself on whose country?', in T. G. Watkin (ed.), *Legal Wales: Its Past, Its Future* (Cardiff, 2001); 'Perhaps my mother'.

73 See Ireland; 'Perhaps my mother', p. 237.

74 *CarmJ*, 8 July 1853. Compare the case of Esther Anthony, *CarmJ*, 7 March 1851.

75 *CarmJ*, 8 July 1853.

[76] 'I wish the English counties could boast of the same minimum of crime as you have in Wales', *per* Pigott B at Carmarthenshire Assizes, *CarmJ*, 20 July 1866. And see D. J. V. Jones, *Crime in Nineteenth-Century Wales*, pp. 1–2.

[77] So, for example, the 1851 census shows that Charles Hill, a borough grand juryman and Mary Ann Thomas, a notorious prostitute, both lived in Lammas Street.

[78] On the question of language, see Ellis Jones, 'Confusion of Babel?', pp. 606ff. The author concludes (p. 608): 'The most important factor in determining the language used in the proceedings of the Quarter and Petty Sessions was the linguistic ability of the magistrates and their attitude towards the native language.' My impression is that at least the vast majority of petty sessions (and all quarter sessions) in Carmarthenshire at this time were conducted in, and not merely recorded in, English.

[79] In this the Carmarthenshire bench again seems to have been following a pattern which may have been typical of an older notion of the role of the Justice of the Peace. See the analysis in G. Morgan and P. Rushton, 'The magistrate, the community and the maintenance of an orderly society in eighteenth-century England', *Historical Research*, 76 (2003), 54.

[80] *CarmJ*, 11 July 1851.

[81] Notable too in this context is the fact that on occasion a JP might intervene as an uninvited witness in a case before him, see the comments of Dr Lewis from the bench in the cases of Coulson Smith, *CarmJ*, 2 March 1866 and David Jones, *CarmJ*, 30 March 1866.

[82] *CarmJ*, 16 January 1852. Note too that intervention could be aimed at dissuading a prosecution from being brought. After a domestic assault it is recorded that 'It is thought that the old woman will be induced by her daughter not to appear against Davis', *CarmJ*, 27 May 1853.

[83] *CarmJ*, 8 August 1851. Such a sentiment is not unique. In a case of stone-throwing by a gang of boys twenty years later no conviction was entered by the court 'solely on the condition that the boys received a good flogging at home' (*The Welshman*, 23 June 1871).

[84] *CarmJ*, 5 September 1851.

[85] See R. W. Ireland, 'An increasing mass of heathens', *Continuity and Change*, 12 (1997), p. 64, and the cases discussed there. Questions of law could lead to colourful disputes amongst the local bench. In a licensing case the angry mayor declared that 'he was going to read five hundred pages that very night before he went to bed, in order to make himself master of a case' (*CarmJ*, 14 March 1851). Not long

afterwards Capt. Phillips stormed out of court in an argument over the construction of a statute (*CarmJ*, 6 June 1851).

[86] Ireland, 'An increasing mass of heathens', pp. 59–60.

[87] See, for example, the comments on the behaviour of PC Buckley, *CarmJ*, 26 December 1851, 2 January 1852.

[88] See Ireland, 'Putting oneself on whose country?', p. 83.

[89] For the concept of the 'total institution' see E. Goffmann, *Asylums* (New York, 1961). I do not suggest that all the characteristics discussed by Goffmann are apparent within institutions at the early stage of their development.

[90] *The Times*, 19 August 1843, quoted in Herbert and Jones, *People and Protest*, p. 129.

[91] See J. and V. Lodwick, *The Story of Carmarthen* (Carmarthen, 1994), p. 196.

[92] Ibid., pp. 94–5.

[93] Ibid., pp. 191–2.

[94] Ibid., p. 146; Spurrell, *Carmarthen*, p. 149.

[95] Although the Carmarthenshire evidence does not exist to consider the particular locality, note too the general link between assisted emigration, both under and outside the 1834 Poor Law provisions, which might on occasions be a way of ridding a locality of trouble-makers, perhaps under threat of prosecution. See on this G. Howells, '"On account of their disreputable characters": parish-assisted emigration from rural England', *History*, 88 (2003), 587, though this analysis suggests that a more positive role for such emigration was the norm.

[96] *The Welshman*, 19 March 1847.

[97] *GJ*, 6 January 1846.

[98] *GJ*, 16 September 1846. The same source shows her to have been recommitted by 6 October of the same year.

[99] *GJ* at that date. If Westlake is willing to trust the magistrates he would apparently trust few others. On the two next days first a policeman (twice) and then Capt. Scott himself, the chief constable, were both sent away when they came to make inquiries about some vagrants from Llansawel.

[100] This volume, p. 182.

[101] Or even the inmate's own clothes, see CRO *QS* Box 10. Convictions in *QS* Box 18 include examples of failing to go to the 'proper ward' in the workhouse, and absconding from it. The meaning of work-house offences, and more generally the relationship between the workhouse and the gaol in response to vagrancy are matters consid-ered in D. J. V. Jones, '"A dead loss to the community": the criminal vagrant in mid-nineteenth-century Wales', *Welsh History Review*, 8 (1977), 312–43.

102   *GJ* for that date.

103   *GJ*, 5 March 1846.

104   *GJ*, 10 June 1846. And note the transfer of Frederic Hammond, 'unwell with venereal' (*FR*, no. 995). Hammond's crime seems to have been motivated by desperation, he having eaten some bread belonging to another and requesting that the police be sent for: *QS* Box 9.

105   R.W. Ireland, 'Confinement with hard labour: motherhood and penal practice in a Victorian gaol', *Welsh History Review*, 18 (1997), 621ff. (*infra*, p. 181).

106   *FR*, no. 607.

107   In 1840 the maximum sum was 5s., the amount depending on the distance to the prisoner's home. In 1842 it was declared to be confined to those who lived outside the town (*Prison Inspectors' Fifth* [1840] and *Seventh* [1842] *Reports*).

108   *GJ*, 14 September 1846. *FR*, records his last residence as Llanegwad, Carmarthenshire.

109   *GJ*, 30 October 1845.

110   *GJ*, December 1845. In 1864 Governor Stephens sent money to await James Dunn's arrival at Swansea following his release (*FR*, no. 989).

111   *GJ* at that date.

112   Not only money might be brought by prisoners to the gaol. John Williams arrived with a box of tools and seven keys (*GJ*, 17 July 1846).

113   *GJ*, 3 February 1846, and note also the order on the same day stopping county pay to two inmates committed for contempt. Payment to traders out of Wilson's funds was ordered by Treasury Chambers: *GJ*, 18 April 1846.

114   *GJ*, 25 June 1846.

115   See the reference to Thomas Phillips, *GJ*, 26 March 1847.

116   See the examples in *QS* Box 8.

117   Ireland, 'Increasing mass of heathens', 59–60.

118   See, for examples, *QS* Boxes 10, 11, 16, 18.

119   See 8 and 9 Vict., ch. 126, section 2 for the provisions. For the Carmarthenshire response see Y. Williams, 'An examination of some of the Lunacy Laws of the eighteenth and nineteenth centuries' (unpublished M.Phil. thesis, University of Wales, 2001).

120   *Prison Inspectors' Third Report* (1837–8).

121   For examples, see the Parish Lunatic Returns for 1863 in *QS* Box 8.

122   J. Lodwick and V. Lodwick, *The Story of Carmarthen* (Carmarthen, 1994), p. 178.

123   *CarmJ*, 4 March 1853.

124   Lodwick and Lodwick, *Carmarthen*, p. 179.

Notes for Chapter 2

1   For the practice, see C. Harding et al., *Imprisonment in England and Wales: A Concise History* (Beckenham, 1985), p. 21.

2   R. Evans, *The Fabrication of Virtue: English Prison Architecture 1750–1840* (Cambridge, 1982).

3   Howard seems to have visited (*pace* Spurrell) three times – in August 1774, September 1776 and May 1778. See *The State of the Prisons* (Warrington, 1777), pp. 468–9, and *An Account of the Principal Lazarettos in Europe* (Warrington, 1789), p. 214.

4   This privilege at this time extended to the ancient London prisons of the Fleet and King's Bench, Lostwithiel and Newcastle; see Howard, *State of Prisons*.

5   W. Spurrell, *Carmarthen and its Neighbourhood* (2nd edn, Carmarthen, 1879), pp. 51–2.

6   R. Suggett, *John Nash Architect–Pensaer* (Aberystwyth, 1995), p. 13.

7   Ironically, Dickens in 'A Visit to Newgate', in *Sketches by Boz* (1839: Mandarin, London, 1991 edn, p. 235) seeks to reawaken interest in this 'gloomy depository of the guilt and misery of London' since, he claims, familiarity has dulled its impact – particularly its relationship to the people within. By 1867, Carmarthen gaol itself was described as a 'repulsive looking building, the doorway of which is hung with sombre festoons of massive manacles' (*CarmJ*, 6 December 1867).

8   *CarmJ*, 16 August 1833.

9   R. Evans, *The Fabrication of Virtue* (Cambridge, 1992), p. 299.

10 CRO Brigstocke 1.

11 For a discussion, see R. W. Ireland, 'A Second Ireland', in R. McMahon (ed.), *Crime, Law and Popular Culture in Europe Since 1500* (Cullompton, 2006).

12 *GJ*, 2 August 1846.

13 Ibid., 19 June 1847.

14 Note that the stocks are still recorded as potential punishment in Llandeilo as late as 1858 and in Llandovery in 1863. See records of summary convictions in these localities, *QS* Boxes 6 and 9.

15 This volume, pp. 170–5.

16 *GJ*, 16 November 1846.

17 Ibid., 5 January 1846.

18 Ibid., 5–11 August 1846.

19 *GJ*, 30 September, 5 October 1846.

20 How shocked must his concerned respectable readers, who by repute included even the Queen herself, have been by Charles Reade's *It is Never Too Late To Mend*, with its exposure of the magistrates' venality. At the first-night performance of a dramatic

version of the novel in October 1865 the audience were outraged. The performance was stopped and one of the actors had to address the audience as to the historical (not contemporary) veracity of the material. See *The Era*, 8 October 1865, quoted in R. Mander and J. Mitchenson, *Lost Theatres of London* (London, 2nd edn, 1976), pp. 139–40.

[21] See *GJ*, 17 November 1845.

[22] Ibid., 1 March 1848.

[23] See *QS* Box 12.

[24] *GJ*, 26 December 1845.

[25] Ibid., 17 July 1848.

[26] We may mention in passing the problems of eligibility of prisoners to write letters and the capacity of prison officials to read or censor them, problems which fall to be resolved in an era when distant communication by prisoners becomes a real and present possibility. See the comments in *GJ*, 9 and 23 March 1846.

[27] It seems that Kidwelly's prisoners were housed in Carmarthen county gaol after the demise of its own. Accounts from the period of the rebuilding of the gaol after the 1865 Prisons Act show separate payments for Kidwelly prisoners transferred to Swansea: *QS* Boxes 11, 12. Note also that Kidwelly was opposed to the extension of the county police to its jurisdiction and went so far as to promise resistance to the imposition of the officers. The dispute eventually involved reference to Whitehall, which ordered the new police into the borough. See the documents in *QS* Box 6.

[28] 32 Geo. III, ch. civ.

[29] CRO Mus. 154, 2 July 1792.

[30] Ibid., pp. 47, 49–50.

[31] See 32 Geo. III, chap. civ, section 14.

[32] 45 Geo. III, ch. cii.

[33] J. Nield in *An Account of the Rise, Progress and Present State, of the Society for the Discharge and Relief of Persons Imprisoned for Small Debts throughout England and Wales* (London, 1802), pp. 72–3, describes the buildings separately but notes of the borough: 'Now consolidated with the County'.

[34] *QS Minute Book (1832–7)*, pp. 32, 34.

[35] Ibid., p. 87. Originally these may have been those convicted by magistrates, not at assize or sessions (*Prison Inspector's Third Report*, 1837–8).

[36] See *First Report of the Commissioners on Municipal Corporations of England and Wales* (1835), p. 214.

[37] Ibid.

[38] *Prison Inspectors' Third Report* (1837).

39 *Prison Inspectors' Fifth Report* (1840).

40 *Prison Inspectors' Seventh Report* (1842).

41 Ibid.

42 *Prison Inspectors' Eleventh Report* (1846).

43 *The Welshman*, 8 January 1847.

44 *GJ*, 10 May 1847.

45 See *Borough Minute Book, Carm. Boro*, p. 403.

46 *GJ*, 12 May 1846. Note too that the house of correction had been brick-faced in the previous month and other cleaning and painting jobs recently undertaken: ibid., 12, 13, 15, 20, 22 April 1846.

47 See the order for 3 yd of blue and 30 yd of yellow cloth, 12 pairs of stockings for women prisoners, fustian for repair of clothing and calico for shifts, 30 October 1847. In the late 1830s the uniform was described as 'party coloured' by Bisset Hawkins (*Prison Inspectors' Third Report* [1837–8]), as it was in 1851 (*Sixteenth Report*). By 1867 a newspaper report describes the uniform as multicoloured but with yellow predominant: *CarmJ*, 6 December 1867.

48 *GJ*, 3 February 1847.

49 *Prison Inspectors' Sixteenth Report* (1851).

50 *GJ*, 11 March 1848.

51 See this volume, p. 142.

52 *CarmJ*, 27 August 1847.

53 For the legislation concerning lock-up houses, see 3 and 4 Vict., chap. 88, section 12; 5 and 6 Vict., ch. 109, section 22. Note also the use of stocks in Llandeilo and Llandovery, see this volume, Introduction, n. 14.

54 *Diary of PC Williams* (CRO Mus. 112), 2, 3 January 1858.

55 *GJ*, 15 November 1845.

56 *QS* Box 2. This may have been a special case, however. Griffiths was ultimately discharged from the county gaol.

57 He did not visit the 'cage' mentioned as existing in Laugharne some years later, see *The Welshman*, 8 January 1858.

58 *Prison Inspectors' Sixteenth Report* (1851).

59 Ibid.

60 Ibid.

61 The process of construction of Poor Law Unions under the 1834 Act to provide institutions to a group of parishes may have been influential in this process.

62 All *QS* Box 21. Willis's report suggests that both the Llandovery and Llandeilo lock-ups were in the same place as before. Llandeilo had had a window repaired in 1872, and some work had been done on Newcastle Emlyn in the same year, when the keeper Samuel Evans was paid £1. 4s. (*QS Misc. Papers*). The Newcastle Emlyn lock-up

was continuing to be discussed in Michaelmas 1876, when plans are being considered for progress (*QS* Box 23).

[63] See *QS* Box 17, which also has a recommendation that there was no need for one at Llangadock.

[64] *QS* Box 25, following a proposal in *QS* Box 17. Presumably remand before a hearing by magistrates is referred to.

[65] For Sheppard see the *Newgate Calendar* accounts. In the next century the fame of John 'Babbacombe' Lee taps into a similar sentiment.

[66] For the value of nails, see P. Priestley, *Victorian Prison Lives* (London, 1985), pp. 122–3.

[67] *GJ*, 17 March 1847; see also the note in respect of Henry Thomas, 30 April 1847.

[68] Ibid., 21 January 1849.

[69] Ibid., 13 November 1849 (4 a.m.), 26 June 1850 (1 a.m.).

[70] Ibid., 24 April 1849.

[71] Tobacco was generally chewed rather than smoked in prison, to preserve secrecy. 'One who has ended it', *Five Years' Penal Servitude* (London, 1878), p. 121.

[72] *GJ*, 27 October 1845.

[73] Ibid., 27 January 1846; see this volume, p. 153.

[74] The order dated 23 August is found pasted in the Journal opposite entries for the beginning of July. The action was prompted by the attempted escape of Thomas Davies (alias Evans) who had access to this yard whilst separately confined on remand within the Lower Trebanda following a previous escape attempt. Davies had been assisted by a debtor, Thomas Lewis, who had thrown a large nail into the yard which Davies had intended to use to secure the door, apparently to buy time as he attempted to scale the wall: *GJ*, 21, 23 August 1847. Lewis is threatened with being reported to the 'Commissioners', presumably the insolvency hearing.

[75] Ibid., 23 June 1846. Remand prisoners were forbidden tobacco from at least 1859. See also Prison Act 1865.

[76] See Davies's trial, *CarmJ*, 26 October 1866.

[77] *GJ*, 8 September 1846.

[78] Ibid., 26, 27 August 1850. The source of the complaint shows the sense of inequality created between prisoners by contraband.

[79] Ibid., 1 January 1846.

[80] Ibid., 24 June 1848, Edward Wickham and John Rees remanded to refractory cell for attempt to smuggle a letter. On 30 October 1845: 'John Smith put in the refractory cell upon Bread and water diet for tearing out a leaf of a hym book and writing a note to be concealed out of the gaol unknown to me to be sent out by Thomas Morris a

discharged Prisoner, which it appears that he has some stoleing property at the Blue Boar in water Street Carmarthen.'

81 Ibid., 2, 3, 5, 7 June 1847.

82 Ibid., 11 April 1846: he was not prosecuted for the escape attempt but received a sentence of transportation for ten years at the summer assizes, 13 July 1846. Note the attempt to rescue a female transport by a man entering the prison (*Prison Inspectors' Eighteenth Report* [1853]).

83 See this volume, p. 150.

84 *GJ*, 12 May 1849.

85 Ibid., 29 May 1850. Vickerman was subsequently given a concurrent six-month sentence for prison breach (see *FR*, no. 310) and yellow cloth purchased thereafter (*GJ*, 1 June 1850), presumably to mark the uniforms of potential escapees. See also *Prison Inspectors' Sixteenth Report* (1851). Rees was replaced by a local policeman, PC Canton (*QS* Box 2, *Gaoler's Report*). Note that suspicious escapes from police custody were not unknown. See *Chief Constable's Report*, January 1862 (*QS* Box 7). The *chevaux de frise* was a protective spiked rail.

86 *GJ*, 4, 5, 6 August 1847.

87 *GJ*, 5 June 1848.

88 See n. 80 above.

89 *GJ*, 25 June 1848.

90 Spurrell, *Carmarthen*, 8 June 1862, 4 January 1866 (pp. 156, 160). Interestingly, these incidents do not appear in reports to *QS*, though the first resulted in a successful escape. Compare this with the regularity of escape *before* imprisonment.

91 *18 Months' Imprisonment*, by D— S— (London, 1883), p. 194; see also the comments in *Five Years' Penal Servitude*, pp. 120–1, where the author attributes the presence of contraband tobacco in prisons to corrupt officers.

92 See, for example, H. Mayhew and J. Binney, *The Criminal Prisons of London* (London, 1862), facing p. 388.

93 There were in total eight children of Williams's marriage (*CarmJ*, 12 December 1845), the rest presumably resident outside the gaol at this time.

94 *GJ*, 8–12 December 1845.

95 *Chaplain's Annual Report*, 1857: *QS* Box 5.

96 The significance of the mulberry is not clear, but Carmarthen was not the only gaol to contain such a specimen.

97 The *Prison Inspectors' Sixteenth Report*, 1851, reveals that the untried prisoners had three cells with four beds in, and one with one bed. The weakness of the cells was revealed in the account of an

escape in 1866 (see *CarmJ*, 5 January 1866). Convicted criminals had three operative sleeping cells.

98 *Third Report* (1837–8). This building was described as 'outside the precincts of the County prison', possibly for tactical purposes, when there were moves to retain it as the lock-up after nationalization (*Chief Constable's Report* and *Visiting Justices' Report*, summer 1877; *QS* Box 25). It was, and remains, outside the old perimeter wall.

99 *Seventh Report* (1842).

100 *Sixteenth Report* (1851).

101 *Twenty-fourth Report* (1859).

102 The photograph (Carmarthen Museum 1975, 0216) is intriguing. It appears to show the prison after the cellular rebuild and Stephens is identified in the donation, by a descendant. The officer seated on the left of the matron (?) in the group looks very much like John Jones in a photograph kindly supplied by Jean Reader, who suggests that such identification requires a date after 1881, though I am not so sure. Stephens certainly retired in 1878. The real mystery is the identity of the women. I think that the majority are prisoners, but the undoubted quality of their uniform dresses, and the keys which the women carry, could be evidence otherwise.

103 *Prison Inspectors' Fifth Report* (1840), though the female cells are described as 'neglected' and the floor 'covered with feathers'!

104 Provision, with a separate access, was by then available for women in the infirmary which had been constructed, following the recommendation of the inspector. The provision of an infirmary was recorded as a 'projected' alteration in 1842 (*Seventh Report*) when Hawkins pointed out that this was a statutory obligation. In 1840 the governor had attempted to persuade Hawkins that 'infirmary rooms' did exist (men had been treated in a ward previously used for lunatics, see *Third Report* [1837–8]). He was not convinced.

105 See too that female prisoners seem to have been moved, as an ad hoc measure, into the Trebanda, a practice which was stopped by the Justices, see *GJ*, 21 May 1847.

106 The governor's house was later moved outside the prison walls, though presumably with a direct connection from the rear to satisfy the 1865 Act. The relocation was probably a consequence of the 1868–72 rebuild, as it appears in its new location in a plan of 1898 (CRO MS 41), with the warden's house still at the prison entrance. The photograph, of uncertain date, is Carmarthen Museum 76 2394.

107 See *The Welshman*, 9 January, 10 April 1857.

108 CRO *QS Minute Book 1852–65*, pp. 201, 206. Originally there

may have been a scheme simply to exchange land with Cawdor, as this seems to be the rationale of CRO Cawdor Maps 41. However, the payment option went ahead (*QS* Box 6), though there seems to have been dispute as to how much was payable in excess of this amount, whether 13*s*. or £1. 13*s*. 4*d*., sums I think in respect of administration. See account of 23 January 1858 (*QS* Box 6) following the discussions at *QS Minute Book 1852–65*, pp. 226, 233.

[109] For details of the debate at quarter sessions see *The Welshman*, 3 July 1857.

[110] Kyrke Penson was the architect of the original plan, but his work may have been subsequently amended by a man called Lindsay. Certainly the description of the finished building differs somewhat from Penson's original design as recorded in *The Welshman* for 9 January 1857. See also the comments in *CarmJ*, 25 October 1861.

[111] *Report*, 2 October 1858 (*QS* Box 6).

[112] *Prison Inspectors' Twenty-fourth Report* (1859).

[113] *Report*, *QS* Box 6 (Michaelmas 1857).

[114] *Letter to Visiting Justices*, 20 August 1859. The dating of the letter is confusing, as the architects plans bear the date 18 August. Williams refers to a letter to the Visiting Justices in his report to quarter sessions for Michaelmas 1859. I suspect the August letter is a copy.

[115] For plans and contract see CRO MS 1–5. A plan to build new refractory cells seems to have been dropped on grounds of expense. Collard was paid three guineas for drawing the plans: CRO *QS Minute Book 1852–65*, p. 293.

[116] For Perry's views see *Carnarvon Committee* (1863), paras 1385–92.

[117] *Prison Inspectors' Twenty-fourth Report* (1859).

[118] Ibid.

[119] See the comments in the *Twenty-ninth* (1864) and *Thirtieth* (1865) *Inspectors' Reports*.

[120] 28 and 29 Vict., ch. 126, section 35.

[121] *Letter from Treasury Chambers*, CRO *QS* Box 9.

[122] Prison Act 1865, Section 36.

[123] *CarmJ*, 27 October 1865. Note that later in the process the chairman of the quarter sessions warned in January 1868 that the rebuild was necessary under pain that the secretary of state was empowered to remove the prisoners, adding (incorrectly): 'Nor does it stop there, for if we do not build the gaol as required by the Act of Parliament, the Government has power to build it for us, and I do not think they would do it at a cheaper rate than we could ourselves. (Laughter and cheers.)' *The Welshman*, 10 January 1868.

[124] *CarmJ*, 5 January 1866. The men were soon retaken, see *CarmJ*, 12 January 1866.

125 *CarmJ*, 12 January 1866.

126 *CarmJ*, 12 January and 13 April 1866.

127 *CarmJ*, 13 July 1866.

128 *CarmJ*, 12 January 1866.

129 These are, I believe, the surviving plans at CRO MS 19.

130 *CarmJ*, 13 July 1866; *QS Minute Book 1866–77*, p. 24.

131 A sum not exceeding £1,300 was agreed to be made available for purchase of the 'High Level of Castle Green, Smithie Cottages and Garden at the South Corner of the Gaol' in Michaelmas 1866. Curiously, a year later this sum is stated to have been £1,500: *QS Minute Book 1866–77*, p. 103.

132 *CarmJ*, 13 July, 26 October 1866. Johnes resigned from the chair in 1872 on grounds of ill health. Four years later he was famously murdered at his home at Dolaucothi by his butler, Henry Tremble, who would have been one of the last of the prisoners in the county's gaol had he not killed himself. See Spurrell, *Carmarthen*, p. 169.

133 *Special Report of the Visiting Justices*, 6 October 1866 (*QS* Box 10).

134 Wesley did indeed preach in the town, on 9 and 16 August 1790, see Spurrell, *Carmarthen*, p. 130.

135 *CarmJ*, 11 January, 12 April, 25 October 1867. The purchase of the Green was to cost £1,300.

136 See *QS Order Book 1866–77*, p. 47, for the power to tender.

137 *CarmJ*, 25 October 1867, *per* Sir John Mansel, who rather underestimated the achievements of a man who helped create the appearance of modern Birmingham. He had become a partner of D. R. Hill, who had designed Birmingham's Winson Green prison. For his career, see B. Little, *Birmingham Buildings: The Architectural Story Of A Midlands City* (Newton Abbot, 1971), and obituary in *The Builder*, 28 July 1900. I am indebted to Sarah Chubb of the City of Birmingham Records Office for her help.

138 *CarmJ*, 12 April 1867.

139 He was also awarded £33 for his expenses in travelling to the various gaols: *QS Minute Book 1866–77*, p. 100; *CarmJ*, 25 October 1867.

140 See section 29. It seems that moneys were borrowed from Morris's bank pending the receipt of funds from the commissioners: *QS Minute Book 1866–77*, p. 174. Note the Carmarthen Justices' confusion at the mechanics of the loan process, *CarmJ*, 3 January 1868, and their making of an invalid receipt in 1870, *QS Minute Book 1866–77*, p. 204. Martin's tender seems initially to have been £15,000: *CarmJ*, 12 April 1867. The rest of the sum is presumably for fittings.

141 It seems that the reduction in the number of cells involved consultation with the secretary of state in advance of the approval's being

granted: *QS Minute Book 1866–77*, pp. 128, 129. *CarmJ*, 10 April 1868, 3 July 1868; Spurrell, *Carmarthen*, p. 163.

142 *Visiting Justices' Report*, 20 October 1869 (*QS* Box 10).

143 One escapee was also transferred. See *CarmJ*, 9 July 1869.

144 For reference to the van and the 'Coach-house', see *QS Minute Book 1866–77*, pp. 344, 437.

145 See, for example, the account for the Borough in March 1870, which shows 19*s.* 6*d.* paid for 'conveying 3 males & 1 female to Carmarthen for Trial & 1 female under sentence from Ditto to Swansea', 7*s.* for 'Omnibus to and from station' and '5*s.* Officers Allowance for One Day'. The prisoners presumably made their own way home, as suggested by a sum of 8*s.* 1*d.* to prisoners 'on discharge' (*QS* Box 12).

146 *FR*, nos 1402, 1403.

147 *CarmJ*, 9 July 1869.

148 'Several' were employed in such labour in the winter of 1869 instead of on the treadwheel: *Governor's Report*, 7 January 1869 (*QS* Box 12). By the time of the 1870 inspectors' report (*Thirty-fourth Report*), only one per day was being employed on the excavations.

149 *Governor's Report*, 7 April 1870. It is possible that the unease concerning separation might explain why the inspector only found one prisoner employed in the work.

150 See *Visiting Justices' Building Committee Report*, 15 October 1870 (*QS* Box 12); *Visiting Justices' Building Committee Report*, December 1870 (*QS* Box 13). Note the laconic comment of Sir James Hamilton for the Visiting Justices in October 1869, '*ex nihilo, nihil fit*': *CarmJ*, 22 October 1869.

151 *Visiting Justices' Building Committee Report*, 27 June 1871 (*QS* Box 15). The expenditure was approved at the sessions. There seems to have been some hesitation over the grant by Johnes as chairman of the sessions, but Sir James Hamilton's endorsement of the prime mover in the Building Committee, Sir John Mansel, carried the day: 'considering that he was not like a young spendthrift who would squander the public money in a harum-scarum way, but that he had plenty of ballast, he [Hamilton] thought the court might give plenary powers to the Committee or rather to Sir John who was "*l'état c'est moi*" to the committee to carry on the work' (*The Welshman*, 7 July 1871). One can only guess at Hamilton's private thoughts when the final account for the rebuilding was presented, though Mansel and the architects were both formally thanked for their efforts in 1873 at the same sessions at which the extent of the bill was revealed: *QS Minute Book 1866–77*, p. 373.

152 *Visiting Justices' Building Committee Report*, 15 October 1870 (*QS* Box 12).

[153] *QS* Box 14.

[154] See *Visiting Justices' Reports*, June 1872, January 1873, April 1873 (*QS* Boxes 15, 16).

[155] *Per* Sir John Mansel, *Visiting Justices' Building Committee Report*, 4 April 1873 (*QS* Box 16).

[156] See the comments in *QS Minute Book 1866–77*, pp. 393, 406, 416, which refer to withholding of money to the contractor and hint at inappropriate subcontracting. Whether the default refers to the failings next mentioned is unknown.

[157] See, for example, *Visiting Justices' Reports*, April and December 1876 (*QS* Box 21, 22) and March 1877 (*QS* Box 21). An attempt to repair the cupola (not the first) 'failed to bear the test of the late boisterous weather', *Visiting Justices' Report*, October 1876 (*QS* Box 23).

[158] *The Welshman*, 6 January 1871. Martin is revealed to be also visiting Glamorgan gaols and the lunatic asylum.

[159] The *Visiting Justices' Report* of 31 March 1877 repeats the problems of the female ward and cupola and notes that the architects have failed to respond to complaints (*QS* Box 21).

[160] *QS* Box 17, and see above, p. 104.

[161] *Report of the Visiting Justices' Building Committee*, 4 April 1873 (*QS* Box 16).

[162] *Report of the Visiting Justices' Building Committee*, 27 June 1873 (*QS* Box 16).

[163] *Treasurer's Account*, 16 October 1873 (*QS* Box 16).

[164] *CarmJ*, 3 January 1868. Martin, the architect of Carmarthen gaol, was also involved with the Asylum and money for it was also borrowed from the Loan Commissioners (*QS Minute Book 1866–77*, p. 272).

[165] See S. McConville, *English Local Prisons 1860–1900: Next Only to Death* (London, 1995), p. 192. See Prison Act 1865 s. 36, but compare s. 65.

[166] *The Welshman*, 6 January 1871.

[167] *CarmJ*, 3 May 1878. Compare the closure and subsequent reopening of Brecon gaol: see McConville, *English Local Prisons*, pp. 193ff.

[168] *CarmJ*, 30 August 1878.

[169] *CarmJ*, 3 May 1878.

[170] *CarmJ*, 30 August 1878.

Notes to Chapter 3

[1] Though note that those at the upper echelons of the administration, the governor, surgeon and chaplain, will not wear a uniform. Their titles and 'respectability' are supposed to be sufficient guarantee of their appropriate symbolic role, to which they may be assumed to be committed.

[2] It is, significantly, the word used in the regulations applicable to the first national penitentiary (see *Rules and Regulations of the General Penitentiary at Millbank*, 1817, p. 338) as well as in the 1839 Act. The 1823 Act used both 'Gaoler' and the functional 'Keeper', whilst 'Gaoler' recurs in the punitive 1865 Act.

[3] For a recognition of the importance of this change, see Reade, *It is Never Too Late to Mend* (London, 1856), p. 162. Note too the other meanings of the term 'governor' at this time, as a political representative and as a mechanical regulator. It is not, I think, too fanciful to see elements of these functions as desirable qualities in the prison version.

[4] Later in the nineteenth century the hangman, like the judge, would travel round the country like the assize judges, another example of the centralization of the control of crime. When Berry, who went about his business in a red Turkish fez, arrived in Carmarthen in 1889 for an execution he was met at the station and followed through the town by a large crowd of local people: see P. Molloy, *A Shilling for Carmarthen* (Fishguard, 1991), p. 146.

[5] Cf. McConville, *English Local Prisons*, pp. 302–3: 'While the prisons were under local government, the surgeon, together with the chaplain, were superior officers, with access to the justices, acting as balances and checks on the authority and actions of the governor.'

[6] The 1823 Gaol Act retained the power of appointment of gaolers to sheriffs, but of other officers to the Visiting Justices.

[7] For an exploration of these tensions and their exploitation, see R. W. Ireland, 'Charles Hunt's haircut: getting down to the roots of a legal adventure', in P. Brand, K. Costello and W. N. Osborough (eds), *Adventures of the Law* (Dublin, 2005), p. 219.

[8] Burnhill replaced William Butterton who had died only six months after replacing Benjamin Waugh in 1825: Spurrell, *Carmarthen*, p. 142.

[9] 1881 census.

[10] The practice of employing Englishmen, and in particular former London policemen, as prison governors is found also at Brecon; see D. Davies, *Law and Disorder in Breconshire 1750–1880* (Brecon, n.d.), p. 66.

11 Above, p. 100.

12 Mrs Westlake was ordered £15 per year in April 1846; see *GJ*, 9 April 1846.

13 *Prison Inspectors' Ninth Report* (1844).

14 £150 per year would be the salary of a respectable tradesman or one on the lower rungs of the professional ladder. I am indebted to Robert Colley for providing me with figures for comparison. The governor was obliged to live in the gaol by section x of the 1823 Gaol Act.

15 *GJ*, 23 April 1847. The JP was Henry Lawrence MD.

16 Ibid., 30 March 1846, a dispute concerning information about some vagrant prisoners.

17 Ibid., 10 March 1847, a dispute with George Thomas over a copy of a commitment. Note also the argument with David Jones, assistant surgeon, over malingering, on which see this volume, p. 139.

18 It seems to have formed part of the early Millbank regime. For Westlake's practice see this volume, p. 197.

19 A prisoner is released by Stephens after 'expressing regret and obedient for the future', *GJ*,1 September 1848. See also *GJ*, 11 July 1849, when the chaplain too was in attendance.

20 Ibid., 26 July 1846: 'The prisoners had new potatoes this Day being the first time this summer.' On 8 October 1846 he reports that boiled rice was served, potatoes being 'scarce and bad'. Three days later he says 'The prisoners had suit Dumplins in lue of potatoes', and rice was served again on the 15th.

21 The magistrates' side of the Gaoler's Journal records a meeting on 7 August at which the governor was suspended until the next quarter sessions; it appeared that 'Mr Westlake had on Thursday 29th July absented himself from the gaol and while absent was drunk and incapable of doing his duty.' Ironically the 28th had seen a meeting of teetotallers in the town, of which *The Welshman* had laconically observed (30 July 1847): 'There was not a very numerous attendance, but the utmost decorum prevailed.'

22 It appears to me that Westlake is not writing the Journal from 24 July until 7 August. He then (ironically, for this is the date of his suspension) writes the Journal for another week and then again from 17 to 19 August. The other hand I presume to be that of William Williams. George Stephens makes his first entry on 4 September 1847.

23 For many of the biographical details of Stephens I am indebted to the personal communication of his great-grandson, David L. Smart.

24 Census 1851.

25 See *Visiting Justices' Report*, 3 April 1874 (QS Box 17).

[26] The question of the pension was inquired into by quarter sessions in January 1848 (see *QS Order Book*). It was still being paid, apparently by the county, as late as 1872 (see *QS Misc. Papers*).

[27] *QS* Box 2.

[28] In this volume, p. 173.

[29] Note, however, that Westlake was not the only Welsh governor to lose his post for misconduct around this time. There was the celebrated dismissal of the governor of Caernarfon, investigated in 1843 (McConville, *A History of English Prison Administration, Vol. 1: 1750–1877* (London, 1981), p. 252) and eventually dismissed in advance of a second inquiry in 1848, see Harding et al., *Imprisonment*, p. 146. The governor of Usk New House of Correction, again investigated previously, was obliged to resign in 1850, see B. Foster, 'The Usk Houses of Correction and the early days of Usk County Gaol', *Gwent Local History* 94 (2003), 20.

[30] It is used in the (*Thirtieth*) report for that year by the prison inspector, though the Prison Act of the same year uses 'prison officer', see section 93.

[31] *Prison Inspectors' Sixteenth Report* (1851).

[32] *QS* Box 2. Williams was at that time earning £1 per week, Rees 15s. They claimed that their counterparts in Brecon and Glamorgan were earning more.

[33] They are mentioned as being worn in the inspector's report of 1859, but not in the previous one from 1857.

[34] In January 1863 the Visiting Justices were proposing to deduct a shilling a week from the turnkeys' pay to cover the cost of uniforms, *QS* Box 8. Note that Williams had once been provided with a greatcoat for a winter trip to Cardiff: *GJ*, 2 January 1847.

[35] J. E. Thomas, *The English Prison Officer since 1850* (London, 1972), p. 41.

[36] Five daughters appear in the 1851 census.

[37] Above, p. 107. Note too that he was drunk whilst in charge of the gaol during Stephens's indisposition at New Year 1848: *GJ*, 2 January 1848.

[38] See the memorial in *QS* Box 2. Williams was being paid a pension of £40 per year in 1872 (*QS Misc. Papers*).

[39] In the 1840s the sole under-turnkey seems to have slept in the gaol, although he may have kept a residence outside. Certainly the prison inspector (*Seventh Report*, 1842) recommended that two turnkeys should sleep within the gaol.

[40] See returns under 2 and 3 Vict. for 1865 and 1869, *QS* Boxes 9 and 11. The (1860s, 1870s?) photograph of Governor Stephens with female prisoners appears to show four uniformed turnkeys. In 1873

there is a 'Chief Warder and one Engineer plus three Subwarders' (*Return*, *QS* Box 15). All of these reports include a female warder as well as the matron. By 1874 one of the male warders may have been dispensed with (or replaced with or reclassified as an 'engineer'?), see *Visiting Justices' Report*, October 1874 (*QS* Box 18). In 1875, and similarly in 1877, the junior officers comprised 'one chief and Two Under Warder [*sic*] a door porter. An Engineer and a female warder' (*Return*, *QS* Boxes 20 and 25). By 1876 six untitled 'subordinate officers' are reported (*Return*, *QS* Box 23).

41 Ibid., see, for example, 28 May and 3 June 1847.
42 See, for example, ibid., 20 January, 7 February, 5 September 1848, which latter occasion notes both Governor Stephens and turnkey David Rees absent taking prisoners elsewhere. Temporary substitutes, if engaged, are not mentioned in the records unless for longer periods – for example, the two weeks of Rees's illness, see 7 February 1848.
43 See *CarmJ*, 8 May 1846.
44 *GJ*, 2 June 1846.
45 Charles Hunt is assigned to care for James Hargrave, ibid., 17 December 1846, their relative roles being reversed on 28 October 1846. Both Ann Awberry and Mariah Thomas were assigned at different times to overlook the insane Mary Hughes, ibid., 10, 16 May 1847.
46 Ibid., 17 November 1845; *CarmJ*, 8 May 1846.
47 Above, p. 120.
48 But see J. Sim, *Medical Power in Prisons: The Prison Medical Service in England 1774–1989* (Milton Keynes, 1990). Equally, it may be argued that the role of the penal revolution in the advancement of medicine is not sufficiently appreciated. It is true that the reformation of punishment provided fewer cadavers for anatomy, but it also provided (in the manner described by Foucault) a captive body of patients. Prison too threw up real issues which would be tested on them. So the 'less-eligibility' principle operating in workhouses and *a fortiori* gaols necessarily posed questions as to how little food, and of what kind, a man could survive on. Not the least surprising thing to emerge from the investigation into the diseases at Millbank in 1823 is just how little was known of such matters: this volume, p. 203.
49 On one occasion three vagrants served their entire sentence before being allowed out of the itch ward: *GJ*, 9 August 1848.
50 John Thomas, pardoned on health grounds in 1863, was suffering from a 'disease of the knee joints', which does not sound potentially fatal (*FR*, no. 955; *QS* Box 8), though the prison inspector (*Twenty-*

ninth Report [1864]), referring to the case, makes it clear that it confined the prisoner to bed. It is noted of John Morris in 1864, discharged in 'a very critical state', that he 'refused to stay longer' (*FR*, no. 972; *QS* Box 9). Rather earlier, John Evans was taken 'very ill' and discharged in a mail coach to Llandeilo within three days (*GJ*, 2, 3, 4, 5 June 1846), whilst Thomas Phillips, 'attacked with paralysis' whilst on remand and taken to trial 'in a sedan', was not prosecuted (ibid., 10, 11 October 1848). Note too that in the case of offenders sentenced to be whipped the surgeon was obliged to inspect them. In Carmarthen this was applicable, as we will see, only to juveniles. For an example, see the case of David Jones, this volume, p. 275, n. 127, though note that in this case the surgeon was from Swansea gaol, Carmarthen being then rebuilt.

51   The edition I consulted was the 7th (London, 1842). Note Zedner's observation (*Women, Crime and Custody*, p. 145): 'The infirmary spanned a[n] ... ambiguous and difficult range of roles: as a means of escaping the rigours of the regime for malingerers; as a source of unprecedented comforts for the enfeebled destitute; and even as a site of moral reform.'

52   See Gaol Act 1823, section 33.

53   Though he claims 35 years' service in the petition against the reduction of his salary in 1850 (*QS* Box 1).

54   For references, see *Prison Inspectors' Third* (1837–8) and *Eleventh* (1846) *Reports*. In this latter Jenkins is referred to as being sixty-two years of age in one place, seventy-one in another. Biographical material supplied by Edna Dale-Jones has him having been born in 1769. The county seems to have been paying separately for medicine by the 1850s, see, for example, *Eighteenth Report* (1853).

55   Visits are declared to take place every other day (*Third* [1837–8] and *Thirty-first* [1866] *Reports*). In 1842 the inspector reports (*Seventh Report*) that the records of the gaol 'prove [the surgeon] to have paid his visits every day'. He records that the assistant visits 'perhaps half as often', but signs in the surgeon's name rather than his own. My impression from the *Gaoler's Journal* is that Jones is the more regular visitor, though. The absence of a reception cell prevents initial examinations, the inspector states (*Eighteenth Report* [1853]), although someone is clearly making decisions on the scabies question. The surgeon is claiming to carry out examinations on reception, discharge and on a weekly basis by 1870: *Surgeon's Report*, January 1870 (QS Box 13) and *Prison Inspectors' Thirty-fifth Report* (1871). The 1842 report had also criticized the surgeon for not keeping a proper journal as required by statute.

56   A special authorization for Jones to visit without the surgeon was

provided by nine JPs in connection with a communication from the Home Office concerning cholera: *GJ*, facing page for 15 November 1848.

57 Rowlands was appointed on 11 March 1850, Davies having apparently filled in since Rowlands's death on 13 January. In the brief period covered by the Gaoler's Journal in relation to his appointment regular visits are not recorded, though whether this is an actual change or an apparent one is not clear. Rowlands had studied medicine at St George's, becoming a member of the Royal College of Surgeons in 1842 and a fellow in 1857. He became a JP in 1861 and died, having served as gaol surgeon for forty years, at the age of eighty-five in 1899. He had been charged, but never prosecuted, in respect of the death of Sarah Jacob. I am indebted again to Edna Dale-Jones for information provided. His own salary was £65 in 1853, but £75 in 1857 and the same in 1865 (*QS* Boxes 3, 5, 9).

58 For this series of disputes and its significance see R. W. Ireland, 'Charles Hunt's haircut', in P. Brand, K. Costello and N. Osborough (eds), *Adventures of the Law* (Dublin, 2005), 224–6.

59 See *GJ*, 7 September 1846, and Jenkins's note of 8 September 1846 pasted on the rear inside cover of the Journal.

60 See M. Davitt, *Leaves from a Prison Diary* (London, 1885, reprinted Shannon, 1972), p. 146.

61 *Surgeon's Report*, January 1875, *QS* Box 19. Compare the case of Winifred Morris in Brecon in 1844: D. Davies, *Law and Disorder in Breconshire*, pp. 49–51.

62 *CarmJ*, 3 December 1867.

63 *GJ*, 13 January 1846. See also 27 August 1846, when Westlake describes Wilson's behaviour as very bad since he had been detected 'faining sick and deceiving the surgeon'.

64 Ibid., 8 February 1847.

65 *Surgeon's Report* (*QS* Box 2): for the disposition, *FR*, no. 132; *Quarter Sessions Order Book 1843–9*, p. 369.

66 For a detailed consideration of Buckley's case see R. W. Ireland, 'Eugene Buckley and the diagnosis of insanity in the early Victorian prison', *Llafur*, 6 (1993), 5. Note too the decision not to prosecute Thomas Phillips, a borough prisoner remanded for trial but 'attacked with paralysis' and discharged having been taken the short distance to trial in the Town Hall 'in a sedan'; *GJ*, 10, 11 October 1848. An unnamed vagrant had her fare paid for her to go to Swansea on the certification of her inability to walk by the surgeon (*GJ*, 29 November 1848), but there is no indication that this was a premature release.

67 *Thirty-seventh Report* (1873). See also the case of Elizabeth Evans, 'removed to Llandovery' from remand on a charge of child murder in October 1868 (*FR*, no. 1271).

68 *QS* Box 7.

69 See Harding et al., *Imprisonment*, pp. 169–71. For a discussion of the chaplain's role see also W. J. Forsythe, *The Reform of Prisoners 1830–1900* (Beckenham, 1987), ch. 2.

70 See P. Rawlings in Harding et al., *Imprisonment*, p. 171, on developments in Brecon, and Foster, 'The Usk Houses of Correction', 13–14. It is a great shame that for Carmarthenshire a number of the chaplains' reports seem not to have been filed with other quarter sessions documents at the time they were submitted (later references suggest that they were made), and that I have no trace of the journal(s?) kept, according to the prison inspector (*Seventh Report* [1842]), 'with great care'.

71 See Gaol Act 1823, section 28.

72 For the details see *Third* (1837–8), *Fifth* (1840), *Seventh* (1842), *Eleventh* (1846), *Twentieth* (1855) and *Twenty-second* (1857) *Prison Inspectors' Reports*; *Chaplain's Reports* 1850, 1853 (*QS* Box 2); *GJ*, 26 April 1846.

73 *Seventh Report* (1842).

74 Again I am indebted to Edna Dale-Jones for biographical details of Williams and Roberts. For the latter's pay claim see his report for 1866 (*QS* Box 10). In 1873 there is a proposal to increase his salary to £140 (*QS* Box 16).

75 *Chaplain's Report*, 1858 (*QS* Box 6): 'the Mahometan, who was convicted of Burglary in March last, professed his conversion to the Christian Faith before his liberation. He learned in gaol to read and write, expressed admiration of the excellency of our religion, and joined in the daily service apparently with devotion.' For Washington, see *FR*, no. 715. He was a shipwright, born in Alexandria. Revd Williams consistently uses the category 'Infidels' to describe non-Christian believers in his reports.

76 See *Chaplain's Report*, 1875 (*QS* Box 20). The British and Foreign Bible Society had given Testaments in eleven European languages, of which the Irish and, more surprisingly, the Norwegian had been made use of. Roberts quotes here from his (otherwise lost) report of 1864:

> A Prison is a World in itself, where we have daily a fresh means of observation of men, mind, manners, habits, Countries, and language; and when I say that we have lately had in our comparatively small Gaol Prisoners from Europe, Asia, Africa & America, natives from the sunny climes of Italy & Spain, Maroons from America, a Quadroon from Manilla, a Native Roman Catholic from the Banks of the Nile, persons of all grades and shades of Religion, and of no Religion, men who have traversed far and wide in the various Zones,

etc., etc.

[77] So the *Chaplain's Report* for 1858 (*QS* Box 6) finds, out of 144 convicted felons and misdemeanants, 46 Church of England, 71 Nonconformists, 22 Roman Catholics, 4 Deists and 1 'Mahometan'. In all three reports by Williams Nonconformists represent the single largest affiliation. Thereafter, though the figures are far from complete, it seems that members of the Church of England assume that position. If I were to suggest a reason for this change it would lie in the result of greater social mobility, or at least the change in numbers of prisoners from outside the immediate locality. A hint of this lies in the report for 1859, in which Williams gives the religion of the deserters from the army as a sub-category of the total. Of 36 of these 17 were Church of England, 17 Catholic and only 2 Nonconformists. This latter class are generally undifferentiated, but Revd Roberts provides a more detailed insight into the Nonconformist affiliations in his report for 1874: 'The Professed Religious Persuasion of 160 Prisoners was 79 Church of England, 16 Independents, 25 Baptists, 7 Wesleyans, 7 Methodists, 2 Presbyterians, 22 Roman Catholics, and 2 were of No Religion' (*QS* Box 18).

[78] *Prison Inspectors' Fifth Report* (1840). He notes that 'About one half the prisoners are dissenters'.

[79] *Chaplain's Report*, 1870 (QS Box 12).

[80] See *Prison Inspectors' Fifth Report* (1840).

[81] See the comments in the *Prison Inspectors' Twenty-seventh* (1862) and *Thirtieth* (1865) *Reports*. Between these two reports the Prison Ministers Act of 1863 (26 and 27 Vict., ch. 79) was passed, making provision for paid ministers from outside the established church. It also provided that the governor should keep a book recording the religion of his charges. There is no evidence that Stephens did keep such a book, though he does note the details in a handwritten addendum to his printed report in that year (*QS* Box 9). Note too that Anne Matthews, whose case is discussed in the next chapter, has her own spiritual needs attended to by Archdeacon Bevan (*GJ*, 31 March 1849). She also received communion from him (*GJ*, 7, 26 April 1849).

[82] *Chaplain's Reports*, 1857 (*QS* Box 5) and 1858 (*QS* Box 6). The use of 'catechizes' in the *Prison Inspectors' Third Report* (1837–8) suggests a similar emphasis under Jones.

[83] The *Prison Inspectors' Sixteenth Report* (1851) is the only source for this observation, so its longevity is unknown.

[84] The *Prison Inspectors' Thirty-eighth Report* (1874) records that, with the exception of juveniles who are taught daily, 'uneducated' are taught only after two months. Again, how far this represents a long-standing practice is unclear.

85 *Prison Inspectors' Sixteenth Report* (1851).
86 See n. 66 above.
87 See *FR*, no. 62. He read the first three chapters of Matthew before release. See also *GJ*, 14 September 1846.
88 In his 1857 report Williams points out the vulnerability of the officers to attack. There is apparently no reference to the 'mutiny' which provoked this observation in any other record. Note his thanks to his 'Brother Officials' in his 1874 report.
89 Note the role of some prison chaplains in publishing their thoughts, a tradition which runs from Nihill to Clay and on to Canon Horsley and Eustace Jervis.
90 *The Welshman*, describing the quarter sessions in October 1857, recorded that the chaplain presented 'a very long, elaborate and able report' (23 October 1857).
91 'The causes of crime I have found to be chiefly ignorance, want of early religious training, idleness, wilful indulgence in sinful passions, drunkenness, and evil associations, but hardly in any case want.' The themes are old, practically a series of Hogarth illustrations, but the confidence with which they are expressed is startling to modern criminological sensibility.
92 The report for 1870 includes figures for both the country of origin and the previous custodial history of the inmates. In 1874 he records 'that the proportion of all Prisoners during the past year supplied by the Principality has been 61.25, whilst that of other Countries has been 38.75'. By 1877 his focus on geographical factors has moved closer, noting of the felons and misdemeanants that 'out of which number of 310 Llanelly has contributed 99, County of the Borough of Carmarthen 48, Newcastle-Emlyn District 26, Llandilo 22, Llandovery 9, and Pembroke Dock 7 military offenders'.
93 See *Prison Inspectors' Thirty-sixth Report* (1872).
94 The chaplain of Usk House of Correction was similarly impressed by the introduction of the separate system, see Foster, 'Usk Houses of Correction', 19.
95 Compare D. Garland, *The Culture of Control* (Oxford, 2001), p. 24: 'A new configuration does not finally and fully emerge until it is formed in the minds and habits of those who work the system. Until these personnel have formed a settled habitus appropriate to the field, enabling them to cope with its demands and reproduce it "as a matter of course", the process of change remains partial and incomplete.'

Notes to Chapter 4

1 *Prison Inspectors' Seventh Report* (1842). Coming so shortly after the Rebecca disturbances the sentiments may seem particularly surprising. As to their accuracy, in terms of security, the reader is referred to chapter 2.

2 Perhaps their absence was fortuitous, for the prison inspector remarked in 1851 (*Sixteenth Report*) that there was no provision for them and they would have to be housed in the female debtors' section.

3 See now R. Dobash, E. Dobash, S. Gutteridge, *The Imprisonment of Women* (Oxford, 1986); L. Zedner, *Women, Crime and Custody in Victorian England* (Oxford, 1991). It should be remembered that the first prisoners ever to occupy a national penitentiary were women, at Millbank in 1816.

4 See Foster, 'Usk Houses of Correction', 29.

5 For the changes see, for example, H. Barty-King, *The Worst Poverty: A History of Debt and Debtors* (Stroud, 1991); G. Rubin, 'Law, poverty and imprisonment for debt, 1869–1914', in G. Rubin and D. Sugarman (eds), *Law, Economy and Society, 1750–1914* (Abingdon, 1984), p. 241.

6 *Sixteenth Report* (1851). He records five ground floor cells and three first floor cells, generally 12 ft × 9 ft × 9 ft. Increased provision seems to have been made thereafter; by 1865 there were eight male and two female cells (*Thirtieth Report*). The *Carmarthen Journal* of 3 December 1863 remarked that the debtors were responsible for the condition of their own cells, but failed to keep them tidy.

7 Note *FR*, no. 849, John Rees, recorded in 1861 as having been in the gaol before as 'a crown debtor for making illicit malt 20 years ago'.

8 In this context it may be instructive to remember the campaign waged by periodicals such as *Seren Gomer* to have Welsh used in the county courts. Their operation could, and increasingly did, deprive persons of their liberty despite their 'civil' jurisdiction.

9 See *CarmJ*, 6 December 1867.

10 See *GJ*, 4 February 1847, and see also 16 June 1846 (£80. 3s.): compare 9 March 1846 (£39. 3s. 10d.), 27 March 1846 (£28. 15s. 11d.), 13 August 1846 (£40), 29 January 1847 (£48. 10s.). Unfortunately I have found no figures to allow of comparison with post-1869 prisoners. The longest period of incarceration found was two years and six months (David Evans: ibid., 4 August 1846).

11 See *Prison Inspectors' Sixteenth Report* (1842). The 1838 report had suggested that lack of alteration to the borough gaol was explicable by the uncertainty over the future of imprisonment for debt.

[12] *GJ*, 14 January 1846.

[13] Ibid., 25 January 1848; see also his discharge, 18 March 1848.

[14] Ibid., 20, 30 October 1847. Williams was a Chancery debtor. The order is made by Henry Lawrence, whose status as a doctor presumably was taken as sufficient authority to alter the diet, though the surgeon's views are not recorded.

[15] J. Nield, *An Account of the Rise, Progress and Present State, of the Society for the Discharge and Relief of Persons Imprisoned for Small Debts throughout England and Wales* (London, 1802), p. 73.

[16] CRO Bowser 192.

[17] *GJ*, 23 February, 9 March 1846.

[18] Ibid., 6 March 1847, and see 19 June 1847, 22, 23 August 1848.

[19] Ibid., 30 July, 5 September 1846, and endpapers. In case of illness those unable to consult their own doctor, or taken suddenly ill, as was William Bowen in June 1849 (26, 27, 28 June 1849), made use of the gaol surgeon. A debtor who died in 1842 had been treated by both his own and the prison doctor.

[20] See the references to Allcock, Feake and Newman, *GJ*, 17, 18 March 1848. Generally speaking only family could visit, other persons being restricted to discussion through a gate in the passageway between the cells and the chapel: *Prison Inspectors' Sixteenth Report* (1851).

[21] *GJ*, Magistrates' side, 22 April 1848.

[22] *Prison Inspectors' Third Report* (1838); *GJ*, 27 March 1847. Note that in the *Seventh Report* of 1842 the inspector records that in the male debtors' provision separate cells and yards were provided for 'master debtors' and poor ones supported by the county.

[23] *Prison Inspectors' Sixteenth Report* (1851). Note a similar revision of rules, again assimilating the debtors to criminals, in Brecon, see D. Davies, *Law and Disorder in Breconshire*, pp. 69–70.

[24] But note also the distribution of coal on St David's Day (*GJ*, 1 March 1847).

[25] *GJ*, 24 December 1846, for example, includes cash of up to £1 to each of the debtors and a load of coal, a load of clay and a shoulder of mutton. The total of benefactions in 1838 was £20. The Poor Debtors' Relief Society was also recorded as active at that time, see *Prison Inspectors' Fifth Report* (1840). The inspector reports in 1861 (*Twenty-sixth Report*) that coal was provided directly by one of the JPs who was a mine owner.

[26] *GJ*, 5, 31 May 1846.

[27] Ibid., 30 January 1847, and 20 May 1846.

[28] The court sat regularly and locally and the governor would attend with prisoners. The court had power to discharge, bail or remand the debtor. Other releases from custody could come in appropriate

cases by order of the sheriff, by *supersedeas*, or application by the creditor. Examples of all these processes are found in Carmarthenshire's records. For the process of the Insolvent Debtors' Court see *GJ*, 16 December 1847, 23 May 1848. Charles Newman's debt was discharged when Governor Stephens himself received the full sum (*GJ*, 20 April 1848).

29 *GJ*, 31 August 1846.

30 Ibid., 5 January 1848: a letter was sent on the question to the secretary of state.

31 This is apparently one of a number of demands which culminate in a complaint being addressed to the secretary of state and the prison inspector (ibid.; *GJ*, 7, 15, 29 April 1847). See also Ireland, 'Charles Hunt's haircut'. The quoits question recalls a splendid recreation in the gaol some years earlier. I quote from the *Carmarthen Journal* of June 1821, for which reference I am indebted to John Davies:

> *Sporting Match.* – On Monday last, James Davies, aged 74 years, and [*sic*] Insolvent Debtor and who has been confined in our County Gaol for the last four years, undertook to run 420 yards, during the time another Insolvent Debtor, would take to eat two half-penny muffins. Davies was started round the Debtors yard, the sun at the time being remarkably bright, and between the old man's anxiety to get the victory, and his eye sight being very bad, he frequently ran against the walls, which created no small merriment among the spectators; even the muffin-eater could not help joining in the fun; and instead of boulting what he had already ground in his mouth, he blew it about like a shower of hail-stones, so that Davies came up to the winning-post in fine style, before his antagonist finished eating one half of the first muffin, consequently he was declared the winner, by the shouts and applause of all present. Considerable bets were pending on this match.

32 Ibid., 16, 23 April 1849.

33 Ibid., 27 May 1847. In fact this inquiry was raised by Henry Lawrence JP, presumably in relation to John Williams's case.

34 In 1873 the incarceration on remand of Dr Hessell provoked letters to *The Times* on the subject from a county prison governor and a prison chaplain which highlight the ambiguous position of this class of prisoner. The correspondence, interestingly, was reproduced in the *Cardigan and Tivy-Side Advertiser* (14 February 1873).

35 For pre-trial procedure see D. Bentley, *English Criminal Justice in the Nineteenth Century* (London, 1998), chs 3 and 4.

36 For Griffiths's trial (the son was not prosecuted) see *CarmJ*, 15 January 1847. For the subsequent proceedings, which included a separate Queen's Bench claim regarding coroners' expenses, see *CarmJ*, 30 April, 18 June 1847. For the altercation at the gaol see *GJ*, 10 March 1847.

[37] See *CarmJ*, 23 July 1847.

[38] Indictable Offences Act 1848, see Bentley, *English Criminal Justice*, p. 33.

[39] Some 337 out of 1,448 remands recorded in the Register result did not result in conviction, through acquittal or failure to proceed with prosecution.

[40] See R. W. Ireland, 'Putting oneself on whose country?', in T. G. Watkin (ed.), *Legal Wales: Its Past, Its Future* (Cardiff, 2001), p. 79.

[41] *Prison Inspectors' Seventh Report* (1842).

[42] *GJ*, 14 April 1849.

[43] *Prison Inspectors' Twenty-ninth Report* (1864).

[44] See *GJ*, 17 October 1846, 30 November 1849, this latter being clearly a post-trial committal.

[45] For an example, see Elizabeth Evans, discharged off remand for child murder in 1868 (*FR*, no. 1271). There are many such cases of post-1848 examinations in the Register, some of which (for example, nos 518, 1071) were then admitted to bail.

[46] *FR*, no. 1388.

[47] *GJ*, 20 November 1848, 5 January 1850. But note that Westlake was unhappy to give details of offenders confined to vagrants to the police without a magistrates' order; 29, 30 March 1846.

[48] Ibid., 4 December 1848, 3 January 1849. This was presumably the search for James Griffiths, arrested in Suffolk; see D. Davies, *Law and Disorder in Breconshire*, pp. 121ff.

[49] *Prison Inspectors' Sixteenth* (1851) and *Twenty-ninth* (1864) *Reports*.

[50] The disruptive Eugene Buckley was held here (*GJ*, 14 August 1846) as was the insane Mary Hughes (21 May 1847), the escapee Thomas Evans (13 August 1847, a policeman being given the key!) and, I believe, on alternate days to keep them apart, the attempted escapees Hugh Harris and Thomas Sloane (25 June 1848).

[51] (1823) 2 B & C 286, 107 *English Rep.* 390.

[52] *GJ*, 10 June 1846.

[53] Compare on this, and also on the use of tobacco, *Prison Inspectors' Third* (1837–8), *Fifth* (1840), *Seventh* (1842) and *Sixteenth* (1851) *Reports*.

[54] See *CarmJ*, 6 December 1867, though note that the newspaper disapproves of the monitoring of conversations, but thinks it not a rule of local origin.

[55] *Sixteenth Report* (1851).

[56] *Fifth* (1840) and *Sixteenth* (1851) *Reports*.

[57] See *GJ*, 25 December 1849.

[58] See chapter 2 above. And note the comment on John Booth at *FR*, no. 676, described despite his acquittal as 'an illconducted fellow'.

59 The *Carmarthen Journal*, thinking Hughes had killed herself, had described her act as 'one of the most cold-blooded and villainous acts of infanticide', 30 April 1847. See also for the case Ireland, 'Perhaps my mother', p. 235.

60 *GJ*, 10 May, 9 June 1847. She is 'fully committed' on 12 May.

61 Ibid., 21 May 1847. The 'other' female prisoners mentioned as there are presumably looking after Hughes.

62 Ibid., 10, 16 May 1847.

63 'When nurses are required for sick women in prison, it is very desirable to select them from among their fellow prisoners, some of whom will mostly be found capable of fulfilling the office, and steady enough to perform it faithfully, under the superintendence of the matron': E. Fry, *Observations on the Visiting, Superintendence and Governance of Female Prisoners* (London, 1827), p. 56.

64 It is interesting that at Hughes's trial evidence of her state of mind was given by the governor, surgeon and the chaplain of the gaol, rather than by independent medical witnesses; see *CarmJ*, 16 July 1847, and this volume, p. 217.

65 Harriet Lewis's case, *CarmJ*, 25 July 1851.

66 Ellen Donoghue's case, *CarmJ*, 4 June 1869.

67 All the cases mentioned here are discussed in detail in Ireland, 'Perhaps my mother', and see also 'Putting oneself on whose country?'.

68 For comments, see Ireland, 'A second Ireland?', in R. McMahon (ed.), *Crime, Law and Popular Culture in Europe Since 1500* (Cullompton, 2007).

69 For the trial, see *CarmJ*, 23 March 1849. For details of her incarceration see *GJ*, 21, 24 January; 21 February; 5, 19, 23, 31 March; 7, 10, 14, 26 April; 31 July; 2, 3, 4, 5, 6 August; 25 October 1849.

70 *GJ*, 18 February 1847; a term of forty days was served.

71 A sentence of seven days; ibid., 15 May 1846.

72 *Prison Inspectors' Thirty-second* (1867–8) and *Thirty-fourth* (1870) *Reports*.

73 *Prison Inspectors' Seventh Report* (1842).

74 Ibid.

75 D. J. V. Jones, 'A dead loss to the community', *Welsh History Review*, 8 (1977), 312–43; and see O'Leary, *Immigration and Integration*, ch. VI.

76 For an interesting discussion of vagrancy and its perceived relationship to other crimes, see R. L. Snowden, *The Magistrate's Assistant and Police Officer and Constable's Guide* (London, 1846), pp. 325ff.

77 D. J. V. Jones, 'A dead loss to the community', 330.

78 On which, see R. W. Ireland, 'The felon and the angel copier', in L. Knafla (ed.), *Policing and War in Europe* (Westport, 2002).

79 D. J. V. Jones, 'A dead loss to the community', 315.

80 This could of course also happen in the town, see, for example, the moving-on of David Bryant, *CarmJ*, 31 January 1851. See also L. Radzinowicz and R. Hood, *The Emergence of Penal Policy in Victorian and Edwardian England* (Oxford, 1990), p. 356.

81 *Prison Inspectors' Sixteenth Report* (1851). Note that a number of vagrants were treated for scabies on admission (*GJ*, 4 October 1846, May 1850, for examples) and on one occasion vagrants were employed 'washing their own clothes' (24 November 1845) rather than working on the wheel, inevitably raising the question of 'less-eligibility'.

82 D. J. V. Jones, 'A dead loss to the community', 322ff.

83 *GJ*, 2 December 1848; *CarmJ*, 6 December 1867.

84 Spellings of Mary Ann Awberry's name are not consistent; in the gaol records she can become 'Marian', 'Miriam'. She also used an alias, Mary Ann Evans (see *CarmJ*, 1 May 1846). A husband and wife called Awberry had been confined as debtors in 1832 (*QS Order Book 1832–7*). For Ann Awberry and others, see P. Molloy, *A Shilling for Carmarthen* (Llandysul, 1991), pp. 98ff.

85 *CarmJ*, 11, 17 January 1851.

86 Ibid., 18 July 1851.

87 *PC Williams's Diary 1859–60* (CRO Mus. 112).

88 *GJ*, 21 August 1846.

89 *CarmJ*, 27 June 1851.

90 *GJ*, 12 May 1846.

91 Ibid., 8, 9, 10 July 1846.

92 Ibid., 1, 2, 3 August 1846. And see this volume, p. 199.

93 Ibid., 31 October 1846; 6, 30 April 1847; 19 June 1848; 28 March 1850 (all Mary Ann Awberry): 30 April 1847; 11, 26 March; 19 August 1850 (all Ann Awberry): 19 July; 2, 9 October 1847 (Mariah Thomas). Compare Zedner's comments on women's behaviour in convict prisons (*Women, Crime and Punishment*, pp. 208ff.)

94 Radzinowicz and Hood, *Emergence of Penal Policy*, p. 231.

95 Ibid., p. 484.

96 I have selected these examples to illustrate that it is not only the 'ticket-of-leave' man who is the object of this process. Habitual drunkenness had been a concern for a long time before the legislation concerning it in 1879, whilst habitual vagrancy was a concern which led to legislation in 1871. To view the particular provisions as evidence of an increased penal 'specialization' or 'medicalization' is to label the process rather than explain it.

[97] M. D. Hill, *Report of the Select Committee on Criminal and Destitute Juveniles* (1852), p. 33, as quoted in J. Bennett, *Oral History and Delinquency* (Chicago, 1981), p. 24.

[98] Ibid., pp. 23ff. H. Mayhew and J. Binney's discussion of the criminal class in *The Criminal Prisons of London* (London, 1862) begins with the statistics of the 1839 Constabulary Commissioners, on which see above, p. 22. And see Radzinowicz and Hood, *Emergence of Penal Policy*, pp. 77ff.

[99] See the report of a murder and robbery in Hull in the *Carmarthen Journal* of 28 May 1852, which assumes that readers will understand the term, or the report of a 'garrotte in Aberavon' in the same publication, 9 December 1853.

[100] For an extended analysis of the issues considered in this paragraph, see Ireland, 'The felon and the angel copier', *passim*.

[101] Above, p. 95.

[102] Ibid. Note, however, the complaints about underfunding in the system in the 1860s: Ireland, 'The felon and the angel copier', p. 67. Not all previous convictions were proved by eyewitnesses; some seem to have relied on documentary evidence alone. But note the problems which this caused to the jury in the case of Samuel Jones at the summer assize in 1851 and the discussion thereof in Ireland, 'Putting oneself on whose country?', p. 65 and n. 10. In October 1858 a previous conviction against Rowland Rowlands was proved by the certificate of the clerk of the peace at Ruthin. Sentenced to five years' hard labour he was, rather surprisingly, removed to Wakefield house of correction; see *QS* Box 6 and *FR*, no. 747.

[103] See above, and the discussion in R. W. Ireland, 'Charles Hunt's haircut', in P. Brand, K. Costello and W. N. Osborough (eds), *Adventures of the Law* (Dublin, 2005), *passim*.

[104] For discussion of the ideas of 'moral panics' and 'deviancy amplification' in contemporary criminology see, for example, J. Tierney, *Criminology Theory and Context* (Hemel Hempstead, 1996), p. 143.

[105] *QS* Box 11, chief constable's order of 16 December 1869. This box also contains copies of the Circulars issued by the Home Office under the 1869 Act.

[106] *QS* Box 13. Roberts was given fourteen days' hard labour.

[107] The conviction of Owen Owens in October 1877 (fined £1 and costs), *QS* Box 25.

[108] See the *Report of the Chief Constable*, dated 29 June 1872, which does not, however, mention any particular statute: 'A prisoner convicted at Radnor and Sentenced to two years' Police Supervision Selected Laugharne Carmarthenshire as his place of residence but I

have not been able to bring him under the Supervision of the Police of this County as he has absented himself.' (*QS* Box 15)

109 It is difficult to tell whether a renewed concentration on the surveillance role of the police in this period played any role in an increasing sensitivity towards the disposition of officers evident in the local records. In March 1870 Chief Constable Scott, using his army rank of lieutenant-colonel, sends an incensed reply to a quarter sessions request for explanation as to the distribution of the county force:

> As for my reasons for the existing distribution I might almost as well be asked how I learned to eat and speak. I think a quarter of a century's experience of the County its inhabitants and the Police and the quantity of Crime would entitle me to form a pretty correct opinion of where the Police are required in each Petty Sessional Division; having regard to the extent of acrage as far as can be obtained, the number of the population, the distance from one station to the other, the means of Communication between them, The probable route of Tramps or Vagrants, guarding against having the Constables Stationed Singly so far as I can avoid it, the means of attending the different Petty Sessions and not forgetting the population bearing in mind that there are some Constables at the Head Quarters who are not sufficiently acquainted with their duties to be stationed alone. (*QS* Box 11)

Notwithstanding this, in the summer there is a petition to have police stationed in Cwm Amman ('there are some worthless characters in the place perfectly lawless in their proceedings'); *QS* Box 12.

110 *QS* Box 9.

111 See the rash of convictions in *QS* Box 19 for 1875.

112 See, for example, the convictions of Henry Davies and George Holmes taken at the Llandeilo fair in November 1871, *QS* Box 15. Four people are so charged at Newcastle Emlyn fair in November 1872, see *QS* Box 16, and four at Llandeilo again in 1874, *QS* Box 19. Similar convictions may be found in Boxes 17 and 19. Box 15 also contains a conviction under section 35, the Larceny Act 1861, for being a suspected person in possession of wood.

113 The Llandeilo town crier was paid 1s. in 1871 to warn people of the threat of pickpockets, *QS* Box 15. The chief constable's report in the same box shows how police were deployed for the occasion.

114 See the deposition of 19 January 1870 in *QS* Box 11, in which the policeman reveals: 'I was on duty at the Llanelly Market – I received information that the prisoner was an habitual thief, I watched her for an hour going up and down the market.' She was sentenced to one month with hard labour. Note also the conviction of Thomas Evans (three months with hard labour) for picking a pocket at Llandeilo railway station after the fair in November 1866. He was apparently working with two women accomplices. (*QS* Box 10).

[115] See the case of Mary Anne Gill and Bridget Mackie, both of whom were sentenced to two months with hard labour. Sergeant Davies visited one lodging house in Ebenezer Street, Swansea ('Ebenezer Street is not a very respectable street, I believe') and then another in Park Street, the respectability of which area seems to have produced some dispute: *QS* Box 15.

[116] Note the comment by Governor Stephens in his report to quarter sessions in April 1871: 'I beg leave to mention the fact that between the period of the last Quarter Sessions in January and the present time, not one prisoner from the entire county has been delivered into my custody, either under sentence or for trial, for Larceny and but for two convicted of Larceny in the Borough of Carmarthen the prison would have had to receive none for that species of offence' (*QS* Box 13).

[117] Compare the case of the 'thimble gentry' working the fair in Carmarthen in 1833, above, p. 92.

[118] J. Stack, 'Children, urbanization and the chances of imprisonment in mid-Victorian England', *Criminal Justice History*, 13 (1992), 113–39 at 126, calculates that the additional reformatory school sentence in the years 1858–75 was restricted to a mere 13 per cent of the total number of children imprisoned.

[119] For the age of criminal responsibility, and different views of the upper age limit of the Parkhurst experiment, see Radzinowicz and Hood, *Emergence of Penal Policy*, pp. 133, 149. Sixteen is used as a defining limit in the Juvenile Offenders Act, 13 and 14 Vict., ch. 37.

[120] *FR*, nos 74 (he is described at the inquest on his victim, three-year-old George Thomas, as a shepherd: see *CarmJ*, 20 September 1844), 926 (Hiram Lane, 'labourer'), 1337 (David Jones, 'farm servant'). Sometimes the youth of the offenders is only too apparent. The last mentioned, convicted of obstructing the railway, was barely visible when he stood in the dock, and was described as 'eccentric, silly and mischievous, but accountable for what he did' by Governor Cox of Swansea, where he had been remanded (*CarmJ*, 11 March 1870). David Joshua, aged nine, convicted of a similar offence, 'cried after admission', *QS* Box 25. Evan Lloyd, though acquitted of the murder on the direction of the judge, was nonetheless presented rather less positively by the local press:

> The prisoner, a heavy and sullen looking youth, stood in the front of the dock with a sulky air, and appeared rather amused than otherwise at the novelty of his position. His history is understood to be one of previous cruelty, taking delight in cutting off the legs of fowls, to see how they would limp without a leg – an exercise that must have prepared him for the deliberate murder of the deceased youth. (*CarmJ*, 21 March 1845)

121 For an example of a conviction for unlawfully employing juveniles, see *QS* Box 11.

122 Radzinowicz and Hood, *Emergence of Penal Policy*, p. 178.

123 Above, p. 77.

124 Compare M. Wiener, *Reconstructing the Criminal: Culture, Law and Policy in England, 1830–1914* (Cambridge, 1990), p. 135: 'If the mid-century reformatory movement marked a new acknowledgment of juvenile weakness and need for special help, this did not entail the repudiation of early Victorian moralism that historians once assumed.'

125 See 10 and 11 Vict., ch. 81. See the extension of the process, but not the age limit for whipping, to those under sixteen by 13 and 14 Vict., ch. 37, and note the presumption against jury trial.

126 *GJ*, 21 August 1847.

127 For Davies see *FR*, no. 185, *GJ*, 29 February 1848, and the subsequent entries at *FR*, 227 and 380. It is interesting that in David Jones's case (see n. 120 above) the whipping was awarded after the jury had recommended that mercy be shown. For whipping inside the gaol the governor and surgeon (or his assistant) would attend, a warder administering the punishment, see the description in *GJ*, 28 December 1849.

128 See *QS* Box 12.

129 See *QS* Box 16. See also the cases of acquittal being announced by the bench on condition of a domestic flogging, *CarmJ*, 8 August 1851, *The Welshman*, 23 June 1871.

130 See the cases of fifteen-year-old Daniel Jones in 1871 (*FR*, no. 1387) and twelve-year-old Theophilus Evans, fined 40s. for attempted theft in 1876, ostensibly under the provisions of *both* the statutes of 1847 and 1850: *QS* Box 23.

131 See the *Report of the Select Committee on Criminal and Destitute Juveniles* (1852–3). For the statutes see The Reformatory Schools Acts 1854 and 1857 (17 and 18 Vict., ch. 86; 20 and 21 Vict., ch. 55, and then 29 and 30 Vict., chs 117, 118). Carmarthenshire's custodial sentences before the Reformatory sentence ranged from ten days (*sic*; *FR*, no. 1326) to three months (no. 727).

132 *Chaplain's Report* (*QS* Box 23).

133 15 January 1847. It is possible that sensibilities had been aroused by the *Report on Juvenile Offenders* of that year.

134 *QS* Box 6.

135 *Chaplain's Report* (*QS* Box 6). For King, see *FR*, no. 727. The details of the disposition of the girl involved, Maryann Williams, have not been discovered. The prison inspectors' *Twenty-second Report* of 1857 had reported that there were then no reformatory schools in Wales.

136 John Joshua in 1876 is reported, however, to have been sent to 'Tysegur Reformatory' (*QS* Box 21). Sarah Evans (*FR*, no. 919) is reported to have gone to 'Redhill House, Bristol', *sed quaere* 'Red Lodge'. For Carpenter see Radzinowicz and Hood, *Emergence of Penal Policy*, pp. 161ff.

137 See *CarmJ*, 11 January 1867. Despite the report the problem seems to have been restricted to the girls; boys continue to be sentenced for three years. The girl mentioned is apparently Eliza Davies (*FR*, no. 1177).

138 *FR*, nos 1033 and 1034, though both had previous convictions. Note too John Evans's family circumstances (see n. 140).

139 Stack, 'Children, urbanization and the chances of imprisonment', suggests more general variables in the use of the measure, but his analysis bafflingly excludes any real consideration of the Welsh experience.

140 See *FR*, nos 919 and 1033, 1247 and 1248. Of those recorded in the *Felons' Register*, no fewer than six of the thirteen receiving the sentence come from the industrial town of Llanelli.

141 *Circular* (*QS* Box 7).

142 *QS Misc. Papers, QS* Box 25.

143 *QS Order Book 1866–77*, p. 73.

144 *QS* Boxes 8 and 26.

145 See *FR*, nos 675, 775, 778. Francis Smith's fellow escapee from Stoke Prior, Peter Bowker (no. 777) was returned to that institution notwithstanding being sixteen at the time of this conviction.

146 The *Felons' Register* provides evidence which unfortunately stops in 1871. It also does not include all the county's juvenile offenders. The picture seems to be of an increased use of reformatory sentences in the 1860s, but with simple imprisonment remaining an option within that period, at least for boys. The last girl to suffer this sentence was Elizabeth Evans in 1859. For labour see, for example *FR*, nos 883, 1387, but compare the thirteen-year-old William Richards, breaking stones before his transfer to Howdre Ganol in 1869, *FR*, no. 1326.

147 See R. W. Ireland, 'Confinement with hard labour: motherhood and penal practice in a Victorian gaol', 18 (1997) *Welsh History Review*, 631. For Bowen see *FR*, no. 1026.

148 The period covered by the *Felons' Register* reveals eleven such cases. This total, of course, excludes other classes of inmate such as debtors and misdemeanants, although it might be unwise simply to assume that similar distributions would occur within these other categories; issues such as length of sentence or relative age may have had an effect.

149 S. McConville, *A History of English Prison Administration, Volume 1: 1750–1877* (London, 1981), p. 332.

150 The *Prison Inspectors' Twenty-ninth Report* (1864) records that no more military prisoners were being sent from Pater Barracks, in Pembroke Dock, as a military prison had opened there.

151 *QS* Box 7 contains a reference to a conviction of a soldier by court martial in 1866 for an 'attempted unnatural offence'. He was sentenced to two years' hard labour and fifty lashes. We have noted, above, pp. 47, 73, the reluctance of Carmarthenshire juries to convict in such cases.

152 For examples, see *QS* Box 9, 6.

153 Above, pp. 146–7.

154 See, for example, *Prison Inspectors' Eleventh Report* (1846); *FR*, no. 101.

155 McConville, *History*, p. 372.

156 *GJ*, 22 October 1845.

157 Ibid., 29 June 1846.

158 Ibid., 8 May 1846.

159 Though resilience, rather than trust, may have been the attraction of setting a soldier to oversee the insane David Lewis (ibid., 25 September 1845); see this volume, p. 218.

160 Ibid., 17 August and 24 October 1847, this latter case being an exemption from solitary on the surgeon's orders.

161 Ibid., 16 May and 16 June 1846. The reasons are not stated.

162 *Chaplain's Report* (*QS* Box 7); above, p. 264, n. 77. Such admixture of religions, repeated on a national level, may possibly have been a factor in the increasing recognition of the role of the Catholic chaplain in prisons.

163 See, for example, the prisoner sentenced to '336 days' for desertion (*QS* Box 24).

164 See *GJ*, 29 July 1846, or *QS* Boxes 6 and 7 for examples.

165 *GJ*, 18 February 1848.

166 Soldiers in solitary confinement were picking oakum in their cells (ibid., 13 February 1846).

167 *FR*, no. 66.

168 At p. 62.

169 Jebb was inspector-general of military prisons as well as being appointed chairman of the directors of convict prisons in 1850. For his views on the value of the capability of comparing experiences in military and civilian regimes, see *Report on the Discipline and Management of Convict Prisons* (1850), p. 64.

170 *QS* Box 24.

Notes to Chapter 5

1 See ch. 4 above. Note, though, that the debtors were once 'employed' picking grass in the yard (*GJ*, 7 September 1846). Individual debtors might employ their trades for the benefit of the gaol (see ibid., 28 November 1849).

2 Ibid., 23, 24, 25, 27 March 1847; *FR*, no. 147.

3 *Prison Inspectors' Third* (1837–8), *Fifth* (1840) and *Seventh* (1842) *Reports*.

4 Compare *Prison Inspectors' Third* (1837–8) and *Sixteenth Reports*, the latter of 1851.

5 *GJ*, 13 January, 4 May 1846.

6 *Prison Inspectors' Thirty-eighth Report* (1874).

7 *CarmJ*, 6 December 1867.

8 *Prison Inspectors' Thirty-eighth Report* (1874).

9 *CarmJ*, 2 November 1832: two 'boxes for the prisoners' presumably formed the only original compartments.

10 *Prison Inspectors' Thirty-eighth Report* (1874).

11 Compare *Prison Inspectors' Third* (1837–8) and *Fortieth* (1876) *Reports*.

12 For Mance, see *Evidence to the House of Lords Select Committee on the Gaols and Houses of Correction* (1835). Mance revealed considerable variation in treadwheel labour across the country, the maximum task being 17,000 ft. For Carmarthen, see *Prison Inspectors' Third Report* (1837–8).

13 *GJ*, 11 December 1846.

14 Ibid., 10 October, 15 November 1849.

15 Ibid., 21 February 1846. The wheel was working again on 17 March.

16 See, for example, ibid., 2 November 1846; 26 February 1848.

17 See, for example, ibid., 10, 11 November 1846; 29 September, 1 October 1849.

18 Ibid., 1 December 1845.

19 Ibid., 26 May 1849.

20 Ibid., 8 May 1846.

21 See, for example, ibid., 23 October 1845; compare 3 August 1849.

22 Ibid., 7 September 1846.

23 Ibid., 3 July, 4 August 1849. For Coupland, see *FR*, nos 228, 294.

24 See *Prison Inspectors' Thirty-second Report* (1867–8). It had been employed also in the borough gaol before its closure; *Seventh Report* (1842).

25 *GJ*, 17 February 1847.

26 Ibid., 12, 19, 20 April 1847.

27 *Prison Inspectors' Thirty-third Report* (1868–9).

28 Ibid. and *Fortieth Report* (1876).

29 *GJ*, 30 January, 12 March 1847.

30 Ibid., 18 February 1846; 17 August 1848.

31 Ibid., 14 May 1850.

32 *Prison Inspectors' Twenty-sixth Report* (1861).

33 *GJ*, 20 May 1846.

34 Ibid., 26 February 1846.

35 Ibid., 14 January 1849. For these prisoners see above, pp. 162–3, 167–9.

36 *GJ*, 8 January 1850.

37 Ibid., 30 June 1846; cf. 30 November 1847, 16 May 1850.

38 Ibid., 14, 16 May 1846.

39 *Prison Inspectors' Twenty-sixth Report* (1861): £5. 12s. as against 10s. 11d.

40 For the rebuilding, see above, p. 121. For the other work, see *GJ*, 8 October 1849; 30 June, 28 July 1846; 29 March 1847; 15 April, June 1847.

41 Ibid., 10 April 1848; 5 June 1850. Compare *Prison Inspectors' Fifth Report* (1840).

42 *GJ*, 30 April 1848, 26 October 1847.

43 *Prison Inspectors' Thirty-second Report* (1867–8).

44 *GJ*, 15, 16, 17 December 1846.

45 Ibid., 10, 11, 12 June 1846.

46 Ibid., 8 October 1846.

47 Ibid., 28 August 1846, but note 'vagrants' washing their own clothes, 24, 25 November 1845.

48 Ibid., magistrates' side, 27 October 1846.

49 *Prison Inspectors' Thirtieth Report* (1865).

50 *CarmJ*, 12 January 1866.

51 *Prison Inspectors' Eighteenth Report* (1851); *GJ*, 19 February 1846.

52 *GJ*, 12 February, 8 April 1847; 30 May, 15 November 1848.

53 Ibid., 6 October 1849; 4 January 1850. For Shaw, see *FR*, no. 246.

54 *Prison Inspectors' Twenty-fourth Report* (1859).

55 *GJ*, 3, 4 April 1847.

56 Ibid., 15 March 1847; see R. W. Ireland, 'Charles Hunt's haircut', in P. Brand, K. Costello and W. N. Osborough (eds), *Adventures of the Law* (Dublin, 2005), p. 225.

57 *Prison Inspectors' Sixteenth Report* (1851).

58 *Prison Inspectors' Third Report* (1837–8).

59 Ibid.

60 *Select Committee on Gaols, First Report* (1835), p. 26, but cf. p. 16.

61 *Prison Inspectors' Third Report* (1837–8).

62 *Prison Inspectors' Fifth Report* (1840).

63 See above, p. 135; *GJ*, 17 November 1845.

64 Ibid., 18 December 1845.

[65] Ibid., 18 November 1845.

[66] Ibid., 26 November 1845.

[67] Ibid., 11 March 1846. It is difficult to assess the extent to which the regime tightened, but figures from the *Prison Inspectors' Reports* for 1842 (*Seventh*) and 1851 (*Sixteenth*) respectively show an increase of 'dark cell' punishments from 7 to 24 in a year against a decline in population over the period. On the 'dark cell' see this volume, p. 198.

[68] See above, p. 6.

[69] *Prison Inspectors' Third Report* (1837–8). René Le Sage's fantasy is in no way indecent, though it does include some criticism of a gaol. It enjoyed some popularity in England, forming the subject of a painting of 1844 by Augustus Egg.

[70] *GJ*, 5 August 1848.

[71] Ibid., 29 August 1848.

[72] This was certainly the case in the 1870s; see *Prison Inspectors' Thirty-eighth Report* (1874).

[73] See the comments in *GJ*, 6 April 1847.

[74] Note ibid., 1 September 1849: John Roberts is released from the refractory cell because he is unwell. But note that in his *Sixteenth Report* of 1851 the inspector sees fit to remind of the desirability of daily visits.

[75] Ibid., 30 September 1848.

[76] Ibid., 12 May 1846.

[77] Ibid., 5 January 1847.

[78] Ibid., 17 December 1848.

[79] Ibid., 8, 9, 10, 11 May 1846.

[80] *Prison Inspectors' Third* (1837–8) and *Fifth* (1840) *Reports*.

[81] *GJ*, 22, 25, 29 November 1845.

[82] *Prison Inspectors' Sixteenth Report* (1851). The plans drawn up in 1866 suggest that there was an exercise yard connected with the refractory cell(s) in the house of correction.

[83] *CarmJ*, 6 December 1867. See *GJ*, 12 June 1849, for an attack.

[84] *GJ*, 20 March 1846.

[85] Ibid., 28 August 1846. For the weather, see the diary at CRO Mus. 622.

[86] For the weather, see ibid. and *GJ*, 10 July 1849.

[87] CRO Misc. Plans 1

[88] See the actions taken against a prisoner later declared insane, *GJ*, 11, 12, 13 June 1849. For handcuffing 'behind', see ibid., 9 June 1848.

[89] Ibid., 19 April 1849.

[90] Ibid., 22 March 1849.

[91] See above, p. 169.

[92] *GJ*, 18, 19 July 1847.

Notes to Chapter 6

1 The debate found many expressions. My own favourite is the opportunistic advert which appears in my own copy of Capt. D— S—'s *18 Months' Imprisonment*, which announces the author's next pamphlet *Advice to Stout People: Showing How I Reduced From 20 Stone To 14 Stone*, the answer to which question seems clear enough to readers of the first work!

2 See the *Report Relative to the System of Prison Discipline etc. by the Inspectors of Prisons* (1843).

3 It might be thought that experience with the army and, in particular, the navy would have established basic nutritional norms, but the fundamental ignorance and confusion apparent in the evidence taken after the Millbank scandal proves otherwise, see the *Minutes of Evidence before the Select Committee on the State of the Penitentiary at Millbank* (1823).

4 See the argument advanced in M. Wiener, *Reconstructing the Criminal: Culture, Law and Policy in England, 1830–1914* (Cambridge, 1990), *passim*.

5 The role of public imagination in the demise of transportation has been considered above, at p. 28.

6 See the *Minutes of Evidence* on the Millbank epidemic.

7 For a summary, see S. Webb and B. Webb, *English Prisons under Local Government* (London, 1922), pp. 138ff.

8 Quoted in ibid., p. 144.

9 *Prison Inspectors' Third Report* (1837–8).

10 *Prison Inspectors' Ninth Report* (1844).

11 *GJ*, 26 December 1845.

12 Ibid., 1, 11, 25, 28, 29 July 1845.

13 Ibid., 15 December 1849; *QS* Box 1, *Prison Inspectors' Sixteenth Report* (1851).

14 *Prison Inspectors' Eighteenth Report* (1852–3).

15 *QS* Box 5, *Prison Inspectors' Thirtieth* (1865), *Thirty-first* (1866), *Thirty-second* (1867–8) and *Thirty-seventh* (1873) *Reports*. For the results of the 1860s reduction, see J. Sim and T. Ward, 'The magistrate of the poor? Coroners and deaths in custody in nineteenth-century England', in M. Clark and C. Crawford (eds), *Legal Medicine in History* (Cambridge, 1994), p. 245.

16 *CarmJ*, 6 December 1867, noted with satisfaction that the cheese was Welsh.

17 *GJ*, 26 July, 8, 11, 15 October 1846.

18 Compare *Prison Inspectors' Third* (1837–8) and *Sixteenth* (1851) *Reports*. By this time it seems to have been highly unusual for

remands to have food brought in by friends. A Justices' order is apparently deemed necessary to authorize this for the celebrated Anne Matthews (above, p. 163), see *GJ*, 21 January 1849.

19 *Prison Inspectors' Thirtieth* (1865) and *Thirty-first* (1866) *Reports*.

20 *GJ*, 24 June 1849.

21 Ibid., 11 July 1846.

22 On this, see the discussion in R. W. Ireland 'Charles Hunt's haircut', in P. Brand, K. Costello and W. N. Osborough (eds), *Adventures of the Law* (Dublin, 2005); see also *GJ*, 13 November 1849; *Prison Inspectors' Twenty-fourth Report* (1859). And see P. Priestley, *Victorian Prison Lives* (London, 1985), ch. 7.

23 *CarmJ*, 6 December 1867.

24 See the minutes of the Carnarvon Committee, paras 1052ff, where Smith goes so far as to urge the adoption of a kind of 'objective' diagnosis of prisoners on a pattern used at Wakefield.

25 *GJ*, 16 February 1847.

26 Ibid., 6 November 1846.

27 Ibid., 6 August 1849.

28 R. W. Ireland, 'The felon and the angel copier', in L. Knafla (ed.), *Policing and War in Europe* (Westport, 2002), pp. 68–9.

29 But note that they had already, before a reception cell was built, entered into contact with other prisoners; *Prison Inspectors' Twentieth Report* (1855).

30 *Surgeon's Report*, *QS* Box 12.

31 See *GJ*, magistrates' side, 10 March 1847.

32 Ibid., 7, 9 June 1846; for Mathias, see *FR*, no. 123.

33 See *Surgeon's Reports*, *QS* Box 6; *FR*, no. 698

34 See the case of Jenkin Jones in this volume, and the unnamed prisoner mentioned in the *Surgeon's Report* of April 1874 (*QS* Box 17).

35 *CarmJ*, 19 July 1850. See Ireland, 'Perhaps my mother murdered me', in C. Brooks and M. Lobban (eds), *Communities and Courts in Britain 1150–1900* (London, 1997).

36 *GJ*, 5 March 1846.

37 *FR*, no. 660.

38 *FR*, no. 385 (as 'Bryan'), *CarmJ*, 9 April 1852. For further discussion, see R. W. Ireland, 'Confinement with hard labour', *Welsh History Review* 18 (1996–7), 621–38 at 631.

39 *Prison Inspectors' Third* (1837–8) and *Fifth* (1840) *Reports*. Note, though, the detentions for the previous crime of attempting suicide of Daniel Jones (*FR*, no. 233) and, though not prosecuted, Rosina Purslow (*QS* Box 15).

40 *FR*, nos 906, 1036, and note the unnamed debtor mentioned in the *Prison Inspectors' Fifth Report* (1840) who died of 'inflammation

and obstruction of the bowels'. John Phillips died of 'natural causes' in 1875 (*Visiting Justices' Report* [QS Box 20]), though note it is not in the *Surgeon's Report*. The chaplain, however, does allow himself a comment: 'I have the satisfaction to say that my hope is that our Brother rests in our Lord Jesus Christ, being delivered out of the miseries of this sinful world.'

[41] *CarmJ*, 27 May 1853.

[42] *Prison Inspectors' Third* (1837–8) and *Seventh* (1842) *Reports*.

[43] For a detailed treatment of the disease in the locality, and observations on both the local medical practitioners and the relationship to central power see H. James, 'Cholera and the public health movement in Carmarthen 1848–1856', *Carmarthenshire Antiquary*, 14 (1988); 83–105.

[44] *Prison Inspectors' Sixteenth Report* (1851).

[45] *Prison Inspectors' Twentieth Report* (1855).

[46] See J. Summers, *Soho: A History of London's Most Colourful Neighbourhood* (London, 1989), pp. 113–17.

[47] *Surgeon's Report*, QS Box 15.

[48] See *GJ*, May–September 1846, *passim*.

[49] This John Evans would appear to have been a misdemeanant. Compare the case of the felon John Thomas whose release from sentence by 'the Queen' is specifically recorded (*FR*, no. 955).

[50] See *GJ*, 28 November 1845: 'J. Jenkins, surgeon, called and ordered me to purchase a few earthen whare dishes for the prisoners that had sore eyes to Bathe there eyes night and morning with luke warm water and each man to use his on dish.' For the combs, see ibid., 25 October 1845, magistrates' side.

[51] Ibid., 10 December 1845; *FR*, no. 62.

[52] *FR*, no. 1202.

[53] Ibid., no. 972 (1864); *Surgeon's Report*, QS Box 9.

[54] *FR*, no. 521 (1855).

[55] Ibid., no. 482 (1855); *Surgeon's Report*, QS Box 4. Compare the case of Ellen King, confined to the infirmary throughout her incarceration and discharged 'in excellent health' (*Surgeon's Report*, QS Box 6).

[56] *GJ*, 11 July 1849.

[57] Ibid., 27 September 1849; *FR*, no. 243.

[58] *Surgeon's Reports*, QS Box 16. For feigning see Priestley, *Victorian Prison Lives*, pp. 173ff.

[59] See above, p. 139.

[60] *CarmJ*, 30 January 1852.

[61] *Lunatic Asylum Visitors' Report*, QS Box 19.

[62] *Surgeon's Report*, QS Box 21.

[63] See above, p. 154, *Surgeon's Reports*, *QS* Boxes 15, 16.

[64] *FR*, no. 933.

[65] *FR*, no. 1255.

[66] *FR*, no. 157; *CarmJ*, 16 July 1847; *GJ*, 11 May, 13 June 1848.

[67] *FR*, no. 499.

[68] See, for example, *FR*, no. 964. The appropriate procedure, which involved certification by the secretary of state, was specified in 3 and 4 Vict., ch. 29 and, with slight differences, 27 and 28 Vict., ch. 29.

[69] *FR*, no. 1086.

[70] See Ireland ,'Perhaps my mother', pp. 234–5.

[71] See *Surgeon's Reports*, *QS* Boxes 17, 18, 24.

[72] *Surgeon's Report*, *QS* Box 17. Compare David Rees in 1875, 'who when brought to prison was eccentric in his conduct but in time he prove [*sic*] to be insane' (*Surgeon's Report*, *QS* Box 20). The means of diagnosis remain unclear. Reporting the insanity of David Howells in 1869, Rowlands simply states that the 'proper means were at once taken to establish the fact' (*Surgeon's Report*, *QS* Box 12).

[73] *FR*, no. 112.

[74] *GJ*, 23, 24, 25, 26 September; 25 October; 3, 8, 11 December 1845.

[75] *Surgeon's Report*, *Governor's Report*, *Lunatic Asylum Report*, all *QS* Box 16.

[76] *FR*, no. 1154.

Notes to Conclusion

[1] See the *Memorandum* of 13 March 1922, and associated letters in CRO Boro. 114.

[2] See CRO CAC/CL/10, 11. The contract for demolition with Henry Strickland of Kilburn was for £90. In June 1951 Strickland, then aged seventy-five, and apparently under the impression that the contract was for ten times that sum, was claiming an unpaid £400 from the council. His accounts had been disturbed by the war, during which he had been 'bommed out. Twice.' The portico was, in fact, broken up, see CRO CC 31.

[3] Of 1,448 remands in the *Felons' Register*, 40 received sentences of transportation, 27 of penal servitude in the period 1844–71.

[4] And notice too the important undermining of localist distinctions in the campaign against borough gaols.

Select Bibliography

This bibliography is not intended to impress the reader by showing how much has been read in the preparation of the text. The works listed here appear either because their importance to the argument means that they appear in a number of footnotes and therefore the reader may be spared having to scour the text for full references, or because they may suggest avenues for exploration by those (whether academic or more general readers, penal or local historians) who may have been interested in the material here presented. I have not listed material, and in particular this relates to archival material (a core component of the treatment offered here), which is available only at specific locations. This, together with other sources such as Acts of Parliament or newspaper reports where references are individual and self-explanatory, is referenced simply in the footnotes. I have, as is traditional, listed more works by myself than is strictly necessary. This is due to vanity.

Official Reports

Reports of the Inspectors of Prisons
(Until 1857 reports relating to Carmarthen county and / or borough gaols are found within the Southern and Western District category, after that date in the Southern. Reports in which Carmarthen is not discussed are not listed here. In the footnotes above the number and year of the report have alone been given for brevity. The references to Parliamentary Papers below are to the report as a whole; individual gaols are located by subheadings therein.)

Third Report 1837–8 [135] xxxi.177
Fifth Report 1840 [255] xxv.721
Seventh Report 1842 [421] xxi.193
Eighth Report 1843 [507] xxv and xxvi.441

Ninth Report 1844 [593] xxix.441
Eleventh Report 1846 [740] xx.461
Thirteenth Report 1847–8 [1001] xxxvi.93
Sixteenth Report 1851 [1346] xxvii.669
Eighteenth Report 1852–3 [1662] lii.113
Twentieth Report 1854–5 [2005] xxvi.1
Twenty-second Report 1857 [2205 Sess. 1] vii.401
Twenty-fourth Report 1859 [2501 Sess. 1] xi.169
Twenty-sixth Report 1861 [2771] xxix.1
Twenty-seventh Report 1862 [2991] xxv.5
Twenty-ninth Report 1864 [3321] xxvi.1
Thirtieth Report 1865 [3474] xxiii.1
Thirty-first Report 1866 [3671] xxxviii.1
Thirty-second Report (1867–8) [4029–1.] xxxiv.203
Thirty-third Report 1868–9 [4214] xxix.1
Thirty-fourth Report 1870 [c.125] xxxvii.1
Thirty-fifth Report 1871 [c.371] xxix.241
Thirty-sixth Report 1872 [c.559] xxxi.1
Thirty-seventh Report 1873 [c.810] xxxii.1
Thirty-eighth Report 1874 [c.1020] xxix.1
Thirty-ninth Report 1875 [c.1261] xxxvii.1
Fortieth Report 1876 [c.1489] xxxv.1
Forty-first Report 1877 [c.1756] xliii.1
Forty-second Report 1878 [c.2030] xli.1
Report of the Select Committee on Secondary Punishments
    1831 (276) vii.559
*First Report of the Commissioners on Municipal Corporations
    in England and Wales* 1835 (116) xxii.1
*First Report of the Select Committee on Gaols and Houses of
    Correction* 1835 (438) xi.1
*Report of the Royal Commission on the Establishment of a
    Constabulary Force* 1839 [169] xix.1
Report on the Conduct of the Governor of Carnarvon Gaol
    1843 (422) xliii.1
Report on the System of Prison Discipline 1843 [457] xxv,
    xxvi.1
Report of the Commissioners of Inquiry for South Wales 1844
    [531] xvi.1
*Report of the Royal Commission to Inquire into the Means of
    Education Available in Wales* (First Part) 1847 [870] xxvii.1

Report of the Select Committee on Prison Discipline 1850 (632) xvii.519

Report of the Select Committee on the State of Discipline in Gaols and Houses of Correction 1863 (499) ix.1

Books and Articles

Beattie, J. M., *Crime and the Courts in England 1660–1800* (Oxford, 1986).

Beddoe, D., 'Carmarthenshire women and criminal transportation to Australia 1787–1852', *The Carmarthenshire Antiquary*, 13 (197), 65–74.

Bentley, D., *English Criminal Justice in the Nineteenth Century* (London, 1998).

Bolwell, J. and Evans, A., *A History of the County Infirmary, Carmarthen, 1847–1948* (Carmarthen, 2005).

Crofton, Sir W., 'The Irish system of prison discipline', in E. C. Wines (ed.), *Transactions of the National Congress on Penitentiary and Reformatory Discipline* (Albany, 1871).

D'Cruze, S., 'Sex, violence and local courts: working-class respectability in a mid-nineteenth century town', *British Journal of Criminology*, 39 (1999), 39–55.

Davies, D., *Law and Disorder in Breconshire 1750–1880* (Brecon, n.d.)

Davies, J., *A History of Wales* (London, 1994).

Davies, R., *Secret Sins: Sex, Violence and Society in Carmarthenshire 1870–1920* (Cardiff, 1996).

——, 'Language and community in south-west Wales c.1800–1914', in G. Jenkins (ed.), *Language and Community in the Nineteenth Century* (Cardiff, 1998), pp. 101–24.

Davitt, M., *Leaves from a Prison Diary; or, Lectures to a 'Solitary' Audience* (London, 1885, reprinted Shannon, 1972).

DeLacy, M., *Prison Reform in Lancashire 1700–1850* (Manchester, 1986).

Dobash, R., Dobash, E., Gutteridge, S., *The Imprisonment of Women* (Oxford, 1986).

Emsley, C., *Crime and Society in England 1750–1900* (3rd edn, Harlow, 2005).

Evans, R., *The Fabrication of Virtue: English Prison Architecture 1750–1840* (Cambridge, 1982).

Floud, R. and McCloskey, D. (eds), *The Economic History of Britain since 1700* (Cambridge, 2nd edn, 1994).

Forsythe, W. J., *A System of Discipline: Exeter Borough Prison 1819–1863* (Exeter, 1983).

——, *The Reform of Prisoners 1830–1900* (Beckenham, 1987).

Foster, B., 'The Usk Houses of Correction and the early days of Usk County Gaol', *Gwent Local History*, 94 (2003), 3–34.

Foucault, M., *Surveiller et Punir*, translated as *Discipline and Punish: The Birth of the Prison* by A. Sheridan (Harmondsworth, 1979).

Garland, D., *Punishment and Modern Society: A Study in Social Theory* (Oxford, 1990).

Gattrell, V., *The Hanging Tree: Execution and the English People 1770–1868* (Oxford, 1994).

Goffmann, E., *Asylums* (New York, 1961).

Goodall P., *The Black Flag over Carmarthen* (Llanrwst, 2005).

Griffiths, A., *Secrets of the Prison House* (London, 1894).

Harding, C., Hines, B., Ireland, R., Rawlings, P., *Imprisonment in England and Wales: A Concise History* (Beckenham, 1985).

Harding, C., and Ireland, R. W., *Punishment: Rhetoric, Rule and Practice* (London, 1989).

Hay, D., in Hay, D., Linebaugh, P., Rule, J. G., Thompson, E. P., Winslow, C., *Albion's Fatal Tree* (London, 1975), pp. 17–63.

Herbert, T. and Jones, G. E. (eds), *People and Protest: Wales 1815–1880* (Cardiff, 1988).

Hines, W. D. (ed.), *English Legal History: A Bibliography and Guide to the Literature* (New York, 1990), pp. 91–5.

Hoppen, K., *The Mid-Victorian Generation* (Oxford, 1998).

Howard, J., *The State of the Prisons* (Warrington, 1777).

——, *An Account of the Principal Lazarettos in Europe* (Warrington, 1789).

Ignatieff, M., 'State, civil society and total institutions: a critique of recent social histories of punishment' in D. Sugarman (ed.), *Legality, Ideology and the State* (London, 1983), pp. 183–211.

Ingram, M., 'Juridical folklore in England illustrated by Rough Music', in C. Brooks and M. Lobban (eds), *Communities and Courts in Britain 1150–1900* (London, 1997), pp. 61–82.

Ireland, R. W., 'Theory and practice within the medieval English prison', *American Journal of Legal History*, 31 (1987), 55–62.

——, 'Eugene Buckley and the diagnosis of insanity in the early Victorian prison', *Llafur*, 6 (1993), 5–17.

——, '"An increasing mass of heathens in the bosom of a Christian land": the railway and crime in the nineteenth century', *Continuity and Change*, 12 (1997), 55–78.

——, 'Confinement with hard labour: motherhood and penal practice in a Victorian gaol', *Welsh History Review*, 18 (1997), 621–38.

——, 'Perhaps my mother murdered me: child death and the law in Victorian Carmarthenshire ', in C. Brooks and M. Lobban (eds), *Communities and Courts in Britain 1150–1900* (London, 1997), pp. 229–44.

——, 'The policeman and the rail: crime and punishment in the paintings of W. P. Frith', *Art Antiquity and Law*, 2 (1997), 381–6.

——, 'Howard and the paparazzi: painting penal reform in the eighteenth century', *Art Antiquity and Law*, 4 (1999), 55–62.

——, 'Putting oneself on whose country? Carmarthenshire juries in the mid-nineteenth century', in T. G. Watkin (ed.), *Legal Wales: Its Past, Its Future* (Cardiff, 2001), pp. 63–87.

——, 'The felon and the angel copier: criminal identity and the promise of photography in Victorian England and Wales', in L. Knafla (ed.), *Policing and War in Europe* (Westport, 2002), pp. 53–86.

——, 'Charles Hunt's haircut: getting down to the roots of a legal adventure' in P. Brand, K. Costello and W. N. Osborough (eds), *Adventures of the Law* (Dublin, 2005), pp. 219–33.

——, '"A second Ireland"? Crime and popular culture in nineteenth-century Wales', in R. McMahon (ed.), *Crime, Law and Popular Culture in Europe since 1500* (Cullompton, 2007).

—— and Breay, C., 'Hard labour on a hard disk: Carmarthen's Register of Felons on computer', *The Carmarthenshire Antiquary*, 29 (1993), 61–6.

James, H., 'Cholera and the public health movement in Carmarthen 1848–1856', *The Carmarthenshire Antiquary*, 24 (1988), 83–105

Jones, D. J. V., '"A dead loss to the community": the criminal vagrant in mid-nineteenth-century Wales', *Welsh History Review*, 8 (1977), 312–43.

——, *Rebecca's Children: A Study of Rural Society, Crime and Protest* (Oxford, 1989).

——, 'Rebecca, crime and policing: a turning point in nineteenth-century attitudes', *Trafodion Anrhydeddus Gymdeithas y Cymmrodorion / Transactions of the Honourable Society of Cymmrodorion* (1990), 99–115.

——, *Crime in Nineteenth-Century Wales* (Cardiff, 1992).

Jones, Dot, *Statistical Evidence Relating to the Welsh Language 1801–1911* (Cardiff, 1998).

Jones, E. Vernon, 'Twelve months in a Victorian gaol', *Carmarthenshire Historian*, 18 (1982), 28–50.

Jones, M. Ellis, 'The confusion of Babel? The Welsh language, law courts and legislation in the nineteenth century', in G. Jenkins (ed.), *The Welsh Language and its Social Domains 1801–1911* (Cardiff, 2000), pp. 587–614.

Jones, Rosemary, 'Popular culture, policing and the disappearance of the Ceffyl Pren in Cardiganshire *c.*1837–1850', *Ceredigion*, 11 (1998–9), 19–39.

Kilcommins, S., O'Donnell, I., O'Sullivan, E. and Vaughan, B., *Crime, Punishment and the Search for Order in Ireland* (Dublin, 2004).

King, P., *Crime, Justice and Discretion in England 1740–1820* (Oxford, 2000).

Langbein, J., 'Albion's fatal flaws', *Past and Present*, 98 (1983), 96–120.

Linebaugh, P., *The London Hanged: Crime and Civil Society in the Eighteenth Century* (London, 1991).

Lodwick, J. and V., *The Story of Carmarthen* (Carmarthen, 1994).

Loughlin, M., *Legality and Locality: The Role of Law in Central–Local Government Relations* (Oxford, 1996)

Mayhew, H., *London Labour and the London Poor* (London, 1851/61).

—— and Binney, J., *The Criminal Prisons of London* (London, 1862).

McConville, S., *A History of English Prison Administration, Volume 1: 1750–1877* (London, 1981).

——, *English Local Prisons 1860–1900: Next Only to Death* (London, 1995).

——, 'Local justice: the jail', in N. Morris and D. Rothman (eds), *The Oxford History of the Prison* (Oxford, 1995), pp. 297–329.

Molloy, P., *And They Blessed Rebecca* (Llandysul, 1983).

——, *A Shilling for Carmarthen* (Llandysul, 1991).

Morgan, G., and Rushton, P., 'The magistrate, the community and the maintenance of an orderly society in eighteenth-century England', *Historical Research*, 76 (2003), 54–77.

Nield, J., *An Account of the Rise, Progress and Present State, of the Society for the Discharge and Relief of Persons Imprisoned for Small Debts throughout England and Wales* (London, 1802).

'One Who Has Endured It', *Five Years' Penal Servitude* (London, 1878).

Owen, J., 'Crime in Victorian Carmarthenshire: the evidence of the Felons' Register', *The Carmarthenshire Antiquary*, 23 (1987), 66–70.

Palmer, S., *Police and Protest in England and Ireland 1780–1850* (Cambridge, 1988).

Parry, G., *A Guide to the Records of Great Sessions in Wales* (Aberystwyth, 1995).

Parry-Jones, D., *Welsh Country Upbringing* (London, 2nd edn 1949).

Phillips, T., *Wales: The Language, Social Condition, Moral Character and Religious Opinions of the People, Considered in their Relation to Education* (London, 1849).

Priestley, P., *Victorian Prison Lives: English Prison Biography 1830–1914* (London, 1985).

Radzinowicz, L. and Hood, R., *The Emergence of Penal Policy in Victorian and Edwardian England* (Oxford, 1990).

Rawlings, P., 'Recent writings on crime, criminal law, criminal justice and punishment', in W. Hines (ed.), *English Legal History: A Bibliography and Guide to the Literature* (New York, 1990), pp. 62–112.

——, *Crime and Power* (Harlow, 1999).

——, *Policing: A Short History* (Cullompton, 2002).

Reade, Charles, *It is Never too Late to Mend* (London, 1856).

Roberts, S., *Order and Dispute* (Harmondsworth, 1979).

Rogers, B., 'Governor Stephens's picture book', in *The Bank Manager and the Holy Grail* (London, 2003), pp. 111–16.

S——, Capt. D——, *18 Months' Imprisonment* (London, 1883).

Sim, J., *Medical Power in Prisons: The Prison Medical Service in England 1774–1989* (Milton Keynes, 1990).

Smith, D., 'The demise of transportation: mid-Victorian penal policy', *Criminal Justice History*, 3 (1982), 21–45.

Spurrell, W., *Carmarthen and its Neighbourhood* (2nd edn, Carmarthen, 1879).

Suggett, R., *John Nash Architect–Pensaer* (Aberystwyth, 1995).

Taylor, T., *The Ticket-of-Leave Man* (London, 1862).

Thomas, J. E., *The English Prison Officer since 1850* (London, 1972).

Thompson, E. P., 'Rough Music', in *Customs in Common* (London, 1991), pp. 467–538.

Webb, S. and B., *English Prisons under Local Government* (London, 1922).

Wiener, M., *Reconstructing the Criminal: Culture, Law and Policy in England, 1830–1914* (Cambridge, 1990).

Williams, D., *The Rebecca Riots: A Study in Agrarian Discontent* (Cardiff, 1955).

Williams, D. J., *Hen Dŷ Ffarm*, translated as *The Old Farmhouse* by W. Williams (Carmarthen, 1987 edn).

Wrightson, K., 'Two concepts of order: justices, constables and jurymen in seventeenth-century England', in J. Brewer and J. Styles (eds), *An Ungovernable People: The English and Their Laws in the 17th and 18th Centuries* (London, 1979), pp. 24–46.

Zedner, L., *Women, Crime and Custody in Victorian England* (Oxford, 1991).

Index